To Rachel and John

Contents

List of Figures and Tables   viii

List of Abbreviations   ix

Preface and Acknowledgements   xi

PART I   THE CONTEXT OF POVERTY   1

1   What is Poverty?   3
2   The Dynamics of Poverty   19
3   Poverty in Europe and Beyond   38

PART II   DEFINITION AND MEASUREMENT   55

4   Defining Poverty   57
5   Deprivation   75
6   Households and Poverty   87
7   Measuring Poverty   101

PART III   SOCIAL DIVISIONS AND POVERTY   119

8   Gender and Poverty   121
9   Racism and Poverty   139
10 Ageing and Poverty   157
11 Disability and Poverty   174
12 The Underclass   190

PART IV   THE POLICY FRAMEWORK   199

13 The Politics of Poverty   201
14 Social Security Policy   214
15 Targeted Antipoverty Strategies   239
16 Poverty, Inequality and the Welfare State   255

References   269

Index   284

List of Figures and Tables

Figures

1.1   Numbers of people living in or on the margins of poverty in 1979 and 1987 (defined as 140% of SB)   16

1.2   Numbers and proportions of the population living in or on the margins of poverty (defined as below 60% average income) in 1979 and 1987   17

2.1   The changing composition of the poorest 10% by economic status between 1979 and 1987 (after housing costs)   25

3.1   The distribution of poverty in Europe   43

4.1   The Engel curve   67

4.2   Inflection points on the Engel curve   67

4.3   Deprivation by logarithm of income as a percentage of SB rates   70

6.1   Income over the life cycle   93

7.1   Pen's 'Parade of Dwarfs'   110

7.2   The Lorenz curve   111

7.3   Intersecting Lorenz curves   113

Table

9.1   Earnings of black and white Britons   146

List of Abbreviations

AA	Attendance Allowance
CAB	Citizens' Advice Bureau
CDP	Community Development Project
CPAG	Child Poverty Action Group
DHSS	Department of Health and Social Security
DIG	Disablement Income Group
DLA	Disability Living Allowance
DSS	Department of Social Security
DWA	Disability Working Allowance
EC	European Community
ECU	European Currency Unit
EPA	Educational Priority Area
ERDF	European Regional Development Fund
ERM	Exchange Rate Mechanism
ESF	European Social Fund
FA	Family Allowances
FC	Family Credit
FES	Family Expenditure Survey
FIS	Family Income Supplement
GLC	Greater London Council
HBAI	Households Below Average Incomes
ICA	Invalid Care Allowance
IEA	Institute of Economic Affairs
IFS	Institute for Fiscal Studies
ILF	Independent Living Fund
IS	Income Support
IVB	Invalidity Benefit
LIF	Low Income Families
LIS	Luxembourg Income Study
LSE	London School of Economics
MA	Mobility Allowance
MSC	Manpower Services Commission
NA	National Assistance
NAB	National Assistance Board
NACAB	National Association of Citizens' Advice Bureaux
NCIP	Non-Contributory Invalidity Pension

NI	National Insurance
OEO	Office of Economic Opportunity
OPCS	Office of Population Censuses and Surveys
PSI	Policy Studies Institute
SB	Supplementary Benefit
SBC	Supplementary Benefits Commission
SDA	Severe Disablement Allowance
SERPS	State Earnings Related Pensions Scheme
TUC	Trades Union Congress

Preface and Acknowledgements

'What thoughtful rich people call the problem of poverty, thoughtful poor people call with equal justice a problem of riches.' — R. H. Tawney, 1913

I set out to write a book about poverty in Britain with Tawney's famous words echoing in my mind. I felt that in one short sentence he had summed up the main issues involved in both the political and the definitional debates about poverty in modern society. After completing the task I had not changed my view on this; and if this book achieves the goals that I set for it, it will be by explaining to those who are new to these debates, or to those who wish to revisit them, why Tawney was right eighty years ago and why we still struggle to come to terms with the implications of his analysis today.

The title of the book expresses these goals. The book is intended as a textbook, providing for students of social policy, sociology and related disciplines an analysis of the various debates which have been conducted in Britain, and beyond, about the problem of poverty, and of the policies which have been developed in response to these. The book therefore discusses research on poverty carried out in Britain and elsewhere; but it is not a report of research and it is not itself based on any new or original research. As we shall see, especially in Part II, both existing research and the academic and political debates which flow from it involve major contradictions and conflicts of view – most fundamentally over the very meaning of the term poverty itself.

Academics and politicians do not agree amongst themselves what poverty is or what should be done about it. Indeed they frequently talk at cross purposes about the size and seriousness of the problem. What all are agreed on, however, is that poverty, where it does exist, is a problem, and a problem which requires policy responses to deal with it. This book is a guide to the various ways in which the problem of poverty has been defined and measured, and to the policies which have been developed in attempts to respond to it. It assumes some knowledge of the social science context of debate about social phenomena, but does not presume any prior acquaintance with writing or research about poverty and related issues. I hope that the understanding that it provides is accessible and self-explanatory. What it does not provide, of course, is any simple answer to the problem itself – beyond that which is implicit in Tawney's early insights.

I should like to thank a few people who helped in the writing of the book. Saul Becker, at Loughborough, read through a first draft and provided helpful comments and suggestions, some of which I have followed. Chris Pond, at the Low Pay Unit, also acted as reader and offered many useful comments. Jo Campling encouraged me to begin a project which I had been thinking about for some time, and helped me to secure the publisher's interest in ensuring that it saw the light of day. Academics writing about poverty are often criticised for talking about, rather than doing anything about, the problem. Writing this has not lessened my commitment to doing something about it; I hope that it might encourage that commitment in some others too.

PETE ALCOCK

The author and publishers wish to thank the following who have kindly given permission to use copyright material:

Ashgate Publishing Ltd for Table 9.1 from *Black and White Britain: The Third PSI Survey* by C. Brown, 1984.

London School of Economics and Political Science for Figure 3.1 from LSE/Welfare State Programme Discussion Paper WSP/60 by A. B. Atkinson.

Oxford University Press for Figures 7.2 and 7.3 from *The Economics of Inequality* by A. B. Atkinson, Figures 2.2 and 3.2, 1983.

Every effort has been made to trace all the copyright-holders, but if any have been inadvertently overlooked the publishers will be pleased to make the necessary arrangement at the first opportunity.

Part I
The Context of Poverty

1

What is Poverty?

Is Poverty a Problem?

'Poverty means going short materially, socially and emotionally. It means spending less on food, on heating, and on clothing than someone on an average income . . . . Above all, poverty takes away the tools to build the blocks for the future – your "life chances". It steals away the opportunity to have a life unmarked by sickness, a decent education, a secure home and a long retirement.' — Oppenheim, 1990, p. 3

'The evidence of improving living standards over this century is dramatic, and it is incontrovertible. When the pressure groups say that one-third of the population is living in poverty, they cannot be saying that one-third of people are living below the draconian subsistence levels used by Booth and Rowntree.' — Moore, 1989, p. 5

Many people, including academics, campaigners and politicians, talk about the problem of poverty; and underlying their discussion is the assumption that identifying the problem provides a basis for action on which all will agree. However, as we can see, people do not all agree on what the problem of poverty is, and thus, not surprisingly, the action they wish to encourage or to justify is not at all the same thing. Most people of course claim that their understanding of poverty is the correct one, based on logical argument or scientific research. But as our exploration of the problem of understanding poverty will reveal, there is no one correct, scientific, agreed definition because poverty is inevitably a political concept, and thus inherently a contested one.

Many commentators perhaps do have a clear idea of what they think should be done about poverty, and thus their description and definition of it provide a justification for this. In political debate the ends and the

3

means – and the terms – are always inextricably intertwined. Thus what commentators mean by poverty depends to some extent on what they intend, or expect, to do about it. Thus academic and political debate about poverty is not merely descriptive, it is prescriptive. Poverty is not just a state of affairs, it is an *unacceptable* state of affairs – it implicitly contains the question, what are we going to do about it?

Therefore the first thing to understand is that poverty is not a simple phenomenon which we can learn to define by adopting the correct approach. It is a series of contested definitions and complex arguments which overlap and at times contradict each other. It is therefore a big phenomenon and a small phenomenon, a growing issue and a declining issue, an individual problem and a social problem. And in understanding poverty the task is to understand how these different visions and perceptions overlap, how they interrelate and what the implications of different approaches and definitions are. In a sense we learn that the answer to the question, 'do you understand poverty?', is, 'it depends what you mean by poverty'.

If, however, we recognise that poverty is essentially a contested concept, why is it that academics and politicians continue to seek an accepted definition or argue that their approach is the correct one? Why not simply sit back and reject them all, arguing that the problem is not poverty, but rather the debates about poverty; and since these cannot be resolved, then there is no problem of poverty with which to be concerned? This may, at least for some of the academically minded, appear an attractive means of avoiding entering into the cut and thrust of political debate. But unfortunately it is not a viable response. We cannot sit on the fence on the poverty problem, or still less deny that the problem exists – at least we cannot once we have entered into the process of debate.

To put it another way, although poverty is a contested problem, it *is still a problem*. As stated above, poverty refers not just to a state of affairs, but to an unacceptable state of affairs. The imperative of action is intrinsic in the concept. Poverty is a problem, or it is nothing. What it cannot be is *not* a problem.

This is not to say that any definition of poverty must require new action now. Some approaches to poverty in Britain in the late twentieth century for instance are based on the argument that no further action is needed because the problem of poverty has already been dealt with by past action. Indeed this is the view popularised by prominent members of government in the late 1980s as revealed by the quotation from

Secretary of State John Moore (1989) at the beginning of this chapter. But it is not an approach which denies that poverty is a problem, nor that action is required in response to this. It is merely an approach which defines poverty as a (relatively small) problem in modern industrial society and restricts the action required in response to that which has already been, or is already being, done. Poverty is still therefore, in principle, a problem and action is still required; and if the action were to be curtailed (for instance, in Britain, if social security payments were to be ended entirely) then presumably the problem could return.

Thus poverty is a problem however it is approached; and when we understand the different approaches we can begin to make judgements about what *we* think the problem is. Poverty is also a basis for action, or policy. Social policy flows from poverty, and debates about poverty have provided a central basis for the development of social policy in Britain, and of course in other countries too.

If the way in which poverty is defined frequently depends on what policies proponents are advancing to deal with it, however, in a sense the policy determines the problem. This may seem like a circular argument – a kind of academic 'chicken and egg' conundrum. But it is really only an acceptance of the interrelated nature of social phenomena in the real world. We are living in a world where academics and politicians are seeking to define the problem of poverty, and where there are a range of policies which have been introduced in response to one or other version of the problem. And of course the introduction of these policy initiatives has had an effect on poverty as previously conceived – some, such as John Moore, even claiming that they have removed it.

This means that an understanding of poverty requires us to undertake too an understanding of the social policies which have been developed in response to it and which have thus removed, restructured or even recreated it. Indeed there are many who argue that poverty is largely, if not entirely, a product of social policies, or social and economic policies, pursued by states in order to control and discipline their citizens. By creating, and then containing, the poor states can control others through fear of poverty, a point to which we shall return shortly. And it is obviously the case that, in Britain in the 1990s, the problems of determining who is poor, how poverty is experienced and how it may or may not be escaped, have been heavily influenced by state policies with a long and complex history.

Identifying Poverty

Poverty therefore is a complex problem and is a product, in part at least of political process and policy development. It is also a political and a moral concept – it implies, and requires, action. Poverty is thus not the same as *inequality*, although the two concepts are interrelated. The most important distinction between the two is that whereas poverty is a prescriptive concept, inequality is a descriptive concept. Inequality *is*, simply, a state of affairs, and whether it is acceptable or not is a matter of opinion. Opinions are hotly disputed about whether, and how much, inequality is acceptable. Certainly there are those who argue strongly that significant inequality is acceptable, and indeed desirable (Green, 1990). But the dispute is about whether particular levels of inequality may or may not be desirable, not about how to define inequality or measure it.

Actually, as we shall see in Chapter 7, there are disagreements about how to measure inequality. But these are technical disagreements about what is counted and how it is counted, not political disagreements about whether inequality exists or whether it is a problem. Unlike poverty therefore, inequality may be a matter for political debate and disagreement, but it is not instrinsically a political problem. And it is for exactly this reason that it has been preferred as a basis for discussion and research by many academics. Investigation of inequality can be a neutral, perhaps even a scientific, exercise in measurement and data collection, the implications of which can be left up to others, such as politcians, to argue about or ignore. Because it avoids the political contestability of poverty a focus on inequality may therefore offer a more attractive option than entering the debate about poverty. Piachaud's (1981a) famous critique of Townsend's major research on poverty in Britain in the 1960s and 1970s (Townsend, 1979), to which we will return in Chapter 4, is in effect adopting such a distancing approach, albeit within a much more complex and technical argument.

But of course for many commentators, and for most of those who will be discussed in this book, it is the political terrain in which the debate about the definition and measurement of poverty is situated which makes it so attractive for study and argument. It is because poverty is not just extreme inequality but unacceptable inequality that it is so important to study it; and it is because the identification of poverty requires policy action to respond to it that both academics and politicians have been concerned to identify it. The moral and the political thrust of poverty research *is* its great attraction, and as such it has attracted some of the most eminent and important academics and politicians concerned with social policy in Britain and elsewhere.

Such a political focus was clearly important for one of the pioneers of modern poverty research, Booth, who undertook a massive study of poverty in London in the 1880s with the clear intention of bringing the scale of the problem, and the intensity of it, to the attention of politicians and policy makers, who would then be forced to react to it (Booth, 1889). This was also the concern, albeit initially on a smaller scale, of the most famous of British poverty researchers, Rowntree, in his study of York in 1889, which was repeated in the 1930s and the 1950s (Rowntree, 1901, 1941, Rowntree and Lavers, 1951). Rowntree paid much attention to arriving at a precise definition of poverty, an issue which will be discussed in more detail in Chapter 4, in order to demonstrate, conclusively he hoped, that those who were poor were unable to provide for themselves and therefore needed support or improvement.

The use of carefully defined and measured research evidence on poverty in order to provoke policy response is an example of the political context of the concept discussed above. It became an approach widely developed by Fabian academics and politicians throughout the twentieth century in order to put pressure on governments, and political parties, to develop social policies to help the poor. Most recently this has included the work of academics, notably from the London School of Economics (LSE), such as Titmuss, Abel Smith and Townsend.

Townsend in particular has developed the argument that poverty continues to exist even in affluent welfare state Britain in the late twentieth century, because poverty is not as narrowly defined as Rowntree previously conceived it, but encompasses the broader notion of relative deprivation within a society of changing norms and customs. This too provides an example of how different definitions of poverty are advanced in order to make the case for new and different policy responses.

More recently still in the campaigning work of organisations like the Child Poverty Action Group (CPAG), the presentation of facts and figures on poverty has been used as part of a constant pressure on governments to change or adapt policies to provide more resources for the poor. For instance CPAG regularly provides updated figures on the 'facts' of poverty in Britain (see Oppenheim, 1990), as well as more considered analysis of the differing aspects of poverty (Golding, 1986), or the impact of government policy (Walker and Walker, 1987; Becker, 1991).

This wide range of academic and political work on poverty has revealed the extent of differences over the identification of the problem of poverty. Different researchers and commentators are clearly operating with different definitions or understandings of the problem. In a book on the 'Politics of Poverty', Donnison (1982, p. 7) attempts to narrow these down into three broad approaches to the problem, by distinguishing destitution, subsistence and relative poverty.

Destitution is extreme hardship or misery. It is conscious suffering which can occur in any society. But it is often taken to mean the problems of starvation, destruction of home and community and, for some, early death, which are associated with poverty on a global scale. This is an acute and catastrophic problem, increasingly brought to our newspapers and television screens in an attempt to secure immediate international action. And sometimes, but not always, some action is provided.

Subsistence poverty is largely what Rowntree understood by poverty: not having enough to get by, or not having enough to meet one's needs. It is also what Beveridge meant by the the evil of 'want', which although it implies some element of choice was intended to convey the notion of needs which had to be fulfilled, and which it was the responsibility of the state, through social security, to meet (Beveridge, 1942).

Relative poverty is the problem of poverty in an affluent but unequal society. Basic needs may be met, but for those at the very bottom many other social expectations cannot be met, resulting in their exclusion from the customary standard of living in that society.

These are obviously quite different conceptions of poverty with quite different consequences for how poverty is identified and what policies might be developed to respond to it. To select one rather than another definition would thus lead to a very different approach to both the problem and the solution of poverty, and this debate will be looked at in some detail in Chapter 4 in a discussion of relative and absolute definitions of poverty.

Recognition of different means of conceptualising and identifying poverty also raises the question of the distinction between *objective* and *subjective* perspective. Whilst academics or politicians may operate with particular definitions of poverty in order to define and identify it, these may not coincide with the views of those people who are thus defined as poor. People at the bottom of the income distribution in Britain may not see themselves as poor, particularly if they make comparisons with those elsewhere in the world who face starvation and destitution, or even with those elsewhere in Britain who are worse off than themselves.

If people do not perceive themselves as poor, then in what sense is it logical, or fair, to treat them as poor? This has led some to suggest that poverty should be identified and defined only by poor people, and only, presumably, as far as they wish to present themselves as poor. Obviously it is important to recognise this subjective aspect to the identification of poverty and to pay attention in research and policy development to the perceptions and views of those who are the intended beneficiaries, or victims, of poverty policy. But there is a danger in adopting wholeheartedly a subjective approach to poverty.

To be poor is, in effect by definition, to occupy an undesirable or negative situation (an unacceptable state of affairs). Those who are poor by some objective criteria may therefore understandably not want to identify themselves in such a negative, exclusionary and even stigmatising fashion. It is not much comfort to admit to poverty, and thus many people may deny it, even though they would welcome the benefits which would flow from policies designed to improve or ameliorate their position. Furthermore poor people often have much lower expectations of social needs and standards when defining poverty. Thus, as will be discussed in Chapter 13, although subjective perceptions are important in developing an understanding of the political context of poverty, they cannnot replace academic and political debate as a means of identifying it.

Creating Poverty

As has been suggested, poverty is to some extent created by, or at least *recreated* by, social and economic policies which have developed over time to respond to or control poverty and those who are poor. Thus the history of policies directed at the poor is a part of the history of poverty itself. And, as Vincent (1991) discusses in his history of poverty in Britain in the twentieth century, this interrelation between poverty and policy has consistently shaped the position of poor people within all aspects of the broader social structure.

Although it is possible to extend the history of poverty as far back as the history of society itself, most of those writing historically about

⇒ INTRoduction

poverty in Britain trace the current development of poverty and poverty policy from the period of the gradual replacement of feudalism by capitalism as the modern economy began to develop in the seventeenth and eighteenth centuries. Indeed, in his book on the history of poverty in Britain, Novak (1988) argues that it is only at this point that poverty is created. This is because at this time the majority of people are separated from the land and become workers, and thus they lose control over the means of producing material support and become dependent upon wages from paid labour. After this those who cannot work for wages cannot support themselves and thus are poor.

Poverty, it is argued from this perspective, is therefore a product of capitalism, and later it is sustained and recreated by capitalism in order to provide a discipline, through fear of poverty, for workers to maintain their commitment to the labour market. For Novak therefore poverty is caused by the logic of the capitalist wage labour market and is maintained by capitalism; it will thus only be eliminated when capitalism is replaced by some other economic system.

There are, however, some serious problems with such a strict Marxist approach to the understanding of poverty, in particular its failure to perceive or discuss poverty within other economic systems and its rejection of any attempts to ameliorate or reduce poverty within capitalism. It is also over-simplistic in its assumption that modern economies such as Britain do experience only a capitalist economic order. Arguably the British economy has only ever been partly capitalist, with elements of feudalism surviving for a while and other forms of state-directed or communal production developing later. And poverty in Britain is a product of such varying economic and other social forces, and not only of the structural exclusion of the capitalist wage labour market.

However the link between poverty and the development, and control, of the wage labour market is an important, indeed a crucial, one. Clearly exclusion from paid labour is likely to be a cause of poverty where there are no, or few, other sources of material support. And at the same time the employers of wage labour will wish to maintain a ready and willing surplus of workers to undertake paid employment at the lowest possible cost. State policies to respond to the problem of poverty have always been directly influenced by such demands, and have created a legacy of policy priorities which have shaped images of the problem of poverty and the needs of the poor.

Thus early laws dealing with the landless poor, dating from 1349, branded them as vagrants and subjected them to controls to prevent unwanted competition for their labour. Through a series of later statutes, in 1530, 1536 and 1547, these controls became more extensive and also began to invoke a distinction between those who were poor and unable to work and support themselves, such as the elderly or sick, and those who were poor but were able in theory at least to support themselves. It was a distinction later represented in the categories of the 'deserving' and the 'undeserving' poor. The latter were assumed to be idle, indolent and possibly criminal and were therefore subject to punitive policies of control designed to encourage, or to force, them into employment and self-sufficiency.

This approach was encapsulated in the Poor Law Act of 1601, during the time of Elizabeth I, the aims of which, according to Golding and Middleton (1982, p. 11) were work discipline, deterence and classification. The Poor Law was the most important policy development dealing with poverty up until the end of the nineteenth century; and it was a development which focused in particular upon control and deterence. This could be seen most clearly in the growth of the institution of the workhouse or Bridewell. Workhouses were institutions to which poor and destitute individuals could be sent to be provided for if they were not providing for themselves. This was a form of poverty relief, but the regime within workhouses was extremely harsh and punitive in order to discourage both present and potential residents from perceiving them to be a desirable alternative to employment and self-sufficiency.

However workhouses could not provide for all the poor, especially in rural areas at times of low wages and high prices. Thus after 1795 the Speenhamland system of topping up by the local parish of agricultural workers' wages to meet higher prices was introduced, and spread rapidly. This was an indiscriminate and costly form of support for the poor, however, and it did not contain direct disciplinary measures of control or encouragement of self-support. It was considered by the Royal Commission on the Poor Law set up in 1832, and in the Poor Law Amendment Act of 1834 'outdoor relief', as Speenhamland payments were called, was ended, parish control of the Poor Law was replaced by central and uniform administration, and the workhouse test of encouragement to self-sufficiency was intended to be invoked for all the poor.

Central to the philosophy of the 1834 Poor Law was the notion of 'less eligibility'. This was the belief that the support provided by the state for the poor should provide for a less eligible status than that of the lowest labourer, in order to encourage all the poor to seek any such employment rather than remain dependent upon the state. As the 1834 report put it,

> The first and most essential of all conditions . . . is that his situation on the whole shall not be made really or apparently so eligible as the situation of the independent labourer of the lowest class (quoted in Novak, 1988, p. 46).

The workhouse test was of course the epitome of the idea of less eligibility, and its punitive regime underlined the punitive attitude towards poverty, or rather pauperism, on which the Poor Law was based and which dominated nineteenth century Victorian attitudes towards the problem of poverty. The predominant assumption was that poverty was the product of the interaction of the twin problems of indolence and vice, and thus state policies should seek to counteract their influences by encouraging self-sufficiency and penalising dependency. That this also enforced labour discipline amongst the workers by putting them in fear of losing their jobs and falling into poverty was also no coincidence. State support for the labour market through social policy, as well as through the laws of contract and combination, was part of the agenda of reform of nineteenth century British government. Despite the protestations of adherence to the ideals of laissez-faire, therefore, early responses to the problem of poverty created a policy framework which produced definite attempts to shape and control the poor.

As will be discussed in Chapter 14, although the gradual replacement of the Poor Law by other forms of insurance-based social security and national assistance in the twentieth century has removed some of the harshest aspects of the workhouse test, the notions of less eligibility and labour market discipline have continued to dominate state policy responses to poverty and to maintain the priorities developed in these earlier forms of state control. Modern social security benefits have consistently been maintained at low levels of payment in order to prevent any competition with low wages, and benefits for the unemployed have generally required recipients to demonstrate that whilst receiving state support they are also seeking employment in the labour market. Thus state policies have continued to be predicated upon support for the labour market and the attempt to divide the poor from the employed.

Employment has never of course in practice been a guaranteed means of avoiding poverty. As Bowley's studies in the early twentieth century were already revealing many of those who were poor then were in full-time work (Bowley and Burnett-Hurst, 1915), and similar evidence of the problem of the working poor is still widespread today (see Low Pay Unit, 1992). Furthermore many of those poor and out of work are far from feckless idlers revelling in dependency. They are looking for, and hoping for, work, but are unable to find it. Thus the distinction between the employed on the one hand and the feckless and dependent poor on the other is a false distinction. But it is a distinction which has maintained an apparent division between the poor and the employed, dividing and classifying those in the lowest classes, and controlling and disciplining the poor at the same time as supporting them.

State responses to poverty which control and discipline the poor have therefore created and shaped particular images of both the problem of poverty and the policy response to it. And how we view poverty and how we change or develop these policies are in part determined by these legacies of history. The divisions between the working and the non-working poor, and between the deserving and the undeserving poor, exercise a strong influence over images of poverty in Britain today. This will be discussed in more detail in Chapter 2.

What has been created is a powerful legacy of what is the problem of poverty and a perception of the poor as separate from those who work and are able to provide for themselves. Poor people's problems are thus seen as largely the product of their own idleness or inability. There is also the fear that overgenerous state support for the poor may only compound this problem by encouraging indolence. And there are overtones of racism: poor people include disproportionate numbers of foreigners who, it is said, have come to Britain to benefit from that generous state support. Donnison's (1982) book on the 'Politics of Poverty' contains a cartoon on the cover which neatly encapsulates these images of poverty that we have inherited from history. It features an obviously poor tramp begging for money in return for which he promises to confirm the prejudices of passers-by. In reply to someone giving him a coin he says, 'Yes. I'm on Social Security . . . . No. I've never done a hand's turn in my life . . . . Yes. I'm of Irish extraction'.

The Extent of Poverty

As we have seen therefore, poverty is a political problem, and thus the nature of the problem is the result of the particular political context within which it has developed. This means inevitably that discussion of the extent of poverty largely takes place within one particular political context, usually within one country; and that comparison of poverty across national political boundaries cannot readily be undertaken. We cannot simply count the numbers or proportion of poor people in Britain in the 1990s and compare them with the numbers in France or the US, or still less Brazil or Ethiopia. What is understood by poverty, and who would be counted as poor in these other countries, will be likely to be very different than in Britain because of their different political and economic circumstances and histories.

Because of the incomparability of definition and measurement therefore, international approaches to the problem, or problems, of poverty have not been widespread, although this is also a product of course of the low level of development of international action on a range of social and economic concerns. Well-publicised cases of destitution or starvation, such as those experienced in Eastern Africa in the 1980s and 1990s, have been the focus of international concern and action. And there are international agencies, such as Oxfam and Christian Aid, who seek to coordinate international efforts to relieve poverty in different parts of the world. But international assessment of the extent of poverty within the third world is relatively under-developed.

Within the developed world, however, measurement and definition are more common and international comparisons of poverty have been made and are being expanded. George and Howards (1991) have recently contrasted poverty in Britain and the US, and the Luxembourg Income Study (LIS), which will be discussed in more detail in Chapter 7, provides an important new source of information about poverty in a wide range of developed countries in the 1980s and 1990s. Mitchell (1991) has utilised the LIS database to contrast income transfer policies in ten welfare states. Furthermore, as will be discussed in Chapter 3, the development of crossnational economic and social policy amongst the member countries of the European Community (EC) has also led to the development of significant investment in the provision of data about poverty and antipoverty policies in all EC countries, and to the development of community-wide policy initiatives to combat poverty, in particular through the three EC poverty programmes. The development of such EC initiatives will provide a European dimension to both poverty and antipoverty policy in all member states in the future, which will be likely to lead to major, even fundamental, changes in debate and policy development in Britain.

Despite such developments, however, it is still the case that most discussion of the extent of poverty in Britain, and in other EC or overseas countries, is focused on the problem within the country, rather than on the broader international context. And certainly attempts to measure the extent of poverty are much simpler when restricted to poverty within one political and economic system. Although, as will be discussed in Part III, both the definition and measurement of poverty within Britain are in practice highly complex and highly contested exercises.

Leaving aside these debates for the time being, however, there is the further problem that even within one country, and despite the continuing impact of past history, the extent of poverty, and the conception of it, also changes over time. In part this is perhaps a welcome feature: the problem of poverty ought to change as new debates and definitions develop and new policies are introduced. However these changes make it extremely difficult to compare past data on poverty with present figures in order to make any comparison or judgement about the effects of changes over time.

This was revealed most graphically in Rowntree's three studies of poverty in York in the 1890s, 1930s and 1950s. Although similar methods were used to survey a similar population, on each occasion changes were in the definition of poverty. As will be discussed in more detail in Chapter 4, these changes were consciously made and readily justifiable, but they did mean that on each occasion different forms of measurement were being taken. When Abel Smith and Townsend (1965) sought to dispute Rowntree's findings on the extent of poverty in the 1950s, their argument was based explicitly on the use of different criteria to define and measure the problem.

Despite these problems, however, some attempts have been made to measure and compare poverty over time. Fiegehen *et al.* (1977, Ch. 3) used a range of definitions and methods to compare changes in poverty from the end of the Second World War to the mid 1970s, concluding that the extent and depth of poverty had reduced over this period. And in an interesting article in 1988 Piachaud attempted to adapt the data from a range of poverty studies to develop a constant relative poverty level which could be used to compare poverty in Britain from 1899 to 1983. Despite the methodological initiatives undertaken by Piachaud, however, his conclusions about changes in poverty levels over time were fairly tentative. Although there was evidence of a significant decline in poverty following the Second World War, trends since then appeared to be fluctuating and revealed increases in poverty levels in the early 1980s, mainly resulting from economic forces.

Recent statistics discussed by the CPAG (Oppenheim, 1990) and Townsend (1991) appear to confirm that the extent of poverty expanded in the 1980s. Oppenheim uses the government's own figures for low-income families, which compare incomes with entitlement to Income Support/Supplementary Benefit (IS/SB), the minimum income provided by the state through social security. However, as will be discussed in Chapter 6, these figures have now been discontinued and replaced by the households below average income figures, which compare households with average income levels. As Oppenheim (1990, pp. 38–43) discusses, there are advantages and disadvantages with each of the approaches, and utilising comparative calculations provided by the Institute for Fiscal Studies (IFS), the CPAG continues to use and compare both methods. And both do reveal significant levels of poverty in Britain, which also increased significantly in the 1980s. Figure 1.1 shows the numbers on the low income family basis and Figure 1.2 shows the numbers on the households below average income basis.

FIGURE 1.1

Numbers of people living in or on the margins of poverty in 1979 and 1987 (defined as 140% of Supplementary Benefit and below)

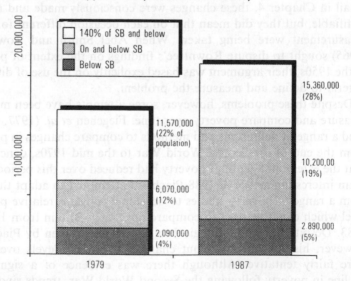

Source: Oppenheim, 1990, Figure 1, p. 22.

FIGURE 1.2

Numbers and proportions of the population living in or on the margins of poverty (defined as below 60% of average income) in 1979 and 1987

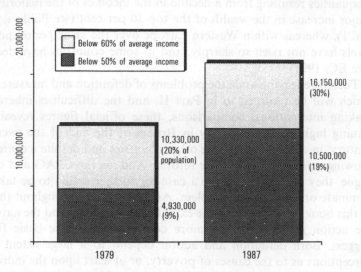

Source: Oppenheim, 1990, Figure 3, p. 28.

On both counts extreme poverty – those below IS/SB level or 50 per cent of average wages – rose from five or six million (9 or 12 per cent of the population) in 1979 to around 10 million (19 per cent of the population) in 1987. And those in relative poverty – those below 140 per cent of the IS/SB level or below 60 per cent of average wages – rose from 10 or 11.5 million (20 or 22 per cent of the population) to 15 or 16 million (28 or 30 per cent of the population). Furthermore figures for 1988–9 reveal that changes in tax and benefit policies in 1988 accentuated these trends, with 12 million (22 per cent of the population) having incomes below 50 per cent of the average at the end of the decade. Despite government claims of growing affluence for all over this period, the 1988–9 figures also show a decline in real terms (against inflation) of 6 per cent in the incomes of the bottom 10 per cent of the population (DSS, 1992).

These are high levels of poverty and, in contrast to earlier evidence of a gradual decline in poverty and inequality since the Second World War, they demonstrate a significant increase, both relatively and absolutely, over a short period of time. They also compare interestingly with developments in other advanced industrial countries. In the US, where similar social and economic policies to those in Britain were pursued in the 1980s under Reagan, there have also been growing inequalities resulting from a decline in the incomes of the majority and major increase in the wealth of the top 10 per cent (see Phillips, 1990, Ch. 1), whereas within Western Europe over the same period poverty levels have not risen so sharply, and in some countries have declined (see EC, 1991).

Therefore leaving aside the problems of definition and measurement, which will be returned to in Part II, and the difficulties inherent in making international comparisons, these official figures reveal continuing high levels of poverty in Britain at the end of the twentieth century, in contrast with some other countries and despite a century of growing affluence and welfare reform. And, as the CPAG and others argue, they continue to create a case for further action to be taken to eliminate or alleviate the problem. As we shall see throughout the rest of this book, however, both the extent of the problem and the nature of the action to be taken are more complex than these basic figures suggest. Both definition and action depend to a large extent upon perceptions as to the causes of poverty, or at least upon the individual and social circumstances in which it arises, and it is to these that we will turn in Chapter 2.

2
The Dynamics of Poverty

Ideologies of Poverty

As we have seen, poverty is a political concept – it does not just describe a state of affairs, it also implies that some action must be taken to remedy it. And the political actions which have been taken, for instance in Britain, have had a cumulative effect in reshaping and recreating the concept of poverty itself. Implicit in the development of both definitions and policies, and the interrelationship between them, however, are assumptions about the impact and the causes of poverty – both who is poor and why they become or remain poor. Informing the politics therefore are ideologies of poverty and images and attitudes which govern how we approach the process of definition, measurement and policy development.

We all perceive poverty, like other social phenomena, through an ideological framework; and for each of us that framework and those perceptions of poverty are unique. However although unique, they are not isolated. Our perceptions and attitudes are governed in large part by broader social influences, in particular the ideologies of powerful social figures and social forces, which receive publicity through the media, through politics, through education and through other social interactions. The public images of poverty are central in determining private perceptions, a relationship which was explored by Golding and Middleton (1982) in research on public and private attitudes to social security dependency and abuse in the 1970s.

Most obviously ideologies of poverty are a product of history – they develop out of past ideologies. Golding and Middleton open their report with a review of the history of social security and poverty policy in Britain over the last few centuries, demonstrating, as we saw in Chapter 1, that current perceptions have been shaped by past perceptions and the policies and practices which have flowed from these. Not surprisingly therefore Golding and Middleton found that perceived divisions between the nonworking and the working poor, and the deserving and the undeserving poor, continued to exercise very powerful influences on public and private ideologies of poverty.

The particular focus of Golding and Middleton's research was on growing fears about social security abuse popularised by the newspapers and by politicians in the 1970s. They explain how media reporting of only one or two established incidents of social security abuse was able to carry the implicit, or at times explicit, message that these were only the tip of the iceberg of widespread social security abuse. Abuse was the product, the media implied, of idle and feckless claimants seeking to enjoy a comfortable living without working, which they were readily able to achieve because of the ineffective administration of an overextensive and overbureaucratic benefits system – and because even for those not actually defrauding the system benefits were so generous that they encouraged a life of indolent dependency, which could even extend to Spanish holidays on the 'Costa-del-Dole' (see Golding and Middleton, 1982, pp. 106–7).

Two particular 'news' stories encapsulated the ideological concern, and preconceptions, which dominated media coverage of poverty and benefits issues during this period. One was the case of a Liverpool claimant, Derek Deevy, who was charged with fraudulently receiving benefits totalling £57, although he claimed to have received over £36 000 in false claims. Among the features of the reports of this case were attempts to portray the apparent ease with which he had duped a naive and ineffective social security system out of tens of thousands of pounds of taxpayers' money. In other words social security support was portrayed as a 'soft touch'.

The other case concerned a genuine claimant in Cornwall who had both a legal and a common law wife as well as twenty children. He was thus claiming an apparently massive social security entitlement and living a life of 'gentle glee' (Golding and Middleton, 1982, p. 92) at the taxpayers' expense. The images portrayed by these two stories were those of an overgenerous and easily outwitted social security system providing, not to alleviate hardship and deprivation, but a comfortable life of idleness which was far more desirable than that enjoyed by many of those at work who, through the growing taxes on their hard-earned wages, were being required by the state to support these people.

It was not only the media who were fanning the flames of anticlaimant hysteria during this period however. MPs too used their high political profile to draw attention to the 'problem' of abuse and to encourage pressure for punitive action to be taken, and government ministers also reinforced the ideological climate of suspicion. In the early 1970s Conservative Secretary of State Keith Joseph had established a committee to investigate the 'abuse of social security benefits' (Fisher Committee, 1973), and later Labour minister Stan Orme established a departmental coordinating committee on abuse (Golding and Middleton, 1982, p. 79). In the 1980s and 1990s these concerns were continued with a number of attempts to 'crack down' on fraud and abuse within social security by the deployment of additional staff on detection work.

Of course the media and the political campaigns against social security abuse were in part a particular product of the social and economic circumstances of the 1970s and 1980s, as Golding and Middleton point out (1982, Ch. 8). These were periods of rapidly growing unemployment and low wages due to economic recession and of a tax burden which was increasing, especially for those lower down the income scale. This was fertile ground for the exploitation of fears about what came to be called 'scrounging'. Golding and Middleton's study revealed the close links in these fears between media and political concerns, and public and private ideologies of poverty – and the consequences which these have for perceptions of the causes of poverty and the policy solutions to it.

Golding and Middleton's research also included a survey of attitudes towards welfare conducted in Leicester and Sunderland in 1977. What this revealed was a high degree of hostility to social security claimants amongst a large proportion of respondents. In particular hostility was directed at scroungers and those, in some cases in very large numbers, claimants who were accused of abusing state support. When asked about who deserved to receive support from social security most respondents mentioned the old and the sick, only 5.9 per cent quoting the unemployed (Golding and Middleton, 1982, p. 169). Furthermore the survey revealed that the highest estimates of abuse and the greatest resentment towards claimants came from those in low-paid, low-skilled employment (pp. 169–72).

Thus attitudes towards poverty reveal the distinctions between the working and the non-working poor and the deserving and the undeserving claimants which are the legacy of the history of poverty and poverty policy in Britain. And they are continually shaped, and reshaped, by ideologies of poverty contained in the media and other public forums, as one of Golding and Middleton's respondents revealed:

There are some genuine ones but the majority just bleed the country
dry. The ones who have not worked for a long time should be made
to do some kind of work and not claim benefit. 80% are scroungers.
It's just what you hear, what's on TV, what's been in the papers over
the last few weeks (fitter's wife, quoted in Golding and Middleton,
1982, p. 173).

The ideological divisions also exploit the contradictory experience of
real economic relations. For instance, it is the low paid in low-quality
jobs, paying taxes and working hard for little reward, who most resent
those apparently benefiting at their expense, although this may be a
notion of 'benefit' ill-informed by knowledge of the realities of
dependency upon social security. Golding and Middleton found that
respondents underestimated family needs and overestimated benefits
levels (1982, p. 188). Such hostility may also rather misjudge the
sources of the real hardships that low-paid workers are experiencing;
for instance even reduced benefit levels would be unlikely to do much
to reduce the burden on ordinary taxpayers or to improve the pay and
conditions of unskilled workers..

Golding and Middleton's survey is not the only evidence of popular
ideologies of poverty in Britain. In 1976 the EC included a survey of
perceptions of poverty in a regular six-monthly opinion survey in
member states (EC, 1977). One of the questions asked was about
perceived causes of poverty. This revealed that in Britain a large
proportion (43 per cent) believed that laziness and lack of willpower
was the main cause, a much higher proportion than in all other
countries where structural causes were more frequently quoted.
Another question asked whether people thought too much or too
little was done for the poor by the state. In Britain 20 per cent said too
much, twice the proportion in any other country, with only Denmark
and Luxembourg registering double figures with 10 per cent.

The EC survey reveals that ideologies of poverty are very much the
product of the particular forces at work in particular societies. They are
the product of particular histories and current circumstances rather
than universal truths (or untruths). And of course as history and
circumstances change so too do ideologies. A repeat of the EC survey
in 1989 found laziness and unwillingness less often cited as causes of
poverty in Britain than in 1976, down from 43 per cent to 18 per cent.
There was also a much higher proportion (70 per cent) believing that
public action to combat poverty was inadequate (EC, 1990), perhaps
suggesting that, after a decade of social security cuts, continuing high

levels of poverty were no longer felt to be entirely an individual responsibility.

Ideologies of poverty provide an important backdrop to both academic and political debate. Academics and politicians may seek to influence popular ideologies, but they also share in them, and share in their reproduction. Golding and Middleton (1982, p. 199) point out that structural explanations of poverty are largely absent from popular debate because perceptions of poverty are linked to experiences of poverty and thus to the individuals who are, or are seen to be, experiencing it. The focus on poverty as an individual experience is also a predominant feature of studies of poverty and explanations of its causes. And although most academic studies do not reproduce directly the simplistic assumption that poverty is largely the result of individual idleness, condoned or encouraged by state largesse, the focus on the question of who are the poor, and the attempts to discern potential causal links between particular social groups in particular circumstances and experience of poverty can, as will be discussed in more detail in Chapter 12, contribute to a misplaced emphasis upon individual or pathological explanations of poverty rather than upon social or structural ones.

Who are the Poor?

It is important to know who is experiencing poverty and to examine whether those in particular social groups or social circumstances are more or less likely to suffer from it. It is also important to be able to see whether this distribution of poverty is similar or different in different societies and whether it varies over time within one society. This is not just a matter of sociological interest either, for the identification of poverty is linked to political action, and the identification of particular individuals or groups as disproportionately experiencing poverty may suggest that policies should be focused or targeted upon them in particular. Although, as we shall see, it is just such an approach which can lead in some circumstances to a pathological view of individual circumstances as the causes of poverty, and individual action on those circumstances as therefore the solution to it.

As discussed in Chapter 1, the history of poverty in Britain is linked to the development of the capitalist economy and the resulting impact of the regime of wage labour. Once removed from the land as a source of support people will be at risk of poverty in a wage-based economy if they do not have either capital resources or a wage (and an adequate wage) from employment. Risk of poverty is therefore related to class status. It is those in the working class, and especially those without recognised skills or qualifications on the margins of the labour market, who are most likely to be unemployed and poor – indeed in a wage economy for the vast majority of people to be unemployed also means to be poor.

Unemployment is also disproportionately experienced by particular categories of potential, or hopeful, workers. Those who are sick or suffer from a disability may find difficulty in securing waged labour because it may be assumed that they cannot perform effectively. Members of minority ethnic groups, in particular black people, may also be excluded from the labour market by the prejudice of employers. Older people are excluded from the labour market by widely held assumptions that after a certain age they would want to, or should be required to, 'retire' from work. All these groups experience particular problems of poverty – this will be discussed in more detail in Part III.

However, as has already been discussed, poverty is not exclusively associated with unemployment. There is no guarantee that all needs will be able to be met from the low wages earned by some workers, especially if there are dependants to support. And thus even those in waged work may be poor, indeed wages not infrequently fall below the state IS/SB levels. This is particularly likely to be the case for temporary or part-time workers based in particular sectors of the labour market, such as catering and cleaning in the service sector. This type of employment is also more likely to undertaken by women, ethnic minority members or those with disabilities; thus reproducing amongst the working poor the social divisions which characterise the distribution of unemployment.

Research on poverty has consistently revealed that pensioners, the sick and disabled, single parents and the unemployed have constituted the majority of the poor in Britain. However the proportions in these different categories have been shifting over time, and in particular in the last quarter of the twentieth century. The numbers of single parents, the majority of whom have always been poor, have grown significantly since the Second World War. And as Figure 2.1 shows, between 1979 and 1987 the proportion of pensioners and sick and disabled declined significantly and the proportion of unemployed grew dramatically. It also shows that the proportion of working poor remained at around a quarter of the lowest decile group (the poorest 10 per cent of the population).

FIGURE 2.1

The changing composition of the
poorest 10% by economic status
between 1979 and 1987
(after housing costs)

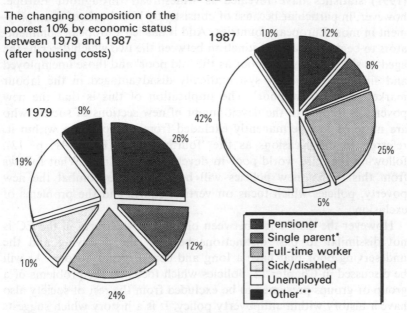

Note: Percentages do not add up to 100% due to rounding

** Single parents not in full-time work. ** Men aged 60–64, widows, students, people
temporarily away from home, people who are unemployed but not available for work.*

Source: Oppenheim, 1990, Figure 8, p. 34.

This shift from old age and sickness towards unemployment in the
distribution of poverty is significant in its resultant increase in the
proportion of the so-called 'undeserving' poor, which may help to
explain the hardening of attitudes towards them revealed by Golding
and Middleton (1982). It is also a move away from what are sometimes
called 'life cycle' circumstances leading to poverty – those which might
affect any or all of us at some time during our lives – towards the
selective experience of poverty by vulnerable groups. We will examine
the life cycle aspects of poverty in more detail in Chapter 6 and discuss
how they lead to different policies to combat poverty by ensuring
horizontal equity redistribution of resources across those at different
stages in their lives, as opposed to the *vertical equity* policies designed
to redistribute resources from the better off to those who are vulnerable
at all or any stages of their lives.

This distinction between groups of the poor, and the changing
composition of the distribution of poverty, is a feature which recent EC

(1991) statistics have revealed is widespread throughout Europe, however, in particular because of consistently high levels of unemployment in most European countries. And it has led European commentators to begin to draw a distinction between the two which describe the aged or sick – life cycle – poor as the 'old poor' and those unemployed and single parents now systematically disadvantaged in the labour market as the 'new poor'. The implication of this is that the new poverty is leading to the development of new sections of society who are more or less permanently excluded from participation within it, referred to on occasions as the 'fourth world' (EC 1991, p. 12), following the third world poor in developing countries. What follows from this is that new policies will be required to combat the new poverty, policies which focus on vertical equity and the problems of exclusion.

However the distinction between old and new poverty in the EC is not dissimilar to past distinctions between the deserving and the undeserving poor that have a long and controversial history. As will be discussed in Chapter 12, policies which focus on the problems of a group or groups presumed to be excluded from the rest of society also have a history within antipoverty policy. It is a history which suggests that the conception of the poor as an excluded class can readily be transformed into a pathological perception of poverty as the problem of that class and their inability or unwillingness to participate with others or to provide for themselves.

Another group of people who are disadvantaged in, and largely excluded from, the labour market and therefore potentially poor are children. Of course in British society we expect children to be cared for by their parents, and thus the assumption is made that children are only poor if their parents are poor. Even if parents do largely care for their children, however, they still need the resources to be able to do this, and the lower their income, and the larger the number of children this must support, the greater the risk of poverty. This means that families with children need more resources than those without in order to avoid poverty, an aspect of the problem of poverty which will be discussed in more detail in Chapter 6. And where parents find it difficult to maintain a high income then the risk of poverty for children will be higher. This is particularly a problem for lone parents who find paid employment more difficult to secure because of the lack of childcare facilities which might free them for paid work. Thus, not surprisingly, as Millar (1989a) for instance discusses, lone parents are disproportionately represented amongst the poor.

The problem of poverty for children in families, as might be expected, has been a particular concern of the CPAG. They have consistently argued that the lack of general support for childcare costs means that families with children are more likely to be poor. For instance Oppenheim (1990, p. 30) reveals that in 1987 the proportion of couples with children in poverty was twice that (20 per cent) of those without (10 per cent) – for single parents the proportion was 47 per cent. As a result of this children are more likely than the rest of the population to be poor. Again in 1987, whilst 19 per cent of the population generally were poor, 26 per cent of children were poor (Oppenheim, 1990, p. 31).

The correlation between children and poverty is an important one. It demonstrates that because of their dependence on their parents and the consequent pressure this puts upon the parents' ability to provide an adequate income, children disproportionately suffer poverty. Of course their childhood is not the cause of their poverty, it is the social circumstances in which children are, or are not, provided for which can cause it. Children are merely the victims.

This is also true of other groups disproportionately likely to experience poverty, such as the elderly or the sick and disabled. Being old or ill is not a cause of poverty either. Nor of course is being unemployed or in receipt of low wages; but for these groups the causal link between social circumstances and experience of poverty is frequently made in ideologies of poverty. As discussed above, unemployment is seen as a cause of poverty because it is associated with individuals who are seen as idle and unwilling to work or provide for themselves. However unemployment is no more a cause of poverty than is childhood, it is merely that given certain social and economic circumstances those who are unemployed are likely to be poor. It is a correlation or a coincidence, not a cause. And this is demonstrated by the fact that not all who are unemployed are poor. Those with capital wealth, pools winners, members of the aristocracy or ex-managers with 'golden handshakes' may be unemployed, but they are not poor.

The confusing of the circumstances of the poor with the causes of poverty is widespread and important. Oppenheim includes in her book a chapter on the causes of poverty, which focuses on unemployment, childhood, sickness and old age; and this confusion is a feature of the individualisation of poverty referred to above; which, in blaming the victims, ignores the fact that who becomes or remains poor is a consequence of structural social forces. What causes poverty therefore is not individuals finding themselves or placing themselves in particular circumstances, but the reasons why those circumstances result in their receiving resources that are inadequate for their needs. It is this relationship which we need to understand if we are to understand the causes of poverty, and attempts to explain this have been as controversial as the attempts to define and measure poverty itself.

The Causes of Poverty

Poverty is not therefore merely the product of individual weakness or failure. Rather, it is the result of social forces – classes and groups and agencies and institutions which operate to reproduce a particular social order in which some are poor. This point is taken up in a book by Ferge and Millar (1987) that includes studies of poverty in a range of different countries in both Western and, the then socialist, Eastern Europe. The authors argue that policies which focus on particular groups of poor people ignore this structural context and process, which they call in the title of the book the 'dynamics of deprivation'.

However Ferge and Millar are aware that this structural context is not a static or unchangeable phenomenon. Indeed their point is that it is a dynamic process which constantly creates and recreates social conditions such as poverty. It is constantly changing, and can be changed, and thus its outcomes too can be transformed. And a recognition of the importance of this dynamic process directs attention away from a focus on poverty and the poor towards the broader social contexts and forces within which they are reproduced.

Thus, the argument runs, social forces produce poverty and therefore in order to understand the causes of poverty we must understand social forces and how they operate to produce it. As Holman discusses in his 1978 study of the explanations of poverty, however, there is disagreement over how social forces operate to produce poverty, and a range of different models of explanation can be derived from amongst the various accounts.

The first category that Holman refers to is 'individuals and poverty'. This includes the pathological explanations of indolence and feckless-ness discussed above. It also includes *genetic* explanations which seek to relate social status with supposedly inherited characteristics such as intelligence, and *psychological* approaches which explain individuals' (non)achievements by reference to acquired or developed personality traits. These are potential explanations of poverty and they do include a dynamic, albeit a largely immutable one deriving from nature rather than nurture. Effectively they reject social or structural explanations in favour of individual ones, and thus they can readily be translated into approaches which seek to blame the victims for their own poverty. Proponents would argue, however, that genetic or psychological approaches do not imply individual blame, they merely establish causal links. But critics who adopt more social, or sociological, explanations question whether the evidence to support those links has been satisfactorily established since, as Holman (1978) discusses, most of those who appear to inherit characteristics associated with poverty do not become poor.

A second category of explanations which also have been interpreted by critics as a case of blaming the victims are those which focus on the family or the community as the cause of poverty. One famous proponent of such approaches, one time Conservative Social Services Minister Keith Joseph (1972), referred to them as including a 'cycle of deprivation' in which the inadequate parenting, lowered aspirations and disadvantaged environment of families and communities became internalised as part of the values of some children as they grew up. Thus when these children themselves reached adulthood their expect-ations, and their abilities, were lowered and they more readily expected, and accepted, the poverty and deprivation of their parents and acquaintances. More sophisticated versions of such an approach have described the families and communities as developing a 'culture of poverty' through which, understandably, people learn to cope with their deprivation; but also, unfortunately, come to accept it (Lewis, 1968).

This is a controversial notion, as will be discussed in Chapter 12, and yet it has been very influential in the development of state antipoverty initiatives 'targeting' resources onto poor families and communities in order to educate or encourage them out of their poverty. This will be examined in more detail in Chapter 15. It is worth noting here, however, that although avoiding ascribing poverty to individuals such explanations still contain a pathological model of poverty creation and recreation. It is the poor themselves who produce and reproduce their poverty, only here collectively through the culture of the family and the community. This does not explain the broader circumstances in which families and communities are situated, nor how they come to be poor in the first place. Nor does it explain how some individuals and families manage to escape the culture and avoid poverty; and yet, as a number of research studies have demonstrated, most children of poor homes do not repeat that poverty, and most of those who are poor have not acquired their poverty from their families or communities (Brown and Madge, 1982).

In modern welfare capitalist countries state policies have been developed to combat or reduce poverty. If, therefore, despite these policies poverty persists then perhaps explanations should look not to the failings of the poor but to the failings of the antipoverty policies and to the agencies and institutions responsible for making them work. If the poor are the victims then the blame must lie elsewhere; agency failure approaches direct it towards those who are supposedly charged with eliminating poverty.

In particular of course this means the social security system, and there are many who have pointed to the failings of social security in relieving poverty (see Alcock, 1987; MacGregor, 1981; Donnison, 1982). For instance many claimants do not receive the benefits to which they are entitled. Benefit publicity is poor and benefit agencies are often hostile and apparently suspicious of the rights of potential claimants. Complex rules on entitlement exclude some in need and even those who do receive benefit may not receive sufficient to meet their needs as they, or others, define them.

Social security policy will be looked at in more detail in Chapter 14; however it is not the only area of policy implementation which may be accused of contributing to the reproduction of poverty. Housing policies, both in the public and private sectors, have obviously failed those poor people who are homeless. Health policies, or the lack of them, may have resulted in sickness and disability leading to poverty. Social services may have failed to assist with, or may even have added to, the problems which have brought individuals and families into poverty. Indeed all agencies, be they state, voluntary or those in the private sector, who provide the range of social services within the welfare state may be accused of failing in their tasks as long as poverty persists amongst their clients, or potential clients.

This may be the fault of those individual officers within these agencies who are experiencing low morale or are falling down on their jobs, or it may be the fault of the structures and operational practices of agencies, which make them unable to achieve success whatever their workers may do. However it may also be the fault of the policies with which the agencies have been charged; or, as some have argued (see Novak, 1984), perhaps a misconception of what such policies are seeking to achieve. Social security systems, for instance, are concerned with controlling and disciplining the poor as well as, or perhaps even rather than, removing their poverty. This is a matter of policy, however, and not merely institutional practice.

A focus on such policy failure, or the failure to develop appropriate policy, is an approach to explaining the dynamics of poverty which moves beyond the level of individuals, communities or agencies – or rather moves to the level of those individuals and agencies who, through political action, claim to be prepared and able to influence social policies and social structures. As MacGregor (1981) argues, policies are the product of political decisions and, as we have discussed, poverty is a political concept. The identification of poverty is linked to political action to eliminate it; thus if poverty remains then politicians have failed either to identify it accurately or to develop appropriate policies in response to it. In such an approach therefore, poverty is the result of political failure, or the failure of political will.

Of course not all politicians would admit that they had failed to eliminate poverty. Indeed as we have seen members of the Conservative governments of the 1980s were outspoken in their claims that poverty, as they defined it, had been eliminated through the policies developed and implemented by previous governments. What this reveals, as we know however, is that political debates about poverty policy cannot be separated from debates about the problem of poverty itself. But this does not negate the value of approaches which seek to explain the causes of poverty within the dynamics of political decision making. Indeed quite the reverse is true.

Who takes political decisions and how their decisions are put into practice are obviously going to be crucial factors in determining the circumstances of people living within that political system, including the poor. There is a powerful logic to the argument that we need look no further than politics and politicians to find the causes of poverty – they run the country, they are responsible for the problems within it.

Sociologists have for long pointed out, however, that no matter how powerful politicians may seem, or may even believe themselves to be, they do not control all aspects of the societies they claim to run. Indeed over many events, both of a day-to-day nature and of major socio-structural importance, politicians have little or no control. Politicians may be prepared to *accept* the blame for the continued existence of poverty but it is far from clear that they are entirely responsible for it.

One of the major reasons why politicians cannot control all aspects of society, or certainly all aspects of welfare capitalist societies like Britain, is the fact that many of the social events in them are the product of economic forces or economic decisions which politicians do not control. Most politicians claim that their aim is to manage the economy, though it is an aim which they would probably readily admit they can at best only partly achieve; and even that partial achievement may depend to a large extent on what they, or we, mean by 'manage'.

Given the structure and operation of a largely market-based economy, within an international market system of growing significance and influence national politicians cannot act freely and cannot change or influence all economic forces. The vagaries of national and international forces therefore can affect people in ways which politicians cannot control. They can create poverty which politicians may have intended or hoped to avoid, and they can reduce poverty without direct political action being taken.

This is obviously the case with the poverty associated with the high levels of unemployment resulting from international economic recession in the 1930s, 1970s and 1980s. And conversely it was also the case for the relatively low levels of poverty associated with periods of boom such as the 1950s. It is not just unemployment which results from economic downturn, however. It is also a cause of lower wages, leading to poverty; of earlier retirement and lower pensions; and perhaps more importantly of pressure to cut public spending on benefits resulting in less state support for the non-employed and employed poor.

Changes in national and international economic forces can, and do, therefore cause poverty. This may suggest a kind of fatalism which assumes that as there is nothing even politicians can do about this, then we must unhappily simply 'grin and bear it' and hope for better times ahead. Recognition of the importance of economic forces does not necessarily imply fatalism however. Economic forces are largely the products of decisions taken by people, and the consequences of these decisions are to a very large extent predictable. And they can, or could, be changed. Indeed they can be changed as a result of pressure from politicians. The point to understand is not that politicians cannot control economic forces, but rather that they *must* seek to control economic forces if they wish to influence the events which economic forces largely determine. Policy responses which merely focus on the consequences of economic forces therefore will, and do, fail; but policies which seek to prevent these consequences by seeking to influence economic forces ultimately can, and will, succeed – a point which will be returned to in the final chapter.

As was suggested in Chapter 1, there are some who argue that the interaction of political will and economic forces cannot solve the problem of poverty because it is this which is its cause. This is the

essence of Novak's (1988) argument. Poverty is
operation of a capitalist wage labour market
labour market needs poverty, or rather poor people ex
fringes of it, to operate efficiently. Fear of poverty acts as a discip.
force on workers and provides evidence that just as hard work and
obedience will bring its rewards, so will idleness or inactivity lead to
punishment. Much the same sort of approach concludes Holman's
(1978) review of explanations of poverty. He refers to it as a structural
explanation in which poverty is merely the converse of wealth within a
stratified society; if we accept the one then really we must also be
prepared to accept the other.

The danger with such structural approaches, however, is that they
can tend to be little more than statements of the obvious. Poverty is the
product of an unequal or capitalist society; therefore only if we change
the society will poverty cease to exist. As an explanation this tells us
everything and nothing, and as a programme for action it is hopelessly
unrealistic. Of course it is the socio-economic structure, and the
political process that reproduces this, which causes poverty. But it is
a complex and ever-changing structure and it is far from immutable.
The structure can be changed, and in particular aspects of it can be
reformed or restructured. The structure of society includes the political
actors, the institutions and agencies, and the families and communities
of other explanatory models. All are in part responsible for the
circumstances in which individuals currently find themselves, and all
can change or be changed in ways which will the alter those
circumstances and the prospects of those individuals.

The search for the cause of poverty cannot therefore be confined
within one or other of these frameworks, it must encompass the
interaction of them all. At the same time therefore the solution to the
problem must involve action and change at a number of different levels
within society. However the action that is taken depends upon who is in
a position of power to act, and how they perceive the problem and its
solution. In practice therefore what is done depends upon the political
ideologies of those in power, and it is to these political ideologies that
we will turn finally in this overview of the dynamics of poverty.

The Politics of Poverty

Understanding different political responses to poverty would ideally
involve an investigation and review of political theories in general and

differing political approaches to welfare in particular. It is not possible in a book on poverty to undertake such an investigation, and to attempt to do so would divert us too far from the primary task of surveying differing approaches towards explaining the dynamics of poverty. What must be recognised, however, is that political approaches to welfare and poverty do differ, and that these differences are situated within broader political theories which offer quite different and competing accounts of both the problems of and the solutions to socio-structural issues. Here, however, we do not have the room to do more than break them down into four broad frameworks, summarising the major assumptions in each and bearing in mind that there are also significant differences of opinion within each and significant overlaps across all the borderlines. The four are neo-liberalism, conservativism, social democracy and revolutionary socialism.

Neo-liberalism has in recent years been associated with the writings of the 'new right' on welfare (see Levitas, 1986), as will be discussed in Chapter 13, and to some extent with the policies of the Thatcher governments of the 1980s (see Gamble, 1989; Johnson, 1990), although in practice neo-liberal thinking has remained a significant, if less prominent, strand in political theory throughout the twentieth century and was presented in the 1940s as a criticism of the postwar welfare state (Hayek, 1944). In general the view of the neo-liberals is that state action should be kept to a minimum in order to avoid interfering with the operation of the market within the economy, and in particular that the state should not meddle in social affairs but rather should leave individuals and families to provide for themselves as and how they wish. Thus their belief is that rather than helping to solve the problem of poverty, state intervention has only made it worse, in particular by encouraging dependency and undermining self-sufficiency.

This argument was outlined in a short and pithy article by the Thatcherite minister, Rhodes Boyson in 1971, and it was later pursued in more depth by the American political scientist Murray (1984). Both argue that the state should not interfere with the dynamics of poverty, and that logically therefore all state support for the poor should be withdrawn. However this extreme position has never been seriously pursued by governments in Britain, including the Thatcher governments of the 1980s, as new right theorists themselves readily concede (Anderson, 1991). Nor has it been pursued in other developed capitalist countries. Of course lack of state antipoverty measures is not uncommon in some developing countries, although this is not generally the product of neo-liberal political theory, and it has not resulted in the absence of poverty. As a recipe for structural change to combat poverty therefore, neo-liberalism is a relatively simple one – reduced state support. What this might achieve however is a more debateable issue.

Conservatism is a loose term used to cover a fairly wide range of political approaches, from those of Conservative governments in Britain, including for the most part the Thatcher governments of the 1980s, to those of European Christian Democrat governments, such as in Germany, Belgium, Denmark and the Netherlands in the 1980s and in France prior to the Mitterrand era. Supporters of Conservatism do believe in the need for state intervention, in particular in matters of social policy, in order to ameliorate or even counteract the problems arising in a predominantly market-based economy. In the case of poverty this means a recognition that it is, at least potentially, a problem requiring state action. However conservatives generally do not wish to see state action interfering too much with the operation of the market economy, especially the labour market, and in particular they do not want social policy to become an expensive drain on public expenditure.

In general therefore conservatives have tended to operate with what is sometimes called a 'casualty' approach towards poverty. The poor are the casualties of the market and their symptoms of suffering must be relieved by the state. This is referred to as 'relieving', rather than 'preventing' poverty, and it leads to measures to target state support upon those individuals or communities who are positively identified as poor. Commentators have called these 'selective' approaches to poverty relief, and contrasted them with the 'universal' approaches preferred by social democrats (see MacGregor, 1981, Ch. 5). And, as will be discussed in Chapter 16, they lead to rather different conceptions of the role of state policy in combating poverty.

Conservatism has been a powerful force in British politics throughout the twentieth century, and especially in the 1980s and early 1990s. And as a result, as we shall see, selectivism has come to dominate the politics of poverty in Britain. This has not been without its problems however – nor its contradictions. For in Britain in particular selectivism has had to compete with universalism within the field of welfare politics, as conservatism has competed with social democracy.

Social democrats include, by and large, the Labour Party in Britain and some of the Liberal Democratic Party. The governments of Scandinavian countries such as Sweden and Norway have also been social democratic ones throughout most of the postwar period. Perhaps the major difference, both in broad political terms and in the field of welfare politics, between social democrats and conservatives is that whereas conservatives operate with a minimal model of social policy when dealing with the casualties of the market economy, social democrats seek to intervene, or interfere, in the market economy in order to prevent the problems occurring in the first place. Thus for them social policy objectives should be related to economic policy measures, a point which will be returned to in Chapter 16.

In the case of poverty this means intervention in the labour market to reduce unemployment and to improve pay and conditions through minimum wages and support for child care, and the provision of comprehensive benefits through social security for those outside the labour market and for additional costs related to such things as child care or disability. Social democrats generally believe in providing benefits on a universal basis to all those who satisfy certain conditions, without imposing a test to determine whether they are poor. However they do generally expect that those able to take employment in the labour market do so; and they may provide both positive incentives, such as state-supported training schemes, and negative incentives, such as availability for work tests as a condition of receiving benefits, in order to encourage them to do so.

Revolutionary socialists, as the name suggests, believe in the revolutionary transformation of capitalist society into socialist society, arguing that this will remove the poverty which in capitalist society results from the operation of a punitive labour market. The failure of the socialist countries of the Eastern Bloc, which became internationally apparent in the 1990s, has significantly undermined the appeal of socialism as a solution to the problem of poverty in capitalist societies, but it has not entirely undermined the revolutionary case. Many argue that these were not in any event proper socialist countries, in particular because they did not pursue collective policies to achieve egalitarian aims but merely reproduced inequalites through state appropriation of wealth and influence.

Crucial to the socialist case is the removal of the capitalist labour market, which they identify as the cause of poverty through unemployment and low pay, and the replacement of this with a system of state-provided support for all, together with a confiscation and redistribution of the wealth of the rich. Although this may seem a distant, even a Utopian, goal there are some who argue that the consistently high levels of unemployment in capitalist countries in the latter part of the twentieth century and the increasingly obvious environmental costs of uncontrolled growth in profit-oriented production, mean that the alternative of a nonproductive, nonmarket social order is becoming ever more attractive (Gorz, 1982 and 1991). And a distribution of basic resources to all, irrespective of labour market position, is now supported by a wider range of opinion than revolutionary socialism alone (see Van Parijs, 1992). Thus whilst revolutionary socialism would still require a radical transformation of the social and economic structure of existing welfare capitalist countries, its vision of a society in which the distribution of resources did not depend primarily upon the labour market is perhaps no longer such a distant prospect.

As we can see, however, the problem with such broad summaries of these different approaches is that they are really only caricatures of a wide range of complex and contradictory political theories and arguments, which in practice frequently overlap and merge. Thus the views of many fit only uncomfortably into one category or another. For our purposes here, however, they do provide a brief guide to the major differences within the approaches to social reform propounded by political theorists and political actors, and they provide a guide to the framework within which political action on the dynamics of poverty is likely to be discussed, and implemented. Part IV of this book will look at the major policies that have been developed to respond to poverty in Britain in the latter part of the twentieth century and assess how successful the differing approaches have thus far been in tackling those dynamics.

3

Poverty in Europe and Beyond

International Comparisons

Although most discussion of the problem of poverty, and certainly most research into it, takes place within national boundaries, poverty is of course an international, or rather a global, problem. There are gross inequalities in the resources available to peoples in different parts of the world and within all countries, and this results in deprivation within relatively affluent countries and in severe deprivation in some less affluent ones when compared with wider international standards. We live in a profoundly unequal world in which the extreme poverty that leads to starvation and early death is unfortunately still quite common.

Such international inequity and extreme poverty are not new phenomena; but the increasing development of international contact through international agencies and international trade are making it an ever more immediate problem for a wider community of nations. And the increasing scope and depth of the communications media are bringing more knowledge of the problem into the homes, and the consciousness, of ever more people. Poverty is thus now an international problem, and politicians and academics are increasingly beginning to realise, and to argue, this (see George, 1988).

Recognition of the international dimension of the problem of poverty, however, brings with it problems of definition and analysis extending beyond the issues which have dominated national debate and research in countries like Britain. As discussed in this book, the problem of understanding poverty in a country such as Britain involves appraising a complex range of debates and assessing confusing, and sometimes seemingly contradictory, evidence. To develop this understanding into an international scale requires an extension and expansion of both theoretical definition and empirical measurement. This is an important development; but it is one which cannot be given adequate attention here. This is primarily a book about poverty in Britain, not about poverty in the world; and whilst it is essential to recognise the wider international context of the problem it is not possible to do justice to the broader issues involved within the confines of a text such as this.

However, because of the increasing importance of international contacts and international cooperation, it is no longer possible to understand poverty in Britain without some understanding of the international context within which British inequality and deprivation is situated, and of the growth of international initiatives in antipoverty policy and antipoverty strategies. In Britain in the 1990s this international context includes in particular the European Community (EC), of which Britain is a member state. Study and debate on poverty within Europe is now well established and EC initiatives to challenge poverty within member states are a significant feature of antipoverty policy. As will be discussed below therefore, the European context of British poverty and antipoverty policy is likely to be of increasing importance in any understanding of the problem and the responses to it.

International comparisons in the study of poverty are therefore increasingly relevant, even though they are inevitably fraught with difficulties. In a survey of poverty rates in a range of OECD countries, Atkinson (1990b) points out that comparisons must take account of the problems of comparability of data across national boundaries, for surveys carried out either independently or by national governments do not use the same bases for definition or measurement in different countries. This is of course a serious methodological and analytical problem, and Atkinson discusses four of the major problems involved in a little more detail. These are the use of different indicators of poverty, the application of different poverty lines to income or expenditure distributions, the adoption of different units, families or households, for measurement, and the choice of different equivalence scales to compare the resources available within units. These present problems in the analysis and comparison of data from research studies within one country; such problems are magnified several times when analysis or comparison seeks to transcend national boundaries.

Nevertheless, as mentioned in Chapter 1, the new Luxembourg Income Study (LIS) does provide an international data base on poverty in a wide range of advanced industrial countries in the EC and beyond. Significant effort has been made within the study to overcome, or at least to recognise, some of the problems of the comparability of data across countries, and within the limits of this the LIS permits academics and politicians in participating countries to contrast levels and distribution of poverty between different nations and assess over time the impact of differing antipoverty policies in differing social contexts, as Mitchell (1991) has demonstrated. This will affect the understanding of the problem of poverty in Britain, and it will surely affect the development of antipoverty policy too. In the 1990s the international, and in particular the European, dimension of British poverty policy is likely to be of more significance than it has ever been in the past.

Poverty in Europe

Despite the existence of wide cultural and political differences, which have often divided Europe over the last hundred years and beyond, the economic and social development of most Western European countries has followed a pattern which provides for closer comparison, and cooperation, than exists between many other groups of countries throughout the world. And since the collapse of Eastern Bloc communism in the late 1980s this pattern is likely to be imported in some form to many Eastern European countries over the 1990s. Thus the growth of capitalism and industrialisation, the development of political democracy and the establishment of welfare states have produced within European countries patterns of poverty and poverty policy which permit a relatively easy comparison between trends and achievements to be made.

The relative homogeneity of Western European socioeconomic structures has been consolidated considerably since the end of the Second World War by the economic and social unity provided by the EC. Initially covering six countries – France, Italy, West Germany, Belgium, the Netherlands and Luxembourg – the EC has expanded to cover twelve countries comprising most of Western Europe, the exceptions being Scandinavia, Switzerland and Austria. As will be briefly discussed, the EC has expanded from being a predominantly economic and trading partnership to become a focus for joint economic and social planning across a wide spectrum of financial and welfare issues, and it is heading towards greater economic and political unity in the 1990s.

In the EC in particular therefore, it is possible to identify common problems of poverty and inequality and common strategies for responding to this, and these can be compared between different nation states with some degree of complementarity. All countries have experienced the impact of industrialisation and the creation of labour markets, although in some countries the size of the agricultural sector of the economy has remained large compared with others. This has resulted in similar patterns to those in Britain of wage poverty and poverty resulting from unemployment, and also in similar family structures in which the impact of this poverty is experienced differently by men and women at different stages of their life cycle. As we shall see therefore statistical comparisons between countries reveal similar patterns of poverty, even though the extent and depth of it varies.

The development of welfare state regimes in all Western European countries has also resulted in a range of similar policies for preventing or relieving poverty. The notion of welfare state regimes has been discussed by Esping Andersen (1990) as a means of contrasting the similarities and differences in the structure of welfare provision in different countries. Drawing on this Liebfried (1991) identifies four models of welfare state regime within Western Europe: the rudimentary (catholic) welfare state associated with the Latin Rim countries, the institutional (corporatist) welfare state associated with Germany, the residual (liberal) welfare state associated with Britain, and the modern (social democratic) welfare state associated with the Scandinavian countries. Mitchell (1991) uses different models of welfare state regimes to contrast income transfer policies across ten welfare states.

Of course these regimes are ideal types, summaries of features which are not replicated precisely in individual countries, for instance Britain does not have an exclusively residual welfare state. But they do represent approaches to social policy which provide for comparison between similar policy development in different countries. This is particularly true of the original six EC nations, which all developed versions of corporatist welfare states with very similar social security and other antipoverty measures based on employment-related insurance benefits with a range of limited safety net measures for those not covered by the major scheme. And, as will be discussed below, the development of EC policy and planning has led to increasing pressures for coordination and harmonisation of social security and antipoverty policy between member states, and these are likely to lead to further convergence of policies in the future.

Despite the similarities in the development of welfare regimes, there are rather different traditions of poverty debate and poverty research in different European countries. As George and Lawson (1980) and R. Walker *et al.* (1984) discuss, in the past this has made direct comparisons between countries difficult, even where overall developments reveal similar trends. Obviously the Luxembourg Income Study

The Context of Poverty

will help to overcome some of these differences in the future. Already, however, the work of the EC, and in particular the central statistical department, Eurostat, has done much to develop a crossnational basis for comparisons of poverty and inequality within EC countries, as can be seen in the papers presented to the EC poverty statistics seminar in 1989 (Teekens and Van Praag, 1990).

In order to provide an empirical basis against which both national and community-wide antipoverty strategies can be assessed, Eurostat has attempted to produce measurements of poverty in EC member states which can be compared across national boundaries and over time (see EC 1991; Atkinson, 1991a). Eurostat's most widely used poverty measure is those below 50 per cent of national average income. This permits crossnational comparisons to be made, whilst recognising the overall differences in standards of living between countries. To make a community-wide comparison between countries of course it would be necessary to adopt a community-wide measure, such as 50 per cent of average income throughout the EC. This would give a rather different distribution of the proportion of Europe's poor in each of the member countries, accentuating the impact of the lower standards of some of the poorer countries.

Figure 3.1 is based upon 1985 information and reveals that, based on a community-wide measure, a larger proportion of poor live in countries such as Italy, Spain and Greece, and a smaller proportion in Germany, France and Britain. This is because the EC poverty line of 50 per cent average income is equivalent to two-thirds of the national average in a country like Spain (Atkinson, 1990b, p. 12). If the German national average were to be applied in Spain then this would create an even higher line, pushing the majority of people in Spain into poverty, by German standards.

These comparisons are made on relative measures. The EC has also been investigating the possibility of developing absolute measures of poverty for the purposes of international comparison. The aim is to determine a European baseline level of living (EBL) using a measure of basic needs – European baseline needs (EBN). Although this is in principle an absolute measure, it is accepted that elements of relativity will need to be built into it to allow for gradual improvement over time as living standards rise (see EC, 1989).

Eurostat have also compared levels of poverty in European countries over time and looked at the impact of poverty on different sections of the population in different countries. These figures show an increase in

FIGURE 3.1 *The distribution of poverty in Europe*

(a) The distribution using national poverty lines

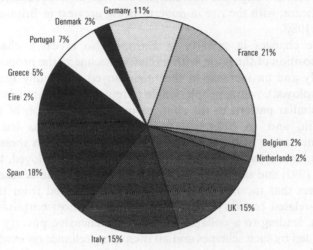

Germany 11%
Denmark 2%
Portugal 7%
Greece 5%
Eire 2%
France 21%
Belgium 2%
Netherlands 2%
Spain 18%
UK 15%
Italy 15%

(b) The distribution using community-wide poverty line

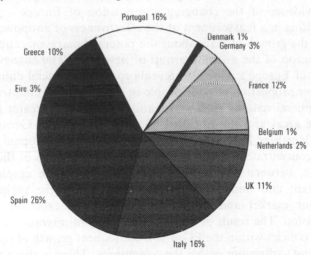

Portugal 16%
Denmark 1%
Germany 3%
Greece 10%
Eire 3%
France 12%
Belgium 1%
Netherlands 2%
Spain 26%
UK 11%
Italy 16%

Note: Luxembourg is not shown separately.
Source: Atkinson, 1991a, p. 16.

the numbers in poverty in Europe between 1975 and 1985 from 44 to 50 million (EC, 1991, p. 3) associated with the impact of economic recession, although the fluctuations between different countries is quite significant, with the rise in poverty being greatest in Britain, especially after 1980.

The changes in poverty in Europe also reveal a change in the composition of the poor, with a relative decline in the proportion of the elderly and an increase in the unemployed (especially the long-term unemployed), young people, single parents and migrant labourers. This is a similar pattern to the changes in the composition of the poor in Britain, and, as discussed in Chapter 2, this has led European commentators to begin to draw distinctions between these groups of *new poor* and the elderly, sick and short-term unemployed, the *old poor* (EC, 1991; and see Room *et al.*, 1989). This problem is accentuated by the fact that the new poor are generally excluded from the employment-related benefit protection provided by most corporatist welfare states, leading to a collapse in the comprehensive poverty prevention provided by such schemes and an increasing reliance on inadequate and loosely structured assistance measures. In Germany for instance the proportion of unemployed people receiving insurance protection fell from 66 per cent in 1975 to 38 in 1984 (EC, 1991, p. 10).

Evidence of the changing composition of Europe's poor is thus resulting in a reassessment of the effectiveness of antipoverty measures and the growth of fears about the potential marginalisation and social exclusion of the growing group of new poor. The changing composition of Europe's poor also reveals spacial and racial dimensions. The higher proportion of poor people in the Latin Rim countries and other peripheral nations such as Ireland is creating a greater gap between these areas and the so-called 'Golden Triangle' of Germany, France and Northern Italy, where industrial growth and well-paid employment are concentrated. A gap is also being created, even in these wealthier areas, between the indigenous labour in secure employment and migrant and immigrant labour, who are on the periphery of the labour market and subject to poverty and exclusion in times of recession. The result of this is a tightening of migration and immigration policies within the EC, and a consequent growth of racist attitudes leading to divisions within the community. There is also a more general fear of what is referred to as 'social dumping', the drift of mobile capital around the community in search of low labour costs in poor areas, and the consequent fear of overall reductions in standards of wages and conditions in the longer term.

As will be discussed below, policy debate and development within the EC is increasingly beginning to focus on the broader trends in the redistribution of wealth and deprivation throughout the community which have been revealed by the improved availability of international comparisons of the experience of poverty. And a general overview of developments in poverty and deprivation throughout the EC is now regularly provided by the recently established EC Observatory on National Policies to Combat Social Exclusion, a term which has been adopted to encourage a wider focus on the problem of poverty as exclusion from social citizenship rights (Room *et al.*, 1991).

European Anti-Poverty Policy

The EC started out primarily as an economic union, indeed it was known initially as the European Economic Community, concerned with the development and the regulation of trade rather than with the determination of economic or social policies within or across member states. Although this primary economic focus has remained of fundamental importance, the EC has become more and more concerned in the latter part of the twentieth century with attempts to intervene in national policy planning to develop community-wide initiatives to which all member states must subscribe. In the 1990s, following the establishment of the single European market in 1992, the aim of the majority of member states is to take such interventionist strategies further in moves towards the forging of greater political union within the EC (see Grahl and Teague, 1990).

This growing concern with social and economic policy planning has been reflected in particular in a range of community initiatives which have sought to respond to the problems of poverty within the EC both directly and indirectly. Although sometimes rather small-scale and limited in their scope and effect, these initiatives have been important in providing new, crossnational approaches towards the relief or prevention of poverty, which are likely to be of increasing significance in all member states as intervention develops in the 1990s.

In general terms social policy planning in the EC has passed through three broad phases (see Brewster and Teague, 1989). Phase I, from 1957–72, was primarily concerned with market development and in particular with the promotion and regulation of labour mobility between EC countries. Phase II, from 1973–83, was primarily concerned with the harmonisation and upgrading of employment practices and in particular the promotion of equal pay and equal treatment between men and women within the community. Phase III, from 1983 onwards, has been concerned with attempts to be more proactive in the establishment of community-wide standards for citizens', or workers', rights through the development of social policy norms, called *L'Espace Sociale* by the EC president, Jacques Delors, and encapsulated in the EC's Social Charter, to which we shall return shortly. As can be seen, the three phases reveal a greater and greater emphasis on interventionist planning, and this is represented in a range of more specific initiatives undertaken under various EC organisations.

One area of specific initiatives which have been important in responding to some aspects of deprivation and growing poverty within the EC is the distribution of EC structural funds. These are EC budgets used to provide support for particular initiatives within member states coming under the broad aegis of the fund. There are three major structural funds: the European Social Fund (ESF), the European Regional Development Fund (ERDF) and the European Agricultural Guidance and Guarantee Fund (FEOGA) (see Teague, 1989). The latter has been used to support rural development schemes such as promoting cottage industries and training displaced farm workers. The ERDF has mainly been used to improve the infrastructure of poorer regions in EC countries, in particular those affected by industrial decline and underinvestment.

It is the ESF which has been most important in terms of more direct antipoverty strategy. Initially its scope and size were limited and it was used mainly to subsidise small-scale project work and to facilitate labour mobility by promoting the formalisation of bilateral agreements between countries to guarantee social security rights for workers from other EC countries. After the early 1970s and the onset of economic recession, however, the operation and direction of the fund were shifted onto a more interventionist footing, in particular in helping member states to combat unemployment by providing support for job creation and training schemes, especially in regions experiencing industrial or agricultural decline. The size of the ESF budget also grew dramatically between the 1970s and 1980s, although after this growth it still only represented about 6 per cent of the community's total budget, and generally the fund would only meet 50 per cent of the cost of individual initiatives or projects. The scope of ESF activities should not therefore be overestimated – even though Britain did relatively well in terms of ESF support in the 1980s this money represented not much more than

10 per cent of the total spent on similar schemes by the government through the MSC (Teague, 1989, p. 48).

In addition to the more general initiatives arising from the operation of the structural funds there have been a series of specific initiatives designed to tackle directly the problem of poverty within the EC, generally referred to as the three EC poverty programmes. These have all been very small-scale initiatives, the third programme being the largest with a budget of 55 million ECUs (£38 million) over five years, less than the annual budget of a large social services department or a university. Nevertheless they have been important symbolically in providing an example of community-wide action to combat poverty, and they have resulted in the development of some interesting new initiatives in project-based antipoverty strategy.

The first poverty programme ran from 1975–80 and comprised a small number of pilot schemes and studies in community development. After these were completed there were no further projects for a period of four years of 'evaluation and reflection' (EC, 1991, p. 15). Then a second programme was established to run for five years, from 1984–9, with a budget of 29 million ECUs. The second programme included 91 local action research projects throughout the twelve member states aiming to build on the actual experience of local antipoverty work, with the results coordinated in academic institutions in Bath and Louvain. This work was supplemented by statistical and attitudinal research carried out on a community-wide basis by Eurostat and the EC survey agency Eurobarometer. The statistical findings have been referred to above (see EC, 1991). The findings of the attitudinal survey, which repeated a similar survey carried out in 1976, revealed that fewer people in the 1980s thought that poverty was the result of laziness or lack of willpower on the part of the poor, and that increased numbers thought that the measures to combat poverty taken by public authorities were insufficient (EC, 1990).

The third poverty programme followed directly on from the second and is planned to run for the five years from 1989–94. The broad aim of the programme is to foster the economic and social integration of the least privileged groups, echoing concerns about marginalisation and social exclusion. This is to be achieved by working *with* poor people in action research projects based on partnership principles. There are 39 projects across the twelve member states, those in Britain being based in Belfast, Bristol, Edinburgh and Liverpool and coordinated by a unit at Warwick University. There is also more general research and evaluation work being carried out through the EC Observatory on Social Exclusion.

As has been said, the poverty programmes are very small-scale initiatives. By targeting limited resources onto a few local areas they can do little to combat the broader problems of poverty within the community, a problem with antipoverty policy which will be discussed in more detail in Chapter 15. However what the action research projects do provide are examples of initiatives to combat poverty and ways of working in partnership with poor people which could be utilised to develop more comprehensive strategies in the future, either at national or community level. Certainly no more than this can be expected of such limited activities in the face of such a major problem.

The increasing focus of the poverty programmes on the problems of marginalisation and social exclusion reflect the increasing awareness of the problem of the so-called 'new poverty' within the EC, and the fears that disparities between core and peripheral workers and regions will lead to growing divisions and to an overall decline in standards resulting from 'social dumping'. These fears extend into the major policy-making bodies within the community and provide an important backdrop to Delors' *L'Espace Sociale* initiative and to the development in the late 1980s and early 1990s of the Social Charter.

The Community Charter of Fundamental Social Rights for Workers, to give it its full title, was developed by the Commission in the 1980s to provide a framework for primarily employment-based rights to be adopted by all member countries in order to guarantee minimum standards across the community. There was hostility to the imposition of such minimum standards from some countries, notably Britain, and as a result of this the original proposals were watered down somewhat in the final version endorsed at the Maastricht Summit in 1991 – although even this was too much for Britain who insisted on reserving the right to opt out of the Charter when it was finally introduced.

The focus on employment-based rights is symbolised in the use of the term workers rather than citizens, and reflects the continuing dominance of economic and labour market concerns within EC social policy planning. However it also reflects a European tendency to identify employment and adequate wage levels as the major means of combating poverty within labour market economies. This is revealed in its most positive form in the aim of extending minimum wage guarantees throughout the community. Statutory minimum wages have existed for some time in countries such as France, the Netherlands and Luxembourg. More recently they have been developed in others, and it is Labour Party policy to introduce them in Britain. Together with measures to create jobs and provide training, especially for the long-term unemployed, minimum wages are seen in Europe as the major means of preventing poverty; and, coupled with employment-based insurance schemes for social security protection, these measures are likely to continue to provide the basis for antipoverty policy planning into the 1990s, despite the growing recognition of the problem of 'new poverty'.

The other important development in EC antipoverty policy which is likely to become of growing significance in the 1990s is the move towards the harmonisation, or 'concertation' as it is sometimes referred to, of social security provisions throughout the member states. The bilateral agreements developed from the 1960s and 1970s have permitted workers moving between member states to receive protection under the different national schemes. However, with the greater integration of social and economic policies envisaged for the 1990s, discussion has begun on the possibility of creating community-wide social security protection. Despite broadly similar structures, however, the social security schemes of EC member states do exhibit significant differences in practice, and harmonisation into one community-wide scheme seems unlikely for some considerable time. Recent discussion has focused therefore upon the possible creation of a separate EC social security scheme, sometimes referred to as the 'thirteenth state', under which the Commission would guarantee a particular set of social security rights for citizens moving from one country to another.

The thirteenth state would provide a potentially powerful vehicle for the development of community-wide institutional structures for combating poverty which could go much beyond the limited initiatives supported by the structural funds and the poverty programmes. They would create pressure upon both the Commission and national governments to contemplate further moves towards harmonisation of policy planning which may prove irresistible as the twentieth century draws to a close. Such pressures would make the European context of poverty and antipoverty policy much more important for all member states than it has been in the past. And this is likely to have significant consequences for poverty in Britain, despite past British reluctance to embrace European policy planning.

Future EC policy development may also be influenced by the changes in Eastern Europe flowing from the collapse of communism within the Eastern Bloc. The reunification of East and West Germany has already led to the need for a significant redistribution of resources within the new German economy which has to some extent upset European economic planning. If EC support, and even EC membership, is extended to the restructuring of Eastern European countries, where high levels of unemployment and deprivation are being experienced, then this may limit the scope for rapid harmonisation across other nations and may put a premium upon new economic and geographical priorities for EC structural initiatives.

The moves towards greater integration and harmonisation within the EC are also likely to have the effect of further segregating European countries from the wider international context. High standards of employment and wages within EC countries are likely to be bought at the expense of maintaining a high overall balance of trade with other countries throughout the world and of excluding from entry into Europe large numbers of migrant or immigrant workers from low-wage third world countries. Integrated Europe may also therefore become 'Fortress Europe', providing relatively high standards for most of its citizens within an increasingly unequal wider international context of poverty and deprivation. Although as discussed above, this is part of a much broader debate about the global context of poverty, of which European protectionism is only one part.

Britain in Europe

Although Britain has been a member of the EC since membership was expanded from the original six nations in 1973, British commitment to and involvement in the idea of an integrated European community has always been somewhat contradictory. In 1975 the Labour government held a national referendum to confirm commitment to membership, and opposition to full participation in EC social and economic policy remained a prominent strand within Labour politics until the late 1980s. In the 1980s members of the Conservative government under Margaret Thatcher also revealed themselves to be reluctant Europeans. During this period Britain was frequently in a minority of one in discussions over both the pace and the extent of European integration. In particular Britain refused to join the European currency control system, the Exchange Rate Mechanism (ERM), refused to support the development of a single European currency, and was unwilling to endorse the Social Charter of workers' rights.

British reluctance to embrace the European ideal can almost certainly be traced back to British imperialism and its commonwealth links with previous colonial nations, and to its geographical and cultural isolation from continental Europe, in particular the closely related original six EC member states. In some circles isolationism may also be based upon beliefs about the alleged superiority of British economic and social policies following the construction of the postwar welfare state. Underlying all these views is an assumption that closer participation in Europe may lead to a threat to British economic development and a levelling down of British standards.

Whatever the historical basis of assumptions about British superiority in social and economic policy, it was clear by the 1980s, however, that they did not have any contemporary foundation. As discussed above, poverty levels in Britain rose faster than in other European countries in the early 1980s, primarily because economic recession was being experienced more acutely in Britain; and British welfare policy has increasingly drifted away from Beveridge's comprehensive ideal towards a residual, means-tested, welfare regime, unlike the corporatist, institutional, welfare states of most of our European neighbours. The Conservative government's opposition to further European integration seemed to be based more and more upon the dogma of nationalism and the supremacy of the British Parliament than on any realistic assessment of future economic prospects. And during this period Labour switched from its opposition to European economic union to a recognition of the superiority of EC economic planning and social protection, and the open embracing of a new future for Britain in Europe.

In the early 1990s economic pressures finally forced Britain to join the ERM, although the conflicts which this produced within the Conservative Party were enough to result in the resignation of Thatcher as prime minister. Her replacement, John Major, took a more positive stance on European cooperation and added Britain's signature to the Maastricht Treaty in 1991, although he insisted on the right to opt out of a single currency and refused to endorse the Social Charter. In 1992, however, economic recession and pressure on the pound forced Britain to leave the ERM, at least temporarily, and more vocal opposition to the Maastricht Treaty both here and elsewhere in the community dampened some of the enthusiasm for more rapid moves towards European union.

Despite any reluctance and the procrastination, however, it is likely that the 1990s will see closer integration within the EC, and within this process Britain will necessarily become more closely tied to its European neighbours. Following the establishment of the EC single

European market in 1992 no British government is likely to contemplate abandoning EC membership, and thus the pressure on future governments to participate in monetary union and to enter discussions about political union will mount as the need to compete within, and to influence the development of, the European marketplace becomes essential to economic prosperity. Competition within the European market is also likely to require adherence to European social policy norms, and so for economic as well as social reasons acceptance of a gradually enhanced social charter seems inevitable. This will put pressure on future British governments to guarantee workers' rights, for instance to job security and equal pay, which conform with European standards, and possibly even to introduce a community-based minimum wage.

In addition to this broad European social and economic context in which British governments will have to operate, there are a growing range of EC initiatives in social and economic policy which will affect all member states and from which Britain may benefit both directly and indirectly. As discussed above, EC social and economic policy initiatives have become more and more extensive and interventionist in scope. These trends are likely to continue towards the end of the century.

Partly because of the severe impact of the recessions of the 1970s and 1980s in Britain, especially in the old industrial regions, this country has been a major beneficiary of EC structural funds, in particular from the ERDF and ESF. Between 1981 and 1985 Britain was, after Italy, the biggest recipient of ESF money, amounting to 244 million ECUs in 1984 (Teague, 1989, p. 47). Although support from structural funds is often conditional upon the provision of equivalent amounts of money from national or regional government in member states, the continued influx of such resources, targeted on areas experiencing economic decline and high levels of deprivation, is likely to be of increased importance in attempts to combat poverty in Britain in the 1990s, not the least reason for which is the limited amount of public money that is likely to be available from national government for such developments.

Britain's continued participation in the EC poverty programmes is also likely to be of importance in maintaining and developing initiatives in antipoverty strategy which can be compared and contrasted across other countries with similar poverty problems. The partnership-based projects in the third poverty programme are of particular significance in pioneering locally based action and research initiatives to work with community representatives in the development of antipoverty measures (Benington, 1991). Although they are very small-scale the EC poverty programmes have been growing in size and scope and, through their support for EC-wide data collation on social exclusion and other problems of deprivation, they will provide a significant framework for future debate about poverty policy at both national and community level.

Of particular significance in the development of community-wide antipoverty policy will be the moves towards the concertation of social security provision within Europe. As discussed above, harmonisation of social security provision to provide a European benefits system appears to be an impossible goal in the foreseeable future. In the past the development of EC social security strategy has been based on bilateral agreements rather than community-wide standards as has been the case in labour market regulation. This trend is to some extent compounded by the operation of the rather obscure principle of 'subsidiarity' in policy development, under which action is not taken at community level if change can be achieved by action at lower levels by national or regional government. This has permitted national governments to forestall some potential community-wide initiatives by undertaking some limited reform to promote more equal access to protection for EC citizens.

Despite the potentially perverse impact of the subsidiarity principle and the significant institutional problems of harmonisation, however, moves towards the integration of social security protection in Europe are to a large extent inevitable as labour mobility, community-wide markets and currencies, and guaranteed social rights in other spheres develop. The thirteenth state proposition is therefore likely to be the precursor to some attempt to guarantee minimum standards in social security protection, at least for some categories of claimants, perhaps mirroring the introduction of a minimum wage for employees.

Certainly moves towards greater harmony and minimum standards within social security provision throughout Europe would be likely to be beneficial for poor people in Britain. The restrictions in insurance-based protection, the reduction in pensions and child benefit support and the increasing dominance of means-tested dependency in Britain have been trends away from the structures of social security protection predominant in most other EC countries, especially those in the wealthier north. Pressures from the Commission and from EC neighbours to reverse these trends would be likely to lead to improvements in social security benefits for many of Britain's poor in the early

1990s. And once again it is likely that any future national government will find such pressures more and more difficult to resist.

Britain's future in Europe therefore will be likely to provide greater international pressure for social and economic reform than the country has ever experienced in the past. Economic and social policy planning will increasingly take place within the EC at a supranational level, and Britain as a member of the community will be required to adhere to this. The result may be a decline in the power and importance of the British parliament in determining significant aspects of welfare policy; but from the point of view of antipoverty initiatives and social security protection this may well result in improved provision for combating poverty in this country. Of course Britain will also increasingly be merely a part of Europe within the broader international stage, and international comparisons of poverty and poverty policy are likely to be restricted to some extent by this relatively limited focus. But even this limited international context will transform academic and political understanding of both the problem of poverty and its potential solution.

Part II
Definition and Measurement

4

Defining Poverty

The Need for Definition

This section of the book deals with the problems of defining and measuring poverty. This chapter and the next will concentrate on a discussion of attempts to define poverty. Arguably it is the issue of definition which lies at the heart of the task of understanding poverty. We must first know what poverty is before we can identify where and when it is occurring or attempt to measure it; and before we can begin to do anything to alleviate it.

As discussed in Part I, however, disagreements over the definition of poverty run deep and are closely associated with disagreements over both the causes of and the solutions to it. In practice all these issues of definition, measurement, cause and solution are bound up together, and an understanding of poverty requires an appreciation of the interrelationships between them all. Nevertheless some logical distinctions can be made, and will have to be if we are to make some progress in analysing the range of theoretical and empirical material which these debates have produced.

The need for definition is in fact recognised by most of the major researchers and commentators on poverty issues. In his major study of poverty in Britain in the 1960s and 1970s, Townsend opened the report with a definition of poverty which was crucial to his approach to the study and the findings it revealed:

Individuals, families and groups in the population can be said to be in poverty when they lack the resources to obtain the types of diet, participate in the activities and have the living conditions and amenities which are customary . . . in the societies to which they belong (Townsend, 1979, p. 31).

In the 1990 CPAG publication, *Poverty: the Facts*, Oppenheim opened with a chapter dealing with the problems of definition which underlay

57

any attempt to present details of poverty to a political audience. Academics and campaigners all recognise the importance of definition to debate about poverty, and most have contributed to a tradition of discussion and argument over definitions which goes back in Britain at least to the end of the nineteenth century and the work of two pioneers of the study of poverty, Booth and Rowntree.

Throughout much of this time, however, the debate on the definition of poverty seems to have been focused primarily upon the alleged distinction between *absolute* and *relative* poverty referred to in Chapter 1. Absolute poverty is claimed to be an objective definition, based upon the notion of subsistence. Subsistence is the minimum needed to sustain life, and so being below subsistence level is to be experiencing absolute poverty because one does not have enough to live on. On the face of it this is a contradiction in terms – how do those without enough to live on, live? The answer, according to absolute poverty theorists, is that they do not for long; if they are not provided with enough for subsistence they will starve, or perhaps more likely in a developed country like Britain, in the winter they will freeze. Indeed every winter significant numbers of elderly people in Britain do die of hypothermia because they cannot afford to heat their accommodation.

The definition of absolute poverty is thus associated with attempts to define subsistence. We need to work out what people need to have in order to survive; then, if we ensure that they are provided with this, we have removed the problem of poverty. This notion of absolute, or subsistence, poverty has often been associated with the early work of Booth (1889) and Rowntree (1901, 1941), although Spicker (1990) and Veit-Wilson (1986) respectively argue that these are mistaken, or oversimplified, judgements and that both in practice employed more complex, relative definitions in their studies. It is also often assumed that absolute poverty was removed by the welfare reforms introduced in Britain immediately after the Second World War, although this too has been subject to wide-ranging debate, as will be discussed below.

In recent times there has been a return to the emphasis on absolute poverty as a result of the growing impact of the new right's contribution to social policy debate in Britain. An early example of this was the work of Joseph and Sumption who claimed that

> An absolute standard means one defined by reference to the actual needs of the poor and not by reference to the expenditure of those who are not poor. A family is poor if it cannot afford to eat (1979, p. 27).

And in 1989 the theme was taken up by John Moore, then secretary of state for social services, in the speech quoted in Chapter 1, which he titled 'The end of the line for poverty' and in which he castigated relative notions of poverty as 'bizarre'.

Absolute poverty is thus contrasted with relative poverty. This is a more subjective standard in that it explicitly recognises that some element of judgement is involved in determining poverty levels, although as we shall see in Chapter 5 the question of whose judgement this should be is a controversial one. Judgement is required because a relative definition of poverty is based upon a comparison between the standard of living of the poor and the standard of living of other members of society who are not poor, usually involving some measure of the average standard of the whole of the society in which poverty is being studied.

Relative definition of poverty is associated in particular with the Fabian critics of the postwar achievements of the welfare state in eliminating poverty in Britain, most notably the work of Townsend (1954, 1979) and Abel Smith and Townsend (1965). Their argument was that although state benefits had provided enough to prevent subsistence poverty for most, in terms of their position relative to the average standard of living in society the poorest people were no better off in the 1950s and 1960s than they had been in the 1940s. Thus in a society growing in affluence, as was postwar Britain, remaining as far behind the average as before continued to constitute poverty. As Townsend put it in the quotation above, relative poverty prevented people from participating in activities which were customary in the society in which they lived.

This notion of participation is not the product only of postwar Fabian thinking however. Commentators as long ago, and ideologically as far apart, as Adam Smith and Karl Marx appeared to recognise and support it. According to Adam Smith:

> By necessaries, I understand not only the commodities which are indispensibly necessary for the support of life but whatever the custom of the country renders it indecent for creditable people, even of the lowest order, to be without. A linen shirt, for example, is strictly speaking not a necessity of life . . . . But in the present time . . . a creditable day labourer would be ashamed to appear in public without a linen shirt (Smith, 1776, p. 691)

and Marx wrote that

> Our desires and pleasures spring from society; we measure them,
> therefore, by society . . . they are of a relative nature (Marx, 1952,
> p. 33).

Of course absolutist critics, such as Moore (1989), argue that relative
differences are merely inequalities, which will exist in any society, and
that the relativist protagonists are using the notion of poverty
illegitimately to redistribute rather than to prevent want. This is a
debate to which we shall return shortly; and, as was suggested in
Chapter 1, it is one which really underlies much of the politics and
policy of poverty prevention or alleviation in modern societies. Once
we examine in more detail what supporters of both absolute and
relative definitions of poverty mean, however, we begin to realise that
the distinction is any case largely a false one. As was mentioned, Veit-
Wilson (1986) has demonstrated how Rowntree, often thought of as
the architect of the absolute definition of poverty, in reality utilised
relative measures. This is because the bald distinction between absolute
and relative poverty is in practice an oversimplification of much more
complex definitional problems.

Absolute and Relative Poverty

Absolute definitions do appear to have some sort of objective logic to
them based around the notion of subsistence – having enough to
sustain life. But this begs the question of what is life. What we require
for life will in practice differ depending upon place and time. For
instance, what is adequate shelter depends upon the ambient climate,
and the availability of materials for construction – even the homeless
poor living in London's 'Cardboard City' in the 1980s arguably were
only able to survive because of the availability of cardboard. Adequate
fuel for warmth also depends upon the climate, the time of year, the
condition of someone's dwelling and their state of health. Adequate
diet depends upon the availability of types of food, the ability to cook
food, the nature of work for which sustinence is required and,
according to Rowntree who allowed more in his basic diet for men
than for women, upon gender. Diet might also depend upon taste;
Rowntree included tea in his basic British diet, although it is of neglible
nutritional value.

Thus different people need different things, in different places,
according to differing circumstances. Differing individual needs will

also be affected by the living, or sharing, arrangements they may have with other individuals in families or households, an issue which will be returned to in Chapter 6. And of course their circumstances will in practice be determined by their ability to utilise the resources they do have in order to provide adequately for themselves. Although Rowntree attempted to use the independent judgement of nutritionists in order to determine a basic diet to act as a subsistence definition of poverty, he still distinguished between *primary* and *secondary* poverty. The former referred to those who did not have access to the resources to meet their subsistence needs, and the latter to those who seemingly did have the resources but were still unable to utilise these to raise themselves above the subsistence level. Although he distinguished between the two, Rowntree referred to both as poverty.

As mentioned, Rowntree also included 'non-necessities' such as tea in his subsistence measure. In a second study in 1936 he also included the cost of a radio, a newspaper, presents for children and holidays. This is not only a recognition that absolute standards may not be the same thing as avoidance of starvation, but also that these standards do change over time. In their review of definitions and measurements of poverty Fiegehen *et al.* (1977) note that there is a tendency for all apparently absolute definitions to raise minimum levels as living standards improve. And of course, as Veit-Wilson (1986) argues, Rowntree's studies of poverty in practice relied primarily upon an arbitrary assessment of lifestyle in York at the time of the surveys, drawn from the judgement of Rowntree and his interviewers.

However we cannot simply conclude from this that absolute definitions of poverty are wrong and relative ones right. There are problems with the relativist case too, many of which are exposed by Sen (1983) in a persuasive attack on the orthodoxy of relativism. If poverty levels change as society becomes more affluent, then it is not clear how the position of the poor can be distinguished from others who are merely less well-off in an unequal social order. This raises the question of where, and how, to draw a line between the poor and the rest, which was taken up in Piachaud's (1981a) critique of Townsend's 1979 study of relative poverty. We shall return to this shortly, but in essence the argument is that any cut-off line is arbitrary and merely involves the imposition of a subjective judgement of what is an acceptable minimum standard at any particular time.

Sen takes this further with the suggestion that if the relative position of the line remained the same, then during a period of recession in which overall standards drop there may be no increase in poverty, or conversely in a very wealthy society people would still be poor if, say, they could not afford a new motor car every year. This, he suggests, is clearly absurd, there must be some absolute measure against which relativities can be assessed. In searching for this Sen returns to Adam Smith's reference to the 'need' for a linen shirt. He argues that this does provide a basis for an absolute, rather than a relative, definition of poverty, because Smith refers to the lack of the shirt as destroying a person's dignity – it is shameful.

It is this experience of *shame* or, as Sen later argues, the lack of capability that it exemplifies, that makes a person poor. The commodities needed to avoid this incapacity would vary from society to society, and within one society depending upon the circumstances of individuals; but the *lack* is absolute and it is this which constitutes poverty. Thus poverty is a separate status which is different from being simply less well-off.

Of course Sen has trouble defining lack of capability. He attempts to base this on a Rawlsian notion of social justice – in which what we are prepared to argue is *just* is the minimum state that we ourselves would accept as tolerable within the existing social order, so that those incapable of achieving such a standard experience social injustice and are therefore poor. But this is always a rather abstract and philosophical approach to social values, which has never been successfully applied to social policy debate or planning. Indeed such a notion of justice is essentially a matter of judgement, or debate, or political preference – and not an objective or scientific fact. For instance Sen implies that starvation is objectively recognisable as poverty, yet as discussed above attempts to arrive at a definition of an adequate diet to avoid starvation have been fraught with disagreements.

Thus absolute definitions of poverty necessarily involve relative judgements to apply them to any particular society; and relative definitions require some absolute core in order to distinguish them from broader inequalities. Both it seems have major disadvantages, and in pure terms neither is acceptable or workable as a definition of poverty. If we wish to retain poverty as a basis for analysis, measurement and ultimately political action, therefore, we need to avoid the disadvantages, or rather to capitalise on the advantages, of both.

In practice most attempts to define and measure poverty do combine both, as Fiegehen *et al.* (1977) note, usually by selecting a poverty standard, expressing it in income terms and then applying it to the income distribution of a particular society in order to reveal the proportion in poverty. The most frequently used such measure in

Britain, as we saw in Chapter 1, is the SB/IS level, as this is clearly an example of what the government regards as necessary at any particular time. It is a readily available definition, it is related to household size with equivalent amounts specified for different household members (see Chapter 6), and, as we shall see, fractions or multiples of it can be used to measure those below the level or just above it. Atkinson (1990a) has discussed the history of the minimum level implied by benefit scales in Britain, pointing out that they do include a mixture of absolute and relative features.

However, as Veit-Wilson (1987) points out, the use of benefit rates to define poverty is tautological. In political terms it cannot provide a definition on which to act as it is already the product of political action. If there are those below it, and most studies of poverty find that there are, then they could be classed as poor; but this does not give a meaningful picture – either absolutely or relatively – of their poverty. And the most obvious problem with such a definition, which was recognised in the ridiculing of so-called relative approaches as 'bizarre' by John Moore (1989), is that if the government were to raise the level of benefit in response to political pressure to alleviate poverty, then the extent of poverty might appear to increase; or if it were to lower the level as a result of a decision to reduce state support, then the numbers in poverty might be reduced. A logical definition ought to operate in exactly the reverse direction.

Thus there have been other attempts to define poverty incorporating in differing degrees both absolute and relative features, but without the tautology associated with the use of benefit levels. These have been developed in Britain and in a range of other countries, in particular in the US. They include *budget standard* methods, drawing on the Rowntree absolutist tradition of a list of necessities, and *deprivation indicator* methods, drawing on the Townsend relativist tradition of deprived lifestyle. There are also variations in between, aiming at some consensually-based definition using income proxies or community-based deprivation indexes. And potentially there is a mixture of all these, outlined by R. Walker (1987), attempting to utilise community involvement in determining democratic budget standards.

Budget Standards

Budget standards approaches to defining poverty are based upon attempts to determine a list of necessities, the absence of which can then be used as a poverty line below which, presumably, people should not be permitted to fall. It is thus absolutist in structure, but, as Bradshaw *et al.* (1987) argue, budgets can also represent socially determined needs. Budget standards definitions are usually based upon the notion of a (weekly) basket of goods. The idea was pioneered by Rowntree in his studies of poverty in York (1901, 1941; Rowntree and Lavers, 1951), where a weekly diet was constructed based on the advice of nutritionists.

Rowntree's was a long and detailed list of goods including, in the 1950 version, 10 ozs of rice at 5½d, 6 lbs of swedes at 1s 3d, 1 egg at 3½d and, of course, ½ lb of tea at 1s 8d. Nevertheless it provided only for an extremely frugal standard of living, as he admitted in 1901,

A family living on the scale allowed for must never spend a penny on railway fare or omnibus. They must never go into the country unless they walk. They must never purchase a halfpenny newspaper or spend a penny to buy a ticket for a popular concert . . . and what is bought must be of the plainest and most economical description (1901, p. 167).

The narrow-minded meanness of this basket of goods approach was expertly exposed in 1922 by Ernest Bevin, then leader of the dock-workers' trade union, in an incident described by Atkinson (1989, p. 27). During an enquiry into dockworkers' pay, evidence as to need had been presented in the form of a minimum basket of goods. Bevin had gone out and bought the recommended diet of scraps of bacon, fish and bread and then presented them to the researcher asking whether he though it sufficient for a man who had to carry heavy bags of grain all day.

Of course baskets of goods need not be so frugal, especially if they are explicitly based on an attempt to define a socially determined standard. There is a long tradition in the US of attempts to define and cost the required living standard for a worker's family, going back to the Bureau of Labor Statistics' (BLS) work of the early twentieth century. The approach has been adapted and developed by other researchers utilising different standards, for instance by the New York Community Council, who maintained a variant of the BLS budget. However there are inevitable problems associated with the use of baskets of goods determined by experts because this involves the imposition of arbitrary, and as Bevin demonstrated, often hopelessly unrealistic, judgements by those who probably have no experience of living on them. They are thus unworkable in practice when compared with the expenditure patterns of real people, as Rowntree's researchers found out (see Veit-Wilson, 1986).

Since budget standards are supposed to represent required expenditure patterns therefore, surely it would be preferable to base them on actual patterns of expenditure rather than on hypothetical expert judgement? This is what the Watts Committee in the US tried to do. Statistical evidence on expenditure patterns was used to draw up different levels of expenditure. There was a 'prevailing family standard', fixed at a median level, but also a 'social minimum standard' at 50 per cent below this and a 'social abundance standard' at 50 per cent above it. Bradshaw *et al.* (1987) compared these to British standards, using purchasing power parities to avoid exchange rate variations, and found similarities between the social minimum standard and SB levels in Britain.

Bradshaw has also undertaken other work in Britain using expenditure patterns and the weekly budgets of people living on SB (Bradshaw and Morgan, 1987) and those of benefit claimants in the north-east of England (Bradshaw and Holmes, 1989). These have demonstrated that weekly budgets derived from expenditure patterns provide inadequate resources for those living at these levels – for example, leaving just 94p a week for a woman to spend on clothing, a diet deficient by 6500 calories and enough money for one haircut a year (Bradsaw *et al.*, 1987, pp. 180–1). These studies provide a picture of the poverty of those living on SB which avoid the tautology of the official definition based on the scale rate. Bradshaw continued this budget standards research in the 1990s through the establishment of the Family Budget Unit, which used expert judgements and expenditure patterns to determine a 'modest but adequate' budget for a British family (Bradshaw and Ernst, 1990). This was then scaled down to provide a 'low cost' budget, which nevertheless produced weekly income figures for families with children about a third greater than IS rates (Yu, 1992).

Before this Piachaud had undertaken similar research to establish expenditure-based budgets for the costs of children (Piachaud, 1979). He then used this to measure the numbers of children in poverty (Piachaud, 1981b). These were politically important findings, especially for the CPAG who published them; but their political appeal was still based upon the assumption that it was possible, and desirable, to determine an objective standard of living against which the situation of real children could then be compared. This is perhaps more acceptable in the case of children, for whom we expect that others will determine their lifestyle, than it is for adults who may legitimately have their own views about what is adequate for them.

Piachaud's and Bradshaw's implicit assumption is that anyone seeing the evidence of the inadequacy of the weekly budget will recognise the existence of poverty – as in Bevin's 'docker's breakfast'. But this is to assume a consensual standard based on average expenditure patterns – that is merely a relative comparison – and thus to assume what is intended to be proved. It is still either a tautological definition or one based only on the judgements of experts (Bradshaw and Piachaud) or non-experts (their readers).

Such a definition also cannot escape Rowntree's primary and secondary poverty dilemma. Most, if not all, real families spend some money on 'non-necessities' such as alcohol and tobacco (see Bradshaw and Morgan, 1987, p. 14). One way to avoid this dilemma may be to adopt what Veit-Wilson (1987, p. 201) calls a 'sociological' approach to budgets and accept that ordinary people's living patterns include non-necessitous expenditure. Therefore the poverty level should be the income at which people, following their ordinary expenditure patterns, would have sufficient for necessities. This is effectively what Rowntree means by his notion of secondary poverty; and still it does not get round the problem of defining necessities, nor the relativities issue of how much non-necessitous expenditure is acceptable as ordinary (keeping pets, running a car, pursuing a hobby?) But it does suggest that some broader averaging out of expenditure patterns and weekly budgets may permit more 'consensual' definitions to be arrived at. This has been attempted in some more detail in income proxy measures.

Income Proxy Measures

When the Watts Committee in the US based definitions of standards on the income levels necessary for various weekly living standards, they were in effect moving towards the use of income levels as a proxy for budget standards or expenditure patterns. The seminal work of Orshanksy in 1965 in the US took this process further in preparing income thresholds for various family sizes to be used as the basis for future poverty research by the US Social Security Administration.

Following the nineteenth century German researcher Engel, she compared the expenditure patterns of families at different income levels, and she found that lower income families spent a greater proportion of their income on necessities. The proportion of income spent on necessities thus declined as income rose and more non-necessities were puchased. This is referred to as the 'Engel curve' (Figure 4.1).

FIGURE 4.1   *The Engel curve*

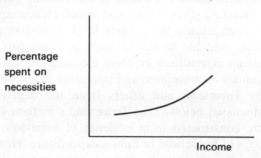

Orshansky argued that average expenditure devoted to necessities could thus be used to determine the poverty level. She suggested that people were in poverty where the household spent more than 30 per cent of their budget on food (Orshanksy, 1969; see Bradshaw *et al.*, 1987, p. 173). This provides an income proxy for poverty, based on the purchase of necessities. And of course the cut-off point need not necessarily be 30 per cent, or the measure need not only be expenditure on food. For instance in Canada a level of 62 per cent of spending on food, clothing and shelter has been used. However instead of fixing the point arbitrarily it could be discerned from the Engel curve itself. Engel curves are not usually a simple curve, but are more of an 'S' shape, representing more complex changes in patterns of expenditure (Figure 4.2).

FIGURE 4.2   *Inflection points on the Engel curve*

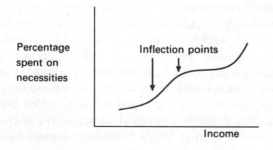

The inflection points, marked by the arrows, are where the marginal propensity to consume more of a particular type of good accelerates or slows down – the 'turn over point'. Above the first point higher income makes a wider range of expenditures possible; later points are likely to represent stages where the variety of new expenditure is exhausted and the quality of goods bought becomes an issue in determining patterns. The turn over point therefore gives the level at which choice replaces need in determining expenditure – the poverty level. Bradshaw *et al.* (1987) claim that it is possible to derive such a point for most household types based on expenditure on food, clothing and fuel.

In practice this is similar in conception and operation to the poverty threshold derived by Townsend and others from thè deprivation indicator approach discussed below. Like Townsend's method it is a *behaviourist* approach, constructed from evidence of behaviour patterns revealed in surveys of household or family expenditure. However it is still dependent upon a judgement by experts as to what constitute the necessities against which expenditure is measured. Other income proxy researchers have sought to overcome this by developing a *consensual* definition of needs and the incomes required to meet them and thus avoid poverty, through asking respondents in the community to make judgements rather than merely surveying behaviour.

Of most significance here is the work of Van Praag and his colleagues at the University of Leyden in the Netherlands (Van Praag *et al.*, 1982). In a series of major social surveys conducted in a number of European countries, they asked respondents what levels of income they would need in order to make ends meet and avoid poverty. And they also asked what cash income respondents would attribute to various standards of living described on a scale from very bad to very good. Fairly complex statistical analysis was then employed to derive poverty lines from the two sets of responses, based on what respondents had said was necessary for an adequate standard – the 'Leyden poverty line' (see Veit-Wilson, 1987, pp. 190–1).

Thus here an income proxy is utilised to define a consensual poverty line, based on the notion of an adequate budget. This is a significant move beyond the arbitrary weekly minimum levels fixed by experts and nutritionists in earlier studies. However it is still dependent upon judgements of adequacy used to fix lines derived from cash incomes specified in responses. This is based on an acceptable welfare function of income levels as applied to each society, and it is still, as Veit-Wilson (1987, p. 193) points out, therefore a political choice – just, of course, as are the levels for benefits such as SB/IS. Some have argued that this element of political choice in determining acceptable levels can be avoided by using deprivation indicators to define poverty.

Deprivation Indicators

Townsend in his work on poverty in Britain in the 1960s was the pioneer of the deprivation indicator method of poverty definition. As with his overall approach to poverty, it is drawn from the relativist critiques of the postwar complacency over the supposed removal of absolute poverty in Britain. In particular this complacency was based on Rowntree's third and final study of poverty in York (Rowntree and Lavers, 1951), which revealed much lower levels of poverty than the previous studies and appeared to confirm the view that welfare state reforms, based on the recommendations of Beveridge, together with growing affluence, had meant that no one in Britain was any longer in need.

Townsend championed the idea that need, or rather deprivation, was relative, as is revealed in the quotation at the start of this chapter from the beginning of his 1979 report on poverty. But he believed that relative need, expressed as exclusion from everyday living patterns, was not a matter of mere arbitrary judgement but could be objectively determined and measured. This was to be done by drawing up a list of key indicators of standard of living, the lack of which would be evidence of deprivation.

In the survey on which the 1979 study was based sixty such indicators, expressed as yes/no questions, were presented to over two thousand households. Around forty of these elicited yes/no answer patterns highly correlated with income. From these Townsend constructed a 'deprivation index' based on twelve indicators, such as the lack of a refrigerator, no holiday away from home in the last twelve months and the lack of a cooked breakfast most days of week, all of which correlated highly with low income (see Townsend, 1979, Table 6.3, p. 250).

The deprivation scores for different households, based on the index and summarised as the modal value for households in each income range, were then compared with the incomes of households, expressed as proportions of the SB entitlement for those households. These were then plotted onto a graph, using the logarithm of income as a percentage of SB entitlement, and here they fell into two clear lines (Figure 4.3).

FIGURE 4.3 *Deprivation by logarithm of income as a percentage of SB rates*

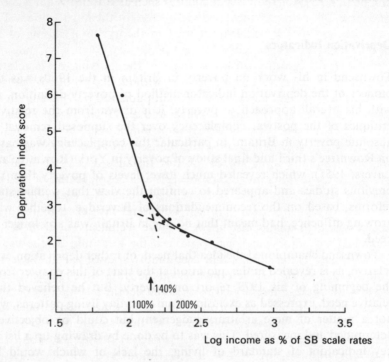

Source: Townsend, 1979, Figure 6.4, p. 261.

One line represented the changing position on the deprivation index of the bottom five income groups as income rose, and the other represented the changing position of the top seven. The bottom five income groups were those with a household income below 140 per cent of SB entitlement.

From this Townsend claimed that the point where the lines met, or to put it another way where the curve 'turned over', constituted a

> threshold of deprivation . . . that is, a point in descending the income scale below which deprivation increased disproportionately to the fall in income (1979, p. 271).

Or more generally, Townsend claimed, here was an objective definition of relative poverty; and the fact that the threshold, or poverty line, was at about 140 per cent of SB entitlement confirmed previous claims by

Townsend and others that those immediately above SB levels would still be in poverty in an affluent country such as Britain. What is more, of course, this also provided a powerful case for the introduction of an easy solution to the problem, at least in theory, by a raising of SB benefit levels by 40 per cent.

This was a ground-breaking step in the pursuit of a relative definition of poverty; but it was not without its problems, nor its critics. The most famous critique was that published by Piachaud in the journal *New Society* (Piachaud, 1981a, and see Desai, 1986). Piachaud criticised Townsend's list of deprivation indicators. Through them it appeared that Townsend was setting himself up as an expert of what was an acceptable standard of life (for instance a cooked breakfast every day) and taking no account of taste as an explanation of the lack of particular indicators (for instance vegetarians who may not choose the Sunday joint, the lack of which Townsend saw as an indicator of deprivation). Piachaud also made a more technical criticism of the statistical technique which had produced the threshold by the use of modal values, as this did not take account of variations around average points which would have left the lines on the graph much less clear cut.

Desai discusses these criticisms in some depth, but he also demonstrates that a reanalysis of Townsend's data which takes them into account still produces the same threshold, thus apparently confirming the validity of Townsend's overall approach. However the approach, and the threshold, are at best a behavioural and not a consensual definition of the poverty line – as with the income proxy measures drawn from spending patterns. And they centrally involve the judgement of experts, in this case Townsend himself, in the determination of acceptable indicators of deprivation from which to derive the line.

These deficiencies were taken into account in later studies, also using the deprivation indicator method, which were sponsored by London Weekend Television for a television series called 'Breadline Britain'. The study was first carried out in 1983 and was subsequently published as a book (Mack and Lansley, 1985). It was repeated in 1990, using the same methodology, and screened as a second series of programmes (Mack and Lansley, 1992). These studies also used a list of indicators expressed as survey questions, but the development and use of the list was much more sophisticated. The researchers asked their respondents whether or not they thought each potential indicator was necessary to avoid hardship; they then asked whether the respondents lacked those indicators *and* whether this lack was due to the lack of resources to purchase them.

From this a list of consensually agreed indicators, similar to but rather longer than Townsend's (Mack and Lansley, 1985, Table 4.1, p. 89), was drawn up to act as an index which avoided the problems both of expert determination of acceptable indicators and of variations in the taste of respondents in choosing to go without. Although, as Veit-Wilson (1987, p. 200) points out, it is really a majoritarian rather than a consensual approach, and thus it may still ignore important cultural differences in living standards within British society.

Just as in Townsend's study, however, the LWT data revealed a threshold between the bottom (four) and the top (eight) groups, although in their case the break occurred at around 135 per cent of SB entitlement level. Interestingly too, in the second survey respondents' judgements as to the unacceptable lack of necessary items had slightly, but perceivably, changed to include such things as a decent state of decoration at home, an insurance policy and fresh fruit; confirming what Townsend had argued, and Rowntree had conceded, that customary standards change as society develops. The 1990 survey also, rather depressingly, revealed higher proportions of respondents suffering from deprivation than in 1983, an increase from 7.5 million to 11 million lacking three or more necessities. These studies thus appear to strengthen the case that objective definitions of poverty lead to pressure for an increase in state benefit levels to alleviate the poverty which they reveal. This is just what you might expect, the cynics could say. And thus the search for an even more elaborate, and potentially less controversial, line continues.

Towards a Democratic Definition

In a discussion of poverty definition covering income proxy measures and deprivation indicator approaches, R. Walker (1987) argues that both are ultimately inadequate as they ignore the more important aspects of the purpose of defining poverty. The political context to poverty definition, as discussed in Chapter 2, is the need for action to eliminate it, and this seems to have been largely avoided in attempts to define poverty. In other words no attempts have been made to discover whether, and if so how much, people would be prepared to pay to eliminate what they define as poverty. And without this dimension, Walker argues, even consensual models are rather limited because they are rather hypothetical.

Perhaps inevitably the questions which are asked in surveys about income or deprivation are rather crude, and, from an uninformed and unprepared public, they are likely to elicit rather crude answers. To construct a fuller picture a more thorough process of public participation in determining poverty levels would be required – 'a democratisation of the budget standard approach' (R. Walker, 1987, p. 222) – based on in-depth interviews with individuals and groups. Such an approach would permit a mixture of income levels and deprivation indicators to be explored in the context of a discussion about the costs and benefits of differing definitions.

Unfortunately, of course, this is likely to produce highly complex and continually changing pictures of poverty, as mixtures of various forms of deprivation rather than any clear and simple income line. As will be discussed in the next chapter, such a complex notion of deprivation is necessary in order to appreciate the various ways in which poor people are excluded or restricted in their lives within a complex, affluent society such as Britain; but this is not the definition of poverty which has traditionally been sought by researchers and politicians in order to be able to measure its extent and develop policies to reduce or remove its effects.

Such a democratic process would also require a political commitment to the removal of poverty thus discovered, which, if the process were institutionalised, would be impossible to resist. Such a commitment is unlikely to be forthcoming in the foreseeable future from governments who have thus far seemed to believe that they have already embarked on the process of tackling poverty through the social security benefit systems and other antipoverty strategies which will be discussed in Part IV.

These are already, of course, the product of democratic processes of one sort via the mandate of electoral democracy. And indeed in more general terms a democratically constructed and genuinely consensual definition of poverty is in effect a negation of the purpose of poverty definition in the first place. As discussed in Chapter 1, attempts to define poverty as a distinct social phenomenon have been developed in order to create political pressure for a recognition of such levels of deprivation as problematic and an acceptance by politicians that something must be done about them.

It is this quest which gives the definition of poverty its social meaning, indeed arguably its *only* meaning. Once the political commitment to investigate the details of poverty in order to eliminate it is genuinely accepted, then the need for definition has gone and we are left with the multifaceted picture of the inequalities and inadequacies experienced in complex modern societies – and in less modern social orders too. We shall return to this more complex picture of deprivation in the next chapter.

5

Deprivation

Experiences of Deprivation

As discussed in Chapter 4, there are problems inherent in all attempts to define poverty, both within absolutist and relativist traditions. In practice most attempts at definition include both absolute and relative elements in an attempt to coalesce the differing aspects of deprivation into a single standard, which can then be measured and perhaps removed. In other words all attempts at definitions of poverty are simplified measures of a broader picture of deprivation, or deprivations. Indeed it is the notion of measurement which is the key to this simplified form since, as will be discussed in Chapter 7, simple phenomena must be identified if they are to be measured, especially if they are to be measured across different societies

However, as is implicitly recognised in the debates over the problems of definition, the simplified standards are really proxies for the more complex webs of inadequacy experienced by the poor or the less well-off – indeed in the case of income proxy measures they are self-confessedly so. What is experienced as poverty, however, is in practice a multifaceted combination of deprivations and unmet needs. The extent of these and their impact on individuals and households will vary from place to place, from person to person and from time to time – and even at different times within one person's lifetime, as will be discussed in Chapter 6.

Thus a full picture of poverty within a society needs to address these fine grains of deprivation, which the simplified definitions and statistical measures necessarily overlook. This involves a recognition of the many forms that deprivation can take in complex societies, and a recognition of the extent to which the experience and impact of these can vary between different sections of such societies. The consensual approaches to poverty discussed in Chapter 4 do not do this, and for the most part they are really therefore majoritarian rather than consensual. Not everyone does agree to the patterns of need that are

75

represented here, and not everyone is covered by them. Needs, and lacks, may vary for different individuals, and in particular for different minority groups or cultural traditions within a wider society – an issue to which we shall return in Part III.

Like the definitions of poverty, however, experiences of deprivation include both absolute and relative aspects. Unmet needs for an adequate diet, adequate shelter and even adequate health clearly involve absolute concepts of needs, which it could be argued should form the basis of state planning to identify and to meet (see Gough and Doyal, 1991). But deprivation also includes the notion of being without things that others obviously have – of separation, non-participation or marginalisation.

This notion of marginalisation, or social exclusion, has now been taken up at a European level through the establishment of the EC Observatory discussed in Chapter 3 (Room *et al.*, 1991). In the first report of the Observatory the authors argue that the concept of social exclusion encompasses a broader focus on the social rights of citizens. Social exclusion is thus the 'denial – or non-realisation – of social rights' (Room *et al.*, 1991, p. 5). Citizenship rights in this context extend beyond the more limited notion of employment rights covered by the Social Charter to include education and training, housing, health, and neighbourhood support. The EC Observatory's concern is thus with the relative aspects of deprivation that have been developed by researchers such as Townsend (1979).

Townsend has probably been the most articulate proponent of the notion of relative deprivation in Britain and beyond. In an article in the *Journal of Social Policy* (Townsend, 1987) he distinguished three different forms of relative deprivation:

1. Lacking the diet, clothing and other facilities which are customary and approved in society.
2. Falling below the the majority or socially accepted standard of living.
3. Falling below what could be the majority standard given a better redistribution or restructuring of society.

He argued that the latter is largely utilised in studies of developing countries, and suggests an attempt to impose relative standards which are not part of current custom and experience.

This raises the issue of the relationship between subjective and objective approaches to deprivation, which has also been the source of some debate. If deprivation is about needs and lacks, then one implication is that it only exists to the extent to which people perceive themselves to have needs which are not met, or are going without things which they think that they ought to have. If you do not need or want something, then in what sense can you be deprived of it?

This subjective dimension was explored by Runciman (1966) in his 1960s study of perceptions of deprivation. He found that many people did not perceive themselves as relatively deprived, over a quarter of his sample saying that there were no others who were better-off than themselves (p. 227). And even those who did experience relative deprivation often compared themselves to those not necessarily much better-off than themselves, for instance, people with no children, people on shift work, university researchers or people able to let out a part of their home (p. 229). In an unequal society such as 1960s Britain therefore, people's sense of social justice was a rather limited one.

Of course this was hardly a surprising discovery. People's knowledge of the standards of others, especially of the luxuries of the rich, are fairly limited – not the least because the better-off do not frequently flaunt their wealth and may even, for a variety of reasons, seek to disguise it. Furthermore we all have to live, and mainly do live, within our current circumstances – we learn to get by. And for many people maintaining alongside this a deep and burning grievance about what they are deprived of is neither comfortable nor healthy.

This point has led to the more general study of the strategies for coping with poverty in affluent societies explored by Coates and Silburn (1970) and incorporated in Lewis's theories of 'cultures of poverty', discussed in Chapter 2 and Chapter 12. However it should not be misinterpreted as implying support for the notion of the 'contented poor'. Townsend also explored subjective perceptions of poverty in his 1979 study and found that although a large number (over a half) of those 'living in poverty' did not feel poor,

> most of them none the less recognised in other ways that they were worse off than people with high or middle incomes, or than they had been themselves in previous life (Townsend, 1979, p. 431).

He also concluded that there was a strong correlation between subjective and objective deprivation.

Townsend has consistently maintained that deprivation can be objectively defined and measured, and that in its focus on the conditions of life, rather than on the distribution of resources, it can be distinguished from the narrower concept of poverty. Further, since deprivation is a major feature of policy debate and an important factor in policy planning, for instance, in the targeting of development resources to deprived groups or deprived areas, which will be discussed in Chapter 15, it is essential that agreed and objective criteria of definition be constructed.

Townsend discusses such criteria in the 1987 *Journal of Social Policy* article. Here, as in his 1979 survey, he distinguishes between material and social deprivation – perhaps in implicit recognition of the absolute and relative dimensions of the phenomenon. He then goes on to outline a list of indicators to be used to determine and measure levels of deprivation, covering such things as diet, home circumstances, working conditions, family activity, community integration and social partici-pation, from which scores could be derived for different individuals or groups. Of course the list of indicators is open to the same challenge of expert judgement, as was the list of indicators used to determine the poverty threshold discussed in Chapter 4. It is an objective measure, but not necessarily a consensual, or even a behavioural, one.

However, the list demonstrates the potentially broader remit of the notion of deprivation. In complex and affluent societies necessities are not just personal needs for food, clothing and shelter; and incomes or expenditure are not the only measures of standard of living. As the concept of social exclusion implies, where we live, where we work, how we work, how we spend our leisure time (if we have any), what services we receive – all these, and not merely our personal or household weekly budgets, affect our lives, and deprivation can extend into any or all of these broader aspects of lifestyle. Indeed it is this broader and richer (or poorer, for some) notion of 'lifestyle', rather than 'standard of living', with which discussion of deprivation has become associated. It is debatable whether lifestyle can be objectively defined and measured; but an understanding of how our lifestyles can alternatively be enriched or deprived is central to an understanding of poverty in affluent societies.

Deprivation at Home and Work

In his 1979 survey Townsend examined a number of the broader aspects of deprivation whilst undertaking his search for the poverty threshold. These included deprivation in housing, environment and workplace. Not having a decent home is obviously an important form of deprivation and one which is widespread, and seemingly chronic, in many affluent societies such as Britain. Townsend distinguishes three aspects of inadequate housing: structural defects rendering housing unfit, lack of basic amenities, and inadequate space or overcrowding. Clapham *et al.* (1990), in a textbook on housing policy, also discuss what they call 'housing disadvantage'. In Britain much of this is the product of the poor quality of the housing stock dating back to the last century.

Old houses inadequately maintained can, and do, decline in quality. Between 1971 and 1981 the number in serious disrepair in England increased by 21 per cent to over one million, and the number of 'unsatisfactory dwellings' rose to over 18 million (Clapham *et al.*, 1990, p. 63). In 1986 as much as 25 per cent of the stock was considered defective, and one and a half million homes were unfit for habitation or lacking basic amenities. Although Hills (1990, p. 13) has argued that these numbers have since begun declining, they are still a significant element of deprivation for those who continue to live in unsafe, inadequate or overcrowded accommodation.

Many of the problems of poor quality housing are distributed across different housing tenures. But tenure differences can add to or accentuate housing deprivation. For private sector tenants there can be the added problem of legal insecurity, especially following the reforms removing Rent Act protection in the Housing Act 1988. And for council tenants there can be the stigma of occupying an increasingly residual and marginalised sector of housing provision. Housing expenditure subsidies from the state have also not been used to remove or ameliorate housing disadvantage (see Hills, 1989), especially in the late 1980s when increasing amounts of money were directed to tax relief on mortgage payments for relatively wealthy owner-occupiers.

Of course the most serious dimension of housing deprivation is homelessness – having no house at all. The number of homeless people has been a serious problem in Britain throughout most of the postwar period, despite the welfare state and the development of public housing. The legislation on homelessness introduced in the 1970s gave a qualified right to a house to some homeless people, although it excluded single people and childless couples. Yet the numbers of those registered as homeless under the law doubled in the decade after its introduction, rising from 50 000 to 100 000. And for those not covered by the legislation homelessness must be endured as a humiliating and debilitating deprivation. Countless thousands now sleep rough in Britain's major cities, with only cardboard boxes and plastic bags as a home. In London, where the numbers are greatest, this public manifestation of deprivation has achieved the notoriety of a pseudonym, 'Cardboard City' – suggesting a permanence which the cardboard itself does not provide.

Such severe housing deprivation brings with it further disadvantages too. Ill health is likely to result from sleeping on the streets. Employment is hard to find when no address can be given to prospective employers. Purchase of household and consumer goods is largely out of the question. And public or private services are mainly irrelevant or even, as in the case of street cleaning, positively threatening. Homelessness is an obvious example of the problems of multiple deprivation, as Townsend and others have called this combination of needs and lacks; but multiple deprivation is not confined to those without homes.

Poor housing may be situated in a poor environment. Townsend also included environmental deprivation in his 1979 survey. Three indicators were chosen: no garden or yard around the house, no nearby safe place for children to play and a state of air pollution in the neighbourhood. Attention to the environmental context of our lives has increased considerably since Townsend's study. In cities in particular, litter and refuse can add to the problems of pollution and safety, as can traffic volume. Leisure space close to home is not the only indicator of this aspect of environmental deprivation either, clearly the larger geographical context of lifestyle is also important. For instance, life in a flat in a densely populated inner city is obviously environmentally poorer than life in a flat in a small town or suburban area with parks or open countryside within easy reach.

This broader geographical context of deprivation takes us into what Townsend refers to as the problem of 'poor areas' (Townsend, 1979, Ch. 15). These are areas where multiple forms of deprivation combine with large numbers of people living on low incomes. They are often found in inner city areas with poor housing, a low quality environment and high levels of unemployment and benefit dependency. Many local authorities are well aware of such area-based deprivation within their localities and may seek to identify such areas in order to channel policy development towards them. For instance, in the 1980s Sheffield City Council called such areas of the city 'areas of poverty', and used this definition to determine the distribution of certain forms of additional services and funding. However areas of poverty should not be misunderstood as geographical proxies for some measure of the extent of poverty or deprivation – some people living in such areas may not be deprived, and many people living outside of them certainly will be. In Chapter 15 we will return to the dangers inherent in using exclusively geographical targeting in order to identify and challenge poverty.

As Townsend also recognised, experience of deprivation is not restricted to where people live; for those who have employment deprivation can also be experienced at work. Some people work in conditions which are considerably more deprived than others, even where pay differentials may not be that great. The working environments of miners and office clerks is an obvious comparison here, even though the former may earn more than the latter. Townsend identified four aspects of deprivation at work: the severity of the job itself (outdoors or indoors, standing or seated), the security of the job, the conditions and amenities of work, and the provision of welfare or fringe benefits.

Most of the problems of deprivation here are pretty obvious, although the issue of fringe benefits has become of much greater importance in recent years. Many jobs, often the more secure, pleasant and better paid ones, now include significant benefits, such as a long holiday entitlement, sickness pay, maternity leave, occupational pensions, travel subsidisation or even free accommodation (for instance No.10 Downing Street, though here security may be a less significant feature!) Occupational welfare provisions like pensions schemes are particularly important for they continue the advantages, and the disadvantages, of differential employment situations beyond the period of the employment contract itself. As Mann and Anstee (1989) discuss, they are of increasing importance in the late twentieth century and contribute to the broader social divisions and deprivations which result from privileged, or non-privileged, access to the labour market. Those in secure positions in the *core* labour market are thus increasingly experiencing different standards from those in short-term, part-time contracts on the *periphery*.

Poor working conditions and poor housing conditions can both contribute to poor health. Clearly experience of poor health is a significant form of deprivation within lifestyle, and if it is serious it can affect the length and quality of life itself. There is a considerable body of evidence to suggest that poor health is associated with other aspects of poverty and inequality, notably the Black Report and the Health Divide Report, sponsored by the government itself but published privately by Penguin (Townsend *et al.*, 1988; and see Blackburn, 1991, Ch. 2). The relationship between health and other forms of deprivation is, however, a complex one – causal links may operate in both directions. Certainly where poor health is serious enough to interfere with employability it is likely to lead to disadvantage in, or exclusion from, the labour market, and as we have seen this is closely associated with experience of poverty and deprivation. Poor health may thus be compounded by other aspects of poverty.

It is nevertheless important to remember that poor health is a form of deprivation itself, whatever its association with other aspects of poverty and inequality of lifestyle. Chronic ill-health is debilitating and restricting, and it can reduce the enjoyment of even those pleasures which are still permitted by it, as diabetics and asthmatics know well. It can also exclude sufferers from a range of activities which others generally take for granted, although as mentioned the problem of exclusion is an aspect of deprivation which is not only associated with ill-health.

Deprivation as Exclusion

As with the EC notion of social exclusion from broader social rights, more recent research in Britain has begun to draw attention to a wider range of forms of deprivation within affluent society than the housing, work and health aspects which have been recognised for some time. Bradshaw and Holmes (1989) in a study of families on benefit living in the north-east of England also discuss problems associated with restricted mobility, no doubt partly encouraged by the local passenger transport authority who helped finance the project.

For those who do not have access to private transport, the lack of reliable, regular and affordable public transport can mean that mobility will be much restricted. And in a society where greater mobility is increasingly necessary in order to meet even basic needs, as local shopping centres are replaced by distant hypermarkets and retail complexes, reduced mobility can lead to other deprivations – in addition to the reduced quality of life experienced by being 'trapped' within the local neighbourhood. This aspect of deprivation is particularly acute in rural areas where public transport is rare, or non-existent, and local services few. Yet it is an aspect which is frequently ignored in studies of poverty or deprivation which concentrate on 'pockets of deprivation' or 'areas of poverty' in inner cities.

The contributors to the CPAG pamphlet, *Excluding the Poor*, edited by Golding (1986), drew attention to a range of other aspects of deprivation which were growing in importance in modern society. Perhaps most important, and most controversial, is the issue of leisure. With reduced working time now a reality for all, albeit differentially distributed, what we do, or do not do, with our leisure time may be an important source of inequality and deprivation. Leisure industries, especially sport and culture or entertainment, are now major features of modern society – indeed they have been the main growth industries in Britain in the latter decades of the twentieth century. Yet access to, and enjoyment of, them is subject to wide differences and deprivations.

Tomlinson (1986) quotes the examples of squash, a rapidly growing and yet expensive and inflexible sport, and *Alton Towers*, a vast but expensive and inaccessible leisure park now copied in many other places, as cases of restricted access to leisure. Leisure is often therefore associated with wealth, hence the inability of the unemployed to benefit from their apparently extensive 'leisure time'. It is also structured by gender, as studies of women's leisure have revealed (Green *et al.*, 1990) – not the least because much of women's leisure time is spent in practice looking after men. Enjoyment of leisure, especially sport, can also be associated with poor health; but as with health it is in itself a clear indicator of lifestyle in modern society.

Lack of access to our increasingly complex and interconnected communications network can also be a source of deprivation in modern Britain. Television, teletext, telephones and now fax machines and electronic mail have come more and more to dominate our lives, or rather the lives of some. And for those without, for instance children with no television at home or lone parents in families with no telephone, they can be a source of social deprivation in the playground or material deprivation in the home.

Along with leisure and communications the other growth industry of the late twentieth century has been financial services – banking, investment, credit, insurance and so on. In particular the development of cheques, credit cards and direct debit cards has transformed the process of buying and selling. For those without access to these facilities therefore, deprivation can be significant. And there are many so deprived. Toporowski (1986) points out that only 69 per cent of adults had current bank accounts in 1985, and for those in social class E (the bottom) the proportion was 41 per cent. Exclusion from access to financial services can also exclude people from the advantages of borrowing and buying on credit, an important means of adding flexibility to consumption, and thus lifestyle, to avoid what might otherwise be significant short-term problems of deprivation.

However the disadvantages of credit can also lead to, or compound, deprivation. Where credit can no longer be repaid it becomes debt, and the problems associated with debt have become more serious and widespread in late twentieth century Britain. Parker (1988), Berthoud and Kempson (1992) and Ford (1991) discuss the problems associated with high levels of multiple debt amongst the less well-off. Such forms of debt are often combined with high rates of interest, thus they cost more, and when unpaid they can lead to pressure and threats from creditors and can cause insecurity and anxiety amongst debtors. Many debts, like mortgages used to purchase owner-occupied housing, are secured against property which is also a home. When these debts cannot be repaid the house can be repossessed to recover the loan. Such repossessions increased tenfold in the 1980s and doubled again to around 40 000 a year in the early 1990s, and yet with the declining value of property at this time they could still leave people owing large sums of money. In circumstances such as these anxiety is acute, and well-founded, and the problems of debt can end in disaster.

Ward's (1986) contribution to Golding's CPAG pamphlet discusses the political dimensions of deprivation in a democratic society. Taking an active part in political organisations may not widely be regarded as an essential part of lifestyle in twentieth century Britain. But it is an essential part of the success of democracy, and those who are excluded from it, either by lack of money, time, knowledge or experience, are deprived of the opportunity to participate in the democratic process. That such non-participation is significantly associated with those groups also disproportionately experiencing other aspects of deprivation – the unemployed, the low paid, women at home, the elderly and ethnic minority communities – suggests that its impact is a significant feature of deprivation – and one with a disturbing self-perpetuating potential.

Another form of deprivation disproportionately associated with those other disadvantages which are commonplace amongst poor groups is the threat, or fear, of being a victim of crime. Having property stolen or damaged, or worse still being a victim of assault or attack, is a severe depletion of quality of life; and the threat of this happening again provides a nagging sense of insecurity which can only fully be appreciated by those who have suffered from it. Crime statistics, and more especially recent surveys asking victims about crime, for instance the Islington Crime Survey (see Young, 1986), have revealed that the highest levels of criminal activity and criminal threats are experienced amongst generally deprived groups living in deprived areas. In one council housing development in Killingworth near Newcastle upon Tyne the problem became so great that the council decided to demolish a block of flats in an attempt to eliminate the problem, even though the recently built flats were structurally sound and there was no obvious local surplus of accommodation (see Cowan, 1988, p. 24).

Again the threat of crime has particular consequences for particular groups. Violence at home is seemingly widespread and is largely directed at women, whose lives can be destroyed by it. Violence and harassment at home and in public is frequently experienced by black and Asian people, for whom it provides a sharp accentuation of the broader deprivations resulting from racism, to which we will return in Chapter 9.

The CPAG book on these new and broader aspects of deprivation was called *Excluding the Poor*, and in one contribution Williams (1986) focused on this wider aspect of deprivation as exclusion. He discussed the EC concept of social exclusion and the suggestion that those denied social rights may exist as a segment of the population separated, in part at least, from the affluent world around them. This notion of the poor and deprived as a separate group within society is a controversial one, however, as will be discussed in Chapter 12. Furthermore, it is frequently linked to discussion of the more punitive overtones of the problem of stigma. In spite of the development of universal state welfare services in postwar Britain, intended in part at least to remove exclusion and stigma by providing equally for all, these have remained central features of welfare services and have been accentuated by the expansion in the scope and impact of selective services in the last quarter of the twentieth century. Services for the poor can easily, as many have pointed out, become poor services – as council tenancies and means-tested benefits exemplify. And where services have been universal, some of the less well-off have often been relatively deprived of them, as Le Grand's (1982) evidence on the use of the NHS and higher education demonstrates.

However, as Titmuss argued as early as 1958, the impact of state welfare support is more extensive than the provision of services and benefits – or rather there are other welfare states providing other benefits, for some. He mentioned in particular the fiscal welfare state providing support through tax relief and the occupational welfare state providing benefits through employment. As we have discussed, the latter is certainly differentially distributed, and of course the fiscal welfare state only benefits those earning enough to pay tax in the first place, excluding those on low wages and benefits. In the latter part of the twentieth century fiscal welfare through tax relief for such benefits as mortgages and private pensions has grown dramatically, providing greater state resources for those already in better housing and more secure employment.

More recently Field (1989) has also drawn attention to the importance of private property ownership and inherited wealth in contributing to improved living standards, or conversely to deprivation. This has become especially important with the spread in ownership of shares, insurance policies and owner-occupied housing. Capital gains from these sources are also largely tax exempt and they can provide significant benefits, for instance on the maturation of insurance policies or on the inheritance of expensive housing. But once again here many are deprived of the benefits of such injections of captial into their standard of living, and once again these are likely to be the same people who are deprived of the range of other improvements in quality of lifestyle discussed in this chapter.

Thus deprivation is a feature of the broader social and economic structure of capitalist or mixed economy welfare states. The wide range of public and private supports and services which make up our modern lifestyle can leave some deprived in many complex and diverse ways from the necessities and the luxuries which the majority increasingly take for granted. This deprivation cannot be pinned down to one factor, or list of indicators, nor can it readily be represented by a given income or expenditure level; and thus it cannot, as will be discussed in Chapter 7, effectively be measured. But it can be studied, both quantitatively and qualitatively, and conceptualisations of need must be open and flexible enough to take account of its many facets, as of course must policies which are designed to challenge and reduce it.

6

Households and Poverty

Individuals and Households

Both poverty and deprivation are concepts used to define and measure differences between people in order to show how individuals living in the same society can have radically different standards of living. And certainly it is individual people who suffer poverty and deprivation, a reality that sometimes feels as though it has been overloooked in some of the complex definitional and statistical debates. However individual people do not by and large live all their lives as individuals, and even as individuals they do not remain the same throughout their lives.

For a start most individuals live with other individuals in families or households, and in families or households they pool their resources to some extent and share their wealth, or their poverty, with other family or household members. Thus if we want to study the effect of poverty on individuals and if we want to develop policies to ameliorate or remove these effects, then we must also study the household or family structure in which people live and in which resources are distributed and consumed. Secondly, individuals' circumstances do not remain the same throughout their lives. As we grow older we move from childhood to adulthood, perhaps to parenthood, and later into retirement; our material circumstances and our chances of experiencing poverty or deprivation are naturally going to be different at different times within our life cycle, in particular because this will affect our abilities to provide resources for ourselves through employment. Thus studies of poverty must also take account of such life-cycle changes.

Finally, of course, our household and family structures will change over our lifetimes. Thus household structure and life-cycle changes are interrelated, and as we move from one household formation to another our chances of experiencing poverty and our experience of poverty itself will vary. So a weekly income of £100 means something rather different if it is received by a single man than if it is received by a couple with two young children; and measures of income which do not take account of this will not tell us much about poverty or deprivation.

Conversely many people in a country like Britain may have no income of their own. Most children do not. But this does not automatically mean that they are materially deprived since they may be members of households where income is shared with them. How the incomes of different household formations and different members of households is defined and measured is therefore an important dimension of the problem of poverty and deprivation.

Household Size and Structure

In a collection of studies comparing the differing needs and resources of different household and family structures, Walker and Parker (1988) point out the importance of both differing household structure and life-cycle changes; and the various contributions to the book take up differing aspects of these issues. The question is also discussed by Townsend in his major poverty survey (Townsend, 1979, Ch. 7). The most important initial issue raised by both is the need to distinguish between households and families, although on many occasions of course the two may overlap and the boundaries between them may not always be clear.

The logical (or sociological) distinction between the two is that unlike households families are constituted by more or less explicit commitments to joint living and sharing based upon emotional, as well as empirical, interdependency. Marriage is the most obvious symbolic representation of this, although families are not only restricted to married couples. They include the dependent children of such couples and usually non-married partners (not necessarily heterosexual) who have made, or appear to have made, quasi-marital commitments. This narrow form of family is sometimes referred to as the *nuclear family*, to distinguish it from broader family and kinship ties between adult parents and children, or adult siblings.

The expectation is that members of families will pool and share resources and will expect, and welcome, interdependency; although, as will be discussed below, this is not always the case. This expectation is also enforced through the law, in particular in the rules covering entitlement to means-tested benefits in Britain, where those 'living together as husband and wife' (together with their dependent children) are treated as an income unit and paid at a lower, couple, rate than two separate individuals would be. The assumption is that two or more together can live more cheaply than one alone; and there is obviously some sense in this. For instance heating and cleaning costs will probably commensurately be reduced. Although how these savings should be measured is a controversial issue to which we shall return shortly in a discussion of equivalence scales.

Reduced living costs such as these, however, will also be experienced by those sharing residential accommodation even if they have no family ties or commitments – hence the argument that households too constitute a basis for a presumed pooling of resources. Since households are not based upon any explicit emotional commitment, then the equivalent of marriage or quasi-marriage cannot serve as a definitional guide; and what constitutes a household can vary enormously. For instance, a household may be based upon a family together with adult children still living 'at home', or aged parents sharing with their adult sons or daughters – in effect forms of extended family. Alternatively a household could be made up of non-relatives living within one house and sharing some living accommodation for convenience, or more usually because of financial necessity, for example, young single adults sharing a rented house.

Obviously there is a distinction to be drawn between family-based or household groupings. Arguably the former have made some inter-personal commitment to sharing resources, whereas the latter probably have not. Although of course the distinction between the extended family household and the single adults household confuses the difference considerably. The distinction is also important when attempting to compare the resources of different groups since households are generally a broader, and larger, category than families. This difference in size is likely to be significant. Having stated a preference for households as a basis for measurement, Beckerman and Clark (1982, p. 17) go on the show that in 1975 3.2 per cent of the population were below SB level using the family unit compared to 2.3 per cent with the household unit. As Piachaud (1988, p. 342) argues:

> It is well known that the extent of poverty based on larger units is less than that based on smaller units since, for example, many poor individuals share households with better-off relatives.

The importance of the distinction was demonstrated most markedly, however, in 1988 when the government introduced a change in the collection and presentation of official statistics covering low incomes.

The change involved a switch from the previous basis of publishing the figures relating to low income families (LIF), which were compared to SB entitlement levels and gave a measure of families in poverty according to this, to the publication of figures relating to households below average incomes (HBAI), which were compared with incomes of other households on order to give a relative measure of income distribution.

The reasons behind the change were complex, and controversial. They stemmed in part from the government's stated opposition to the use of SB/IS scales as a poverty benchmark, an argument discussed in Chapter 4. But they also involved the more debatable claim that sharing within households was commonplace (DSS, 1988). Critics of the change were concerned not only with the principles behind this assumption, but also with the practical effect the changed basis for calculation would have on official statistical measures of poverty and inequality – especially as the government refused to publish the old data as a comparison.

In order to compare the changes resulting from the switch the Institute for Fiscal Studies (IFS) compared the figures under the new HBAI measure in 1988 with what these would have been under the old LIF measure if this had still been used (Johnson and Webb, 1990). Their analysis showed that the switch from family to household basis reduced the percentage of people with low incomes and thus produced a measure which appeared to demonstrate reduced inequality, resulting from the assumption of greater levels of income sharing. They also discussed the other changes introduced in the 1988 measures, for instance, the switch from *normal* to *current* income, to which we shall return in Chapter 7. But they concluded that the switch from family unit to household had 'by far the greatest effect' (p. 13).

Thus the difference between household or family measures is important, not just in the assumptions which different measures make about how we organise our domestic lives – which of course must be assumptions only – but also in the consequences these have for the extent of poverty or inequality which the different measures reveal. Researchers have for some time therefore tried to develop ways of including within statistical measures some mechanism for taking account of the reduced cost of pooled resources in families or households, so that comparisons can be made between the circumstances of those living in differing domestic arrangements. This has been done through the development of equivalence scales.

Equivalence Scales

Equivalence scales are an attempt to express in proportional terms the presumed reduced costs of living experienced by members of households sharing resources. They have been widely used in studies of poverty: for instance Rowntree's first 1899 survey (Rowntree, 1901) was based upon an equivalence scale drawn from presumed dietary needs, under which the amount allowed for children in a household was estimated at between a third and a quarter of that for an adult. Thus a household containing one adult and one child would require an income between 1.25 and 1.33 times the income of a single adult household to achieve the same standard of living.

The most well-known and widely used equivalence scales today are the SB/IS scale rates, where the lower rate for a couple compared with two single persons and the reduced rate for children produce an equivalence scale, using a base of 1.0 for a couple, of 0.49 for a third additional adult in a household, 0.38 for a 16–17 year old, 0.32 for a child of 11–15 and 0.21 for a child under 11. These are of course arbitrary fractions based upon the judgement of governments, who set the scales every year; but as established scales they at least give a consistent basis for comparative analysis.

Thus the change in the equivalence scales resulting from the move from the LIF to the HBAI basis for government statistical recording in 1988 aroused further controversy because of the change in equivalence values which accompanied it. The HBAI figures are based on a different and more complex equivalence scale, with finer gradations of changes for third and fourth adults and children with different ages. The more complex scale is not necessarily superior. It is debatable whether the marginal costs of additional household members and children with different ages can be so closely determined. But the main problem of the change is the lack of consistency it introduces, especially as the IS equivalence scales remain within the benefit system itself.

How to determine equivalence scales is a controversial issue. Fiegehen *et al.* (1977, Ch. 7) discuss different models and the consequences of these. They used behaviouristic measures, based on the 1971 FES, to determine the costs of different household members such as children. They then compared the scales based on these expenditure patterns to those assumed in the SB rates and found that in practice there was little difference between the two.

Budget standard approaches have also been used to compare the needs of family members, especially children, with the resources implied in the equivalence scales incorporated into SB/IS. For instance Bradshaw and Holmes (1989) examined families living on SB, Roll (1986) focused on the costs of babies, and, most well-known, Piachaud (1979, 1981b) looked at the costs of children. All concluded that costs are greater than the amounts allowed in the benefit rates. But Piachaud, for example, found that the estimated costs of children did vary with the age of the child, as did the SB equivalence scales, suggesting that even if overall the rates were too low the equivalence ratings were fairly accurate.

The great advantage of equivalence scales, as both Atkinson (1983, Ch. 3.3) and Fiegehen *et al.* (1977, Ch. 7) discuss, is that they permit households or families of different structures or sizes to be compared, in particular in terms of changes in expenditure patterns at different levels of income. Thus analysis utilising Engel curves, the points in income scales at which expenditure on items of need changes, can be constructed and comparisons made between families of different types. Fiegehen *et al.* use this to show how Engel curves vary for households with and without dependent children, confirming our commonsense expectation that for households with children expenditure on necessities claims a higher proportion of income, especially at low income levels.

Different equivalence scales for children of different ages suggest that the cost of living increases as we get older. For children this is obviously so, but in practice needs and resources vary considerably with age in adulthood too. And changes in needs and resources throughout our life cycles is an important feature of both poverty and inequality.

Life Cycle Changes

By and large income changes over an individual's lifetime are a product of changes in earnings capacity. On average the pattern of income over a lifetime takes the form of an inverted U, earning capacity grows in early adulthood, reaches a plateau in middle age, and then declines with old age and retirement (Figure 6.1).

In fact the decline does not go completely back to zero in old age due to the effect of retirement pensions. And entitlement to a pension, particularly a generous, earnings-related occupational pension, can

FIGURE 6.1 *Income over the life cycle*

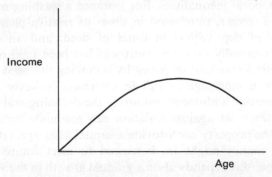

significantly reduce the decline into poverty in old age. This means that the steepness of the decline will vary between different individuals depending on their employment status during adulthood, with non-manual workers generally experiencing a shallower decline as they get older due the retention of well-paid jobs with incremental salary scales and the enjoyment of occupational pensions.

It is clear from this that pensions can be regarded as a form of deferred income and their impact on life-cycle wealth and poverty demonstrates the importance of regarding income as a resource over time, as well as when it is actually received. The ability to save and defer spending can operate to even out periods of relative poverty within the life cycle and can therefore mitigate to a considerable extent the deprivation associated with low income, if this is a temporary or a predictable event.

Saving for the metaphorical 'rainy day' is in practice a major feature of the balance between individual income and expenditure, which can have a significant effect on the extent and the experience of poverty. The American academic Sherraden (1991) has argued that saving and the acquisition of 'assets' is more important than income in determining, and preventing, poverty. As will be discussed in Chapter 7, this means that studies of poverty need to pay attention to the cumulative and lifetime effects of periods of low income or deprivation, rather than utilising only snapshot measures of current circumstances. And thus, as Atkinson (1983, 1989, Ch. 1) has argued, studies of poverty which are based upon a longer 'accounting period' in which income is measured are likely to reveal a lower overall rate of poverty.

It is not just monetary savings, such as pensions, annuities and insurance policies, which can mitigate poverty over time, however.

Spending and investment in consumer durables, especially housing, can also even out temporal inequalities. For instance a washing machine and a fridge or a freezer, purchased in times of relative plenty, can reduce problems of deprivation in times of need; and an owner-occupied house, especially once the mortgage has been paid off, can significantly improve standard of living by removing the need to pay rent. Even where a mortgage is still in existence, however, owner occupation can provide additional resources, the declining real cost of the repayments when set against inflation can gradually reduce the actual cost, and the property can provide a capital asset against which further sums of money might be borrowed to meet future needs, although, of course, this depends upon a gradual growth in the value of such property. Where this does not happen, as in the recession of the early 1990s, high mortgages on houses falling in value resulted in repossession and bankruptcy for some recent buyers, turning capital investment into future deprivation.

Thus although income and wealth can be spread by individuals throughout their lifetime to mitigate the problems associated with periods of deprivation, the success of such strategies is never guaranteed. And, as we might expect therefore, poverty too can have a debilitating effect over time. Inability to save and invest now means that resources are not there to be drawn on in the future. This can accentuate any deprivation due to low income later in life, a problem experienced by many older pensioners in the 1980s and 1990s who did not have the benefit of the wide range of occupational and private pension schemes which are now available when they were perhaps earning enough to pay into them. And debts inherited from earlier periods of life only compound this.

There have not been many studies which have attempted to investigate the effects of the experience of periods of poverty on chances in later life. Atkinson *et al.* (1983) studied the children of the families in York interviewed in Rowntree's last study there (Rowntree and Lavers, 1951), and found that there had been some mobility away from poverty by some families, but only some. In the US, however, 'panel studies', which follow individuals at regular points throughout their lifetime, provide an important basis for this type of approach to be developed, as R. Walker (1991) discusses; and as we shall see in Chapter 7, this kind of research will soon be possible in Britain too.

This raises the further issue of the differences between all individuals in particular cohorts across societies over time, arising as a result of demographic changes and reforms in social and economic policy and which are carried through into later life. Policy changes have obviously influenced the situation of the current cohort of pensioners mentioned above, especially those retiring before the initial introduction of the State Earnings-Related Pension Scheme (SERPS) in 1978 and thus unable to benefit from earnings-related additions to their state pensions.

Demographic changes are perhaps less obvious; but in practice they may be more significant. For instance a downturn in the birth rate will be represented fifteen or twenty years later by a reduced number of school leavers entering the employment market. And this may well mean enhanced employment prospects, and hence reduced poverty prospects, for these young adults, irrespective of any individual efforts or talents on their part or any policy changes introduced by government. Conversely those born during the periods of so-called 'baby booms' may face greater difficulties in providing for themselves as they grow older.

Other demographic changes, such as changes in marriage and divorce rates, and age at childbirth, will also affect individuals' earning capacity and income, and thus spending needs and spending and saving patterns. This raises the more general issue of changes in household and family structure over time, which is a long established feature of discussion and analysis of poverty and inequality. As discussed above, differences in household structure will affect the circumstances of household members. However such structures are not static. Inevitably they change over time, and this family aspect of life cycle changes is crucial in influencing the impact of poverty and deprivation.

In his pioneering work on poverty, Rowntree (1901) identified five periods of alternating want and relative plenty through which a labourer would pass: childhood, early working adulthood, parenthood, working life after children had grown up and old age. In their discussion of such changes O'Higgins *et al.* (1988) identified ten life cycle groups between which family structures vary in ways that are likely to impact on standard of living, and they then used FES data to compare the circumstances of a sample of different groups. They concluded that the principles behind Rowntree's model of alternating periods remained as relevant in the latter part of the twentieth century as at the beginning of it, although with changed economic and social circumstances periods of differing resources and needs may have become more complex. For instance, with widespread owner-occupation, families may rely upon two incomes to pay for the costs of setting up a household during early adulthood, before children are born, after which they will survive for a period when the children are young with only one income (see R. Walker, 1988).

O'Higgins *et al.* (1988) also included an eleventh group, lone parents, who are also now more likely to be poor. Townsend (1979, Ch. 22) too identified lone parents as a group potentially experiencing deprivation. And, as Millar (1988, 1989a) discusses, lone parents are predominantly mothers and most have become lone parent families following matrimonial breakdown.

Of course matrimonial breakdown is not a life cycle event experienced by all, and it was certainly ignored in Rowntree's five periods of life cycle need and plenty. However, it is experienced by an increasing proportion of the population of Britain, with more than one in three marriages expected to end in divorce in the 1980s and 1990s. And, as Millar (1988) demonstrates, it is a life cycle change with a significant impact on income and wealth. Townsend (1979, Ch. 20) and Glendinning and Baldwin (1988) point out that this is also true of chronic sickness and disability, an issue to which we shall return in Chapter 11.

Unemployment too may have household and life cycle consequences. For instance Cooke (1987) discussed the effect of male unemployment on families which appeared to result in wives withdrawing from paid work as well as their husbands. Given Walker's argument above about the importance of two incomes for families during certain periods of the household life cycle, this is likely to have an impact beyond the immediate period of lost income from wages.

One of the significant features of life cycle periods of relative deprivation is that they are to a large extent predictable. They could thus be prepared for and the relative deprivation associated with them prevented or mitigated. This can be done at an individual level, for example through a private pension scheme. But more significantly it can be done at a social level by directing resources towards predictable periods of need.

This idea of the redistribution of resources across the life cycle is referred to as *horizontal equity*, as contrasted with *vertical equity* which is redistribution between rich and poor at similar periods of their lives, or irrespective of life cycle needs. This was recognised as a basic, if not the basic, feature of social security protection by Beveridge (1942), who based his benefit proposals on Rowntree's analysis of poverty. Social security should, according to Beveridge, be designed to provide for periods of need – from the cradle to the grave – using an insurance model under which contributions made in times of employment would provide for benefits at times of need. The advantage of collective protection through social security is that it can provide for periods of need which may not be predictable at an individual level, for instance marital breakdown. This was included in Beveridge's original proposals but was omitted from the postwar national insurance scheme because of government fears that this might encourage marriages to break up.

Beveridge was quite clear, however, that it was children, and the associated costs of caring for them, which was the most important predictable case for horizontal equity, and he supported the use of a universal state benefit to provide for this – Family Allowances. Family Allowances have now been replaced in Britain by Child Benefit. Both, however, have received widespread support as a means of achieving some measure of horizontal equity between households (see Henwood and Wicks, 1986; Brown, 1988; and Parker and Sutherland, 1991). However the value of universal child support has not remained constant throughout the postwar period and, as Piachaud (1982a) has shown, this has led to a decline in the relative living standards of families. Universal benefits such as Child Benefit have also never been sufficient to equalise fully the deprivation effects of child-rearing. And, as Piachaud has also pointed out (1982a, p. 19), they do not compensate for the loss of income from second earners if childbirth leads to one adult family member (usually the woman) leaving paid employment.

Thus, as O'Higgins *et al.* (1988) argue, although they are largely predictable, life cycle changes have not by and large resulted in adequate horizontal redistribution to prevent the poverty and inequality associated with them. Indeed, especially for families with children, in the 1980s the distinctions between groups at different stages of their life cycle became more acute. This aspect of relative poverty has always been a major concern of the most important postwar antipoverty campaign group, the Child Poverty Action Group, as their name implies. And CPAG has always been a strong supporter of Child Benefit, as will be discussed further in Chapter 13.

Intrahousehold Transfers

Different household and family formations therefore result in different needs and expenditure patterns, and these also vary over time. Equivalence scales are a means of comparing different households or families by formalising assumptions about the reduced needs and expenditure which result from the sharing of resources within the household. However the comparisons based on reduced costs due to sharing in households are founded upon two important assumptions, both of which can be subject to critical debate. The first assumption is that sharing or aggregation of resources does take place within households, and that this interdependency is non-problematic. The second is that two or more people can live less expensively than one and maintain the same standard.

The assumption of *aggregation* is a longstanding feature of both academic analysis and policy development. And it is obviously not without foundation. For instance, although most children have no income of their own we know that most parents expect to use their incomes in order to provide for their children. However it is far from clear whether all parents share all their resources with their children on an equal basis, and commonsense suggests that it is most unlikely that they do. When it comes to sharing between adults the assumption of equal sharing is even more questionable.

Obviously discovering reliable information about the distribution of incomes within households is problematic, a point to which we shall return shortly; but recent studies which have attempted to do this suggest that unequal sharing is likely to be the norm. Piachaud (1982a, p. 481) concludes that, 'the distribution of incomes within families is highly unequal'. In a series of ground-breaking papers Pahl (1980, 1984, 1988) described the different patterns of income distribution within families, some of which were clearly unequal both in shares of income and control over expenditure.

Given their relative exclusion from the labour market, and their weaker position within it, it is usually women who are the less equal partners in such divisions, and, as we shall see, this is usually associated with their greater responsibilities for caring work. One startling example of the depth of this inequality was Graham's (1987) finding that over a half of the women questioned in a survey of separated lone parents felt that they were better off after separation, dependent on state benefit and living on the 'poverty line', than they had been when they were sharing with partners with higher earnings.

One of the reasons why the women in these families felt poor was because they did not control the resources – it was not their income which provided for the family and they could not by and large determine expenditure. This feeling of dependency is a central feature of inequality within households, and it is compounded by the assumptions about aggregation and sharing of living costs incorporated into benefit policy (see Alcock, 1987, Ch. 3). It is a social and an emotional as well as a material inequality, and it is a significant yet widely overlooked feature of poverty amid affluence to which we shall return in Chapter 8. Even where married women are in paid employment, family inequalities are not necessarily removed for, as Morris (1989) shows, their income is generally lower and more likely to be spent on supplementing an inadequate housekeeping budget.

Of course poverty and inequality within households is not exclusively a female problem. The enforced dependency contained in policies which aggregate family and household incomes also has consequences for sick and disabled adults forced to rely upon others at home, and for young unemployed adults, now up to the age of 24 under IS regulations, assumed to be able to share their households with others.

The second assumption underlying the household basis for poverty measurement is that of the reduction in living costs associated with sharing. Again there is obviously some basis for this, heating can be shared, as can furniture and many other household items. But many of the reductions supposedly associated with shared living are indirect savings based upon unpaid work performed within the household, usually by women. Piachaud (1987) contrasts the cost of oven-ready chips with home-prepared chips, the end result is more or less the same but one costs more to the household in terms of money and the other more in terms of time. For the go-getting executive we know that 'time is money', but the equation is equally valid for the housewife at home.

The standard of living of many households is maintained by, usually women's, unpaid labour at home cooking and cleaning. This is a substitute for a reduced family income, but at a cost to the family member performing the work. As Lister (1990) argues, this loss of time, 'time poverty', is a significant deprivation in the lives of many women and which is disguised within the household measure of income and expenditure.

Where unpaid work at home extends to caring for other dependents, such as children, the costs in time rise astronomically. In a well-publicised pamphlet Piachaud (1984) estimated that this averaged out at around fifty hours a week for the ordinary young child. This is more than the average working week in paid employment and a significant feature of a broader conceptualisation of the intrahousehold distribution of resources.

Both direct (cash) and indirect (emotional dependency, loss of control and time poverty) costs of intrahousehold distribution have often been ignored in studies of poverty. Indeed it is only fairly recently that research has attempted to discover information about such distributions. Although it hardly provides a justification, this may in part be due to a recognition of the difficulties inherent in securing reliable data about such a potentially sensitive issue. Pahl's work was based on qualitative interviews with very small samples of households. The results were revealing, but they were not necessarily representative. Conducting large-scale quantitative research within households is likely to be difficult, if not impossible, to organise however.

Nevertheless Jenkins (1991) has argued that it may be possible to develop new dimensions within existing quantitative analysis to represent better the hidden costs of sharing, for instance by manipulating equivalence scales. But the attempt to undo the problems of aggregation by assumption within existing studies of poverty and deprivation may be a tall order, and certainly much work would need to be done to demonstrate the feasibility of this. However even awareness of the problem can begin to minimise its implications, and in both qualitative and quantitative research there is no longer any justification for not addressing the issue of intrahousehold equity at the same time as that of household structure more generally.

7

Measuring Poverty

The Problem of Measurement

As suggested in Chapter 1, for most academics as well as most politicians the purpose of attempting to define poverty is in order to be able to measure its extent within societies, or across societies, with the implication being that where the extent of poverty is great then it will be the focus of concern and policies may be developed to remove or ameliorate it. It is primarily because of this policy context that the task of defining poverty is, of course, so problematic. And for the same reason the question of measuring poverty is fraught with difficulties and disagreements too.

Fundamental to the debate over measurement, as in the debate over definitions, is the question of whether what is being measured is some separate category of poverty or merely some predetermined aspect of the broader measurement of levels of inequality, such as a line or threshold drawn towards the bottom of the income or wealth scale, below which inequality is argued to be, or presumed to be, unacceptable. We shall return shortly to this question of how to draw up a line to be measured. However the issue is further complicated, as Ringen (1988) has pointed out, by confusion over the use of both direct and indirect measures.

The emphasis upon relative deprivation and standard of living in determining poverty levels, developed by Townsend (1979), Mack and Lansley (1985) and others, focuses attention upon expenditure, or more accurately consumption, as a measure of poverty. But most studies of poverty, particularly those seeking to establish the numbers below a given poverty line, including Townsend and Mack and Lansley, use income as a measure. Ringen's argument is that income cannot be used as a proxy for consumption since many aspects of consumption are not determined solely by income, notably the consumption of non-commodified welfare services

This is an important point; and, as is conceded by Donnison (1988) in a reply to Ringen, crude attempts to equate cash inequalities to poverty are not acceptable either in academic or political circles. However, as discussed in Chapter 4, there have been some more sophisticated attempts to establish a link between income levels and consumption patterns, for instance via the notion of a threshold of deprivation. And if the limitations of these are borne in mind, it may nevertheless be feasible to use income measures to make some assessment of numbers in poverty according to certain definitions.

In fact the problems involved in the measurement of income and/or consumption extend well beyond the difficulties pointed to by Ringen. There are many other inconsistencies between different measures resulting from the means by which data is collected, analysed and presented, some of which we shall return to below. However these problems do not mean that, and should not be used to suggest that, we cannot arrive at any useful measures of poverty or inequality. As Atkinson in particular has consistently argued and demonstrated (for instance Atkinson, 1983, 1989), if care is taken to recognise the problems involved, there is quite a lot we can say about the extent of poverty and inequality in Britain, and across other advanced industrial countries too.

Much of the work on measuring poverty has been quantitative in nature, using statistical techniques to count the numbers of people in poverty or to measure the extent of inequalities. Indeed in Britain in particular this arithmetic tradition has a long and well-established history in academic circles and political debate, stemming from the seminal studies of Booth (1889) and Rowntree (1901) at the end of the nineteenth century.

However, quantitative measures provide us with a rather limited picture of the extent of poverty and inequality in society. These limitations were graphically illustrated in the interchange between Bowley, one of the British pioneers of poverty measurement, and Bevin, the trade union leader and later foreign secretary, in 1920 over the 'docker's breakfast' discussed in Chapter 4. As Bevin's biographer pointed out, the trade union leader's (qualitative) measure of the meagre diet of bread, bacon and fish was worth 'volumes of statistics' in its effect on public opinion (Atkinson, 1989, p. 38). The qualitative measure tells us what the volume of statistics could never do: how poverty is measured in real life terms. Qualitative data is thus as important as statistical data analysis in the measurement of poverty, and we will return shortly to a brief discussion of the role of qualitative studies in poverty research.

Quantitative Measures

The great advantage of quantitative measures, however, is their scale and their anonymity. A statistical survey, if it is large enough and if the sample of respondents providing the data is sufficiently carefully chosen, can provide an objective, and arguably scientific, picture of the broader group or society from which it has been selected, particularly if the standard measures of the statistical significance of the data have been reached. As we suggested above therefore, quantitative measures have always been at the centre of poverty research and measurement in Britain. These can be based upon existing statistical information collected by government or other agencies for different purposes, or they can be based on original data collected directly by researchers using survey methods to question a sample of the population. Both approaches have been widely utilised in poverty and inequality research in Britain.

The main sources of existing data are government statistics; collected by government departments or the Central Statistical Office (CSO). In particular these include the 'Blue Books', national income and expenditure blue books produced by the CSO from inland revenue data and other official sources, which provided a more or less consistent source of data from 1952 until the mid 1970s. Since 1957 the government has also conducted a regular family expenditure survey (FES) based on information about the expenditure patterns of a relatively large sample of the population.

It was an early version of the FES which was used by Abel Smith and Townsend (1965) in their famous study, *The Poor and the Poorest*, which demonstrated that high levels of poverty persisted in Britain despite the introduction of the welfare reforms of the postwar period. Extracts from these, and other official sources, provide the basis of the annual statistical reports on *Social Trends* and *Economic Trends*. Since the 1970s the DHSS, later the DSS, has also been utilising this data to publish the details of families with low incomes relative to state benefit, and now the HBAI figures discussed in Chapter 6. The most comprehensive official statistics dealing with incomes, including low incomes, however, were those produced by the 'Royal Commission on the Distribution of Income and Wealth', the Diamond Commission, who produced regular reports culminating in 1980 when they were discontinued by the Conservative government (Royal Commission, 1980).

The great advantages of government statistics, of course, are that access to them is free and they carry the authority of their official status. They are thus used widely by academic researchers and political campaigners. For instance the CPAG has established a strong tradition of analysing and publicising official statistics on poverty and inequality in order to demonstrate, using the government's own figures, the limitations of policies aimed at reducing poverty (see Oppenheim, 1990).

Despite their apparent authority, however, there are limitations within the official statistics which need to be borne in mind in any attempts to utilise them as a poverty measure. For instance the FES sample is only about one in 2500, it covers only those in households (thus excluding the homeless or those in institutions), it has a roughly 30 per cent non-response rate, and given the way the data is gathered it is very likely to understate income. Thus not everyone, or everything, is covered; and poverty and low incomes in particular may be under-represented in the figures.

It is partly because of limitations such as these, therefore, that some researchers have sought to collect their own quantitative data about poverty and deprivation, although original data also has the advantage of being able to cover a breadth and depth of detail not included in government and other official statistics. Some of the most significant studies of poverty have thus been based on surveys conducted by, or on behalf of, the investigators themselves. Rowntree (1901, 1941) and Townsend (1979) employed research workers to interview respondents and collect data. Mack and Lansley (1985), through London Weekend Television, used a contract research agency (MORI) to conduct a survey for them. And in a later study of poverty in London, Townsend (Townsend *et al.*, 1987) combined a survey of a sample of the population with cooperation and consultation with representative bodies in local councils and the now abolished Greater London Council (GLC).

Of course all the problems of sample size, non-response, and so on apply to originally collected data too. But control over the construction of questionnaires and samples of respondents allows a much greater range of data to be collected and analysed, as was demonstrated in Townsend's major 1960s and 1970s survey (Townsend, 1979). However collecting original data is costly, and Towsend's study in particular struggled with a budget which, though large by some research standards, was barely adequate for the task to which it was addressed.

Despite these problems some very useful and significant studies have managed to collect original data without relatively large budgets by using various opportunities arising from other activities. For instance Coates and Silburn's (1970) classic study of poverty in an inner city area of Nottingham (St Ann's) was based on data collected by Workers Educational Association students and undergraduates at Nottingham University as part of their social studies curriculum.

One of the broader limitations of originally collected data, however, is its compatibility with other data from other studies, either of different populations or at different times. One of reasons why Abel Smith and Townsend (1965) were able to discover higher levels of poverty in Britain in the 1950s than those revealed in Rowntree's final 1950 survey in York (Rowntree and Lavers, 1951) was because their work was based upon a different, and more extensive, source of data. Thus the difference was arguably as much to do with how the data relied on was collected as it was to do with different levels of poverty and inequality in British society itself. Over time this problem of comparability of data is indeed a large one, as Piachaud (1988) discusses. Although, as he showed, adjustments can usually be made to the data to reveal some comparability if this is approached carefully.

If we want to make comparisons between levels of poverty and inequality in different countries, then the problems of comparability of data grow even greater, as mentioned in Chapter 3. Even in official statistics there are differences in policy over what information is collected, and differences in culture and convention over how this is done and how it is analysed and presented. At times this problem may have seemed insurmountable, but the increasing activity of the EC has led to a significant commitment to international comparability within Europe and to growing pressure within Europe for the collection of crossnational statistical information through Eurostat, the Commission's statistical service. Such information is available on a comparable basis for all EC member states in the 1980s in the *Final Report of the Second European Poverty Programme* (EC, 1991).

More recently a major international collaborative venture in the collection and analysis of data on incomes has begun with the support of the government of Luxembourg. The Luxembourg Income Study (LIS) is a large and long term commitment to establish and develop a database on income levels and poverty in a wide range of advanced industrial countries (see Smeeding *et al.*, 1990). Initially seven countries were involved (Canada, Israel, Norway, Sweden, Britain, the US and West Germany), but soon others joined in. Data is provided by each country and then adapted by the research team to give some measure of compatability. The British data is that from the FES in 1979 and 1985.

The great advantage of the LIS is that it provides a database which researchers and analysts from different countries can use and adapt for their own purposes. What makes this feasible now of course is the use of new technologies in information storage and retrieval on computers and microcomputers. The development of computer-based information technology has transformed, and much enhanced, the use of quantitative measures of poverty and inequality. Computerised data can be much more speedily collected and analysed and, even more importantly, it can be readily transferred, adapted and reanalysed any number of times.

Users of the LIS can request data direct from the computer base using information links and can then analyse the data received as they wish, although obviously a fee is charged for this service. This accessibility and transferability of computer-based data is a trend which has been supported strongly in recent years by Atkinson, the leading British expert on quantitative measurement of poverty and inequality (for instance Atkinson, 1989. p. 38). As he argues, if such data can be made accessible to other researchers, then they can analyse it using their own poverty lines or poverty measures, thus avoiding the problems and disagreements discussed in Chapter 4.

With the assistance of Sutherland, Atkinson has developed such a database as part of the LSE Welfare State Research Programme (TAXMOD), which can be used to measure the effects of potential changes in taxes and benefits on income distribution in Britain and can be adapted to respond to specific questions or assumptions made by different users (Atkinson and Sutherland, 1984).

Adaption and reanalysis of data, however, is constrained by the basic structure of the information available. As with all computer-based data, we can only get out what we have put in. This poses obvious limitations on the international comparisons which can be made using the LIS for instance. In Chapter 6 we discussed the differences between the family and the household as a basis for measuring income. Although the LIS data includes family-based measures for all the initial countries in the study, it does not contain household data for all, so only limited comparisons can be made.

The household/family distinction is obviously an important variable in structuring data in quantitative studies; but there are also others. In spite of Ringen's criticisms most surveys measure income. But what is income? And in particular over what time period should income be measured? For instance a distinction can be made between *current* weekly income, that is the income actually received during the week of the survey, and *normal* income, that is income taking account of potential fluctuations or eccentricities in weekly income.

For instance incomes recorded in the FES are the last-earned weekly income in circumstances where the head of household has been out of work for less than twelve weeks. Beckerman and Clark (1982) demonstrated that on 1974–5 data this made a significant difference to the numbers consequently assumed to be below the poverty line: on the normal income basis there were 5 per cent, but this rose to 6.8 per cent if current income only were used.

However the choice is not restricted only to these two measures. For some purposes arguably it would be more appropriate to use monthly rather than weekly income as the 'accounting period', as this is sometimes called, or even to use an annual income measure as is more commonly the case in US statistics. But even an annual basis will ignore the cumulative effects over time on incomes of savings and investments, as discussed in Chapter 6. As R. Walker (1991) has pointed out in a survey of US statistical measures using differing accounting periods, the longer the period the lower the incidence of poverty likely to be recorded. However it is not just the overall incidence of poverty which varies according to the period adopted; the spread of poverty throughout the population also changes. Although most spells of poverty are quite short and affect a relatively wide range of the population, there is a smaller core of people experiencing the more serious poverty associated with longer accounting periods.

However even with longer accounting periods there are problems of exclusion, for instance of those experiencing periods of poverty which began before the research measurement started, or those whose periods of poverty extend beyond the completion of the data collection. To take account of this, and of the more general problem of the cumulative effects of changes over long periods of time, one-off or snapshot surveys will always be inadequate. Changes over time need to be measured over time, or to put it in more technical terms the 'window of observation' needs to exceed the accounting period.

This can be done by using what are called panel studies, which measure income and expenditure, and other characteristics, of a sample of correspondents at regular intervals over a long period of time. These have been more widely used in the US than in Britain, for instance the University of Michigan Panel Study of Income Dynamics, which has collected data on a sample of respondents annually since 1968 (see R. Walker, 1991). However in the late 1980s a major panel study was established in Britain with Economic and Social Research Council support at Essex University, using a sample of 5000 households (12 000 individuals) to be interviewed annually on a range of issues including income and expenditure up to the year 2000. As this becomes established it will provide a major enhancement to poverty measurement in this country, revealing patterns in income and expenditure change which could not be discovered using snapshot surveys.

In addition to the problem of what to count as income is the debate over where to draw the poverty line in quantitative studies. Obviously there is the definitional problem here which was discussed in Chapter 4, as well as Ringen's point about the appropriateness of income measures to determine levels of poverty. But nevertheless poverty lines are drawn, and where they are drawn does have important consequences for the conclusions which flow from them. We have already discussed some of the consequences of the move from the LIF to the HBAI figures in government statistics in Britain in the 1980s. In her 1990 pamphlet, Oppenhiem explains why CPAG continued to use both the SB/IS line of the LIF figures and the 50 per cent of average income line of the HBAI figures in their measurements of poverty. As she points out both have advantages and disadvantages, although by both measures there were roughly similar numbers of people in poverty in Britain in 1987 (10.2 million on or below SB level and 10.5 million below 50 per cent average income; Oppenheim, 1990, p. 42). Both of these figures had risen significantly since 1979.

Counting the numbers of people, or households, below a poverty line is also contentious however. For this 'head count', as it is sometimes called, does not reveal the extent of poverty of individuals or households. That is, it does not tell us how far they are below the poverty line. Obviously there is a significant difference between say ten million people being just below the poverty line and five million people being more than 50 per cent below it. In the latter case fewer are 'in poverty', but their experience of poverty is much more serious.

Thus the depth as well as the breadth of poverty – or the poverty gap as it is sometimes called – may also need to be measured in order to determine levels of poverty. As Beckerman (1980) argues, the distinction is not only of academic importance, it can also have an important effect on policy planning. The policies and resources required to lift a large number of people just a short way over the poverty line would be rather different from those required to raise the incomes of a smaller number much further. As will be discussed in Chapter 14, social security policies in Britain have mainly been aimed at reducing the poverty gap; yet most quantitative studies of poverty are attempts to determine a head count of numbers below the poverty line.

The importance of the poverty gap measure is that it can give us a clearer indication of the scale of relative poverty when compared with the broader distribution of resources. It is really a version of a measure of inequality, expressed in relation to a poverty line drawn within the overall income distribution. In practice of course, as discussed in Chapter 4, this is what all definitions of poverty are, and thus all quantitative measures of poverty are primarily measures of inequality onto which definitions of poverty are mapped.

In order to do this definitions of poverty must be expressed in a form which can be applied as an indicator of poverty to a statistical database of income or expenditure. In most cases this takes the form of algebraic formulae, which can then be applied to the data to reveal the numbers and proportions of the poor. This use of indicators is a complex science, generally referred to as econometrics, and it requires an understanding of algebra which is likely to be beyond most social scientists. Atkinson is the most important and widely read exponent of econometric approaches to poverty measurement and he discusses some of the conceptual and practical issues involved in this in two famous papers reproduced in 1989 (Atkinson, 1989, Chs 1 and 2). The use of algebraic formulae permits us to make measurements of poverty, according to different definitions, from data on income or expenditure inequality. Thus they can help to turn definitions into measures. However mathematics cannot overcome the problems associated with definition itself, discussed in Chapter 4.

Measures of Inequality

It is measures of inequality which are therefore at the heart of quantitative studies of poverty. Measuring inequality and changing patterns of income or expenditure distribution provides us with the broader picture of relativities of wealth and deprivation into which discussion about where to draw the poverty line can be inserted. Thus in order better to understand debates about poverty we need to spend a little time examining how measures of inequality operate and what kind of information they provide.

The most graphic demonstration of the power of inequality measures is Pen's famous 'Parade of Dwarfs' (Pen, 1971). In a fascinating popularisation of the distribution of income in British society, Pen characterised the spread of incomes as an hour-long parade of people whose height was symbolic of their relative place in the distribution of resources in society, with average income being represented by persons of average height. As the title of the paper suggests, under this representation the vast majority of people were dwarfs – only twelve minutes before the end of the hour did persons of average height appear. But after that, in the last ten minutes, heights grew dramatically, with doctors and accountants seven to eight yards high, and finally at the end a few people who were a mile high or more. Seen in this way the measurement of inequality is indeed staggering. Pen also presents it as a graph, which reveals in visual form the fact that so many are below the average, and that a few are far above it (Figure 7.1). The political importance of the relationship between inequality and poverty measures becomes much clearer when we recognise that the large majority of people receive below average resources.

FIGURE 7.1 *Pen's 'Parade of Dwarfs'*

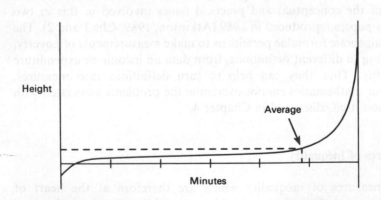

Source: Pen, 1971.

A more conventional, and adaptable, way of expressing the distribution described in Pen's parade is through the construction of what are called Lorenz curves. These are used to represent, in simple graphical form, the distribution of incomes in a particular country against what would be a hypothetical distribution of completely identical incomes. They are discussed by Atkinson (1983, pp. 15–17), who provides the following example based on the distribution of income in Britain in 1978–9 (Figure 7.2).

FIGURE 7.2 *The Lorenz curve*

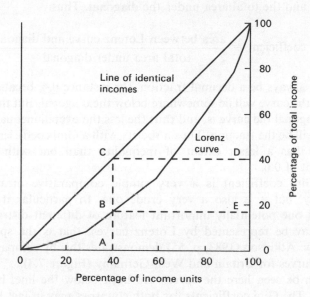

Source: Atkinson, 1983, Figure 2.2, p. 16.

The curve representing distribution in Britain lies below the straight line representing hypothetical identical income levels. Thus if all incomes were equal, 40 per cent of income units would receive 40 per cent of total income – line ACD. In fact, however, distribution is not equal, it follows the curve below the line, and thus 40 per cent of people receive below 20 per cent of income – line ABE. The trajectory of the curve below the line thus expresses the extent of inequality in the society. The further away from the diagonal line the curve is, the greater the extent of inequality; thus a curve below that in Figure 7.2

would show 40 per cent of the population getting much less then 20 per cent of income.

Lorenz curves not only have the advantage of expressing measures of inequality in a simple, visual form; they can also allow comparisons to be made easily between different distributions (and thus inequalities) in different societies (see Atkinson, 1983, pp. 54–5). Thus if the US has a Lorenz curve below that of Britain, then we can say that in general it is a more unequal society. This relationship can also be expressed in numerical form by calculating from a Lorenz curve a figure known as the Gini coefficient. This is the fraction which represents the relationship found in the graph between the area between the curve and the diagonal and the total area under the diagonal. Thus:

$$\text{Gini coefficient} = \frac{\text{area between Lorenz curve and diagonal}}{\text{total area under diagonal}}$$

This will always be a decimal fraction, for instance 0.4, because in all societies the curve will lie somewhere below the diagonal. But the closer to the diagonal the curve is, and thus the less the overall inequality, the smaller will be the fraction. Thus a society with a Gini coefficient of 0.4 generally has a lesser extent of inequality than one with a Gini coefficient of 0.6.

The Gini coefficient is a very simple comparative measure of inequality, but it is also a very crude one. In particular it cannot represent one potentially important feature of different distributions which may be represented by Lorenz curves, that is the spread of inequality. Atkinson (1983, p. 55) demonstrates this by comparing the Lorenz curves for Britain and West Germany (Figure 7.3).

As can be seen here the curves are both below the line, but they intersect. The Gini coefficients for both countries may in fact be more or less the same, but the distribution of income in each is significantly different. Thus according to Atkinson, there were more people in West Germany with low incomes than there were in Britain, but conversely those in the middle in West Germany enjoyed a comparatively higher relative position to those in the middle in Britain.

Measures of inequality therefore concern not just the relationship between those at the top and those at the bottom. They also tell us about the relationships between all those in between, and here patterns may, and do, vary significantly between different countries, as expressed by the intersection of comparative Lorenz curves. This is a similar distinction to that between the head count and poverty gap

FIGURE 7.3   *Intersecting Lorenz curves*

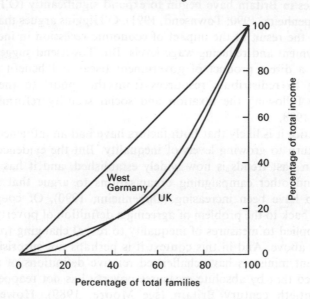

Source: Atkinson, 1983, Figure 3.2, p. 55.

measures of poverty referred to above – both are important and may lead to important differences in policy to respond to the patterns they reveal. Of course distributions will also vary within one country over time, particularly if policy measures are introduced aiming to reduce, or increase, the extent of inequality. And measures of inequality compared over time can tell us something about the success or failure of such policies.

It is generally assumed that in Britain, as in most other advanced industrial societies, the impact of taxation and welfare policies over the last century or so has reduced overall levels of inequality (see Rubenstein, 1986; Soltow, 1980). This is probably true, although more recent measures suggest that the reduction in relativities has not been so marked in Britain since the establishment of the welfare state after the Second World War. In particular the relative position of the bottom 50 per cent of the population has remained, relatively speaking, more or less static throughout the postwar period, although overall levels of affluence have risen (Royal Commission, 1979, p. 75).

More importantly perhaps, as we discussed in Chapter 1, more recent evidence suggests that despite earlier trends towards greater equality, since the mid 1970s, and especially during the 1980s, inequalities in Britain have begun to expand significantly (O'Higgins, 1985; Oppenheim, 1990; Townsend, 1991). O'Higgins argues that this is primarily the result of the impact of economic recession in increasing unemployment and reducing wage levels. But Townsend suggests that it is also a direct product of government fiscal and benefit policies operating to redistribute resources from the 'poor' to the 'rich', especially following the taxation and social security reforms introduced in 1988.

In practice it is likely that both factors have had an influence on the recent return to growing levels of inequality. But the evidence of the reversal in past trends is now widely established, and it has led the CPAG and other campaigning organisations to argue that poverty levels too have been increasing (Oppenheim, 1990). Of course this brings us back to the problem of agreeing a definition of poverty which can be applied to measures of inequality to reveal changing trends, as discussed above. And in this context it is perhaps not surprising that government ministers have challenged relative definitions of poverty and argued that by absolute measures poverty has not reappeared in late twentieth century Britain (see Moore, 1989). However, as suggested above, measures of poverty do not just involve quantitative analysis of statistics, they involve examining what these mean for the real lives of real people. To gain a fuller understanding therefore of poverty and inequality in Britain in the 1980s and 1990s, or at any other time, we need to use qualitative measures in addition to statistical surveys.

Qualitative Measures

Any understanding of poverty requires a focus not just on overall numbers and trends; the individual experience of poverty must also be witnessed and described. And although quantitative measures of poverty have dominated much of British poverty research and debate, there is also a strong history of qualitative descriptions of the experience of poverty which have given life and meaning to the fairly dry tables and graphs of the arithmetic tradition.

Both Rowntree and Booth included descriptive material on the standard of living of the local people covered by their surveys, further underlining the mythical nature of claims that they were operating only with crude notions of absolute poverty. Townsend in his major 1960s and 1970s survey of poverty in Britain specifically focused part of his research, and a chapter of the book based on the study (Townsend, 1979, Ch. 8), on what he called the impact of poverty. For instance, here is an extract from the description of the impact of poverty on a young family suffering disability and with a handicapped child:

> Mr and Mrs Nelson, 35 and 32, live with their three sons of 13, 9 and 6 in a four-roomed council flat in a poor district of Oldham, overlooked by a rubber factory belching smoke all day long and near a canal. They believe the flat is a danger to their health. 'One bedroom is so damp that it stripped itself'. The living room has a fire but they can only afford a one-bar electric fire to heat the bedrooms because they are terribly damp. The fire is taken from one room to the next. At Christmas the bedroom window was smashed by a brick. Because the family cannot afford new glass, the room gets too cold and the boys sleep in one bedroom, (Townsend, 1979, p. 305).

More recently CPAG's review of the experience of poverty in the 1990s, *Hardship Britain* (Cohen *et al.*, 1992), used interviews with people living in poverty to provide a depressing picture of the struggles in their lives. For instance:

> The family have no telephone, vacuum cleaner, electric kettle, or freezer and their fridge is in poor condition, as are all their other household goods. Although they try to give the children two hot meals a day, and often feel obliged to give them fruit and sweets (even though this stretches their budget), their lifestyle is in all other respects spartan. For example, the Chaudrys do not have a set of warm winter clothes or two pairs of all-weather shoes for everyone; the children get no treats and the family cannot afford to go and visit friends and relatives in other towns (p. 19).

As with the CPAG review of poverty in Britain in the 1990s, some of the most interesting and most significant qualitative analyses of poverty have been based largely, or entirely, on descriptive material. These include the early works such as Mayhew's *London's Poor* or Orwell's *Road to Wigan Pier*, and more recent works such as Harrison's (1983) *Inside the Inner City* and Seabrook's (1984) *Landscapes of Poverty*. They also include a range of smaller studies published by organisations like the CPAG and focusing on particular aspects of poverty, such as McClelland's (1982) *A Little Pride and*

Dignity looking at child care costs, or on poverty in particular localities, such as Evason's (1980) *Ends That Won't Meet* examining poverty in Belfast. Qualitative studies generally seem to have more evocative titles than do statistical analyses.

Of course qualitative studies are generally not large scale, and the descriptions they offer cannot claim to be representative of poverty in any scientific sense. Despite their popular persuasive power therefore they can more readily be dismissed by critical academics or unsympathetic politicians, although in practice of course politicians are perhaps more likely to be influenced by popular opinion, or by attempts to manipulate it, than they are by statistical rigour.

However, qualitative data can be linked directly to quantitative measures to harness the complementary strengths of measurement and description. This has been attempted in particular in budget standards studies such as Bradshaw and Morgan (1987) and Bradshaw and Holmes (1989). In these studies descriptions of meagre weekly budgets, monotonous daily menus and dreary and unfulfilling lives accompany attempts to quantify these into a measure of poverty. For instance one mother interviewed in Bradshaw and Morgan could afford only one dress every five years and one pair of shoes every eighteen months. The family could not afford a holiday away from home, a newspaper, a trip to the cinema, tools for the garden or even a haircut (except once a year). Such deprivation can be measured quantitatively, but an important part of what is being measured is lost in the process.

The development of new information technologies has transformed qualitative measurement of poverty as well as quantitative measurement of it. Here it is the development and growth of television and video which has been the powerful influence, however. Television and video descriptions of poverty, either real or fictional, can be taken as moving and talking pictures right into the homes of a mass audience.

There have been a number of influential, qualitative televised studies of poverty. Perhaps the most famous was the fictional 1960s drama on the homelessness and poverty of a young family entitled 'Cathy Come Home'. However probably the most important example of this new genre of qualitative research presentation is the television series for which Mack and Lansley's (1985 and 1992) important studies of relative poverty were undertaken in 1983 and again in 1990. The studies were originally commissioned by London Weekend Television and were screened as a series of television programmes called 'Breadline Britain'. Like the survey itself, the programmes were largely based on interviews with respondents conducted in their own homes.

These were screened as a series of vignettes in which the people described in their own words their struggles to manage on the breadline. They made for harrowing viewing and presented to a wide audience the human costs of the statistical measures of poverty detailed in the survey, although, given the late night screening time, the audience was probably not as wide as it might have been earlier in the evening.

'Breadline Britain's' use of television to present the qualitative aspects of poverty research has since inspired other researchers to use video programmes as a supplement to, or even a replacement for, published written reports on poverty, inequality or social policy. For instance in 1990 members of the Social Security Research Consortium produced a video based upon the findings of their research into the impact of the Social Fund on clients of rights and advice agencies, and this was presented to, amongst others, members of parliament in both the Commons and the Lords.

The use of poor people's own descriptions of their deprivation on television or video raises the broader issue of the role of poor people's determination of and control over the qualitative measurement of their poverty, and the presentation of this to the wider world. There is a strong element of paternalism in all academic studies of poverty and deprivation, which is most clearly revealed in qualitative descriptions or depictions of the lives of the poor. And it is argued by some, in particular by the one-time academic and now community worker in Glasgow's Easterhouse estate, Bob Holman, that the poor should be permitted, or encouraged, to speak for themselves about their experiences of poverty. Autobiography should replace biography, it is argued, not necessarily because it is a more accurate or convincing message, but because it places the power and control over the message in the hands of those experiencing the problem.

This raises a broader issue still, however, about the politics of poverty more generally, about whose problem poverty is and who should, or could, be expected to define it and determine how it is to be tackled. And it is an issue to which we shall return in Chapter 13. Clearly however, self-description is, and should be, an important element within qualitative studies of poverty; and some studies, usually based within local community groups or campaigning organisations, have sought to present personal accounts of poverty to a wider audience. For instance in 1989 the Sheffield branch of CPAG produced a report entitled 'Out of Sight and Out of Mind' as part of a range of activities to publicise the problems of poverty within the city.

Unfortunately most studies such as this take place with little or no funding, and they are therefore usually very limited in scope. However the Joseph Rowntree Foundation has agreed to earmark trust funding for antipoverty action work with local groups of poor people, and the research accompanying the Third European Poverty Programme, discussed in Chapter 3, now includes specific provision for working with local groups representing poor people and their communities. This may, through the relatively generous resources of the EC, be able to provide a much larger audience, and a more influential voice, for self-descriptive approaches to the measurement of poverty in the future.

Part III
Social Divisions and Poverty

8

Gender and Poverty

The Feminisation of Poverty

Most attempts to measure poverty use household or family income or
expenditure as the basis for counting or calculating the extent of
poverty, as discussed in Chapter 6. Even where individual income is
used, measurement then tends to treat all individuals similarly as
recipients of income without comparing their different circumstances
or obligations. Insofar as this is explained or justified, and generally it
is not, the assumption is that whilst income and expenditure are
matters of public knowledge and concern, and thus amenable to public
scrutiny and measurement, households and family circumstances and
obligations are private matters which cannot, or should not, be the
focus of public research.

We will return later to the significance of this alleged public/private
divide in structuring our knowledge and perceptions of individual and
family poverty. It is increasingly widely recognised, however, that
differences in individual and family circumstances are crucial in
determining the impact and extent of poverty, and that rather than
being excluded or ignored they should be a central feature of any
understanding of poverty. This is particularly true of the differences
associated with gender.

The predominant focus on household and family income has
obscured, or in Millar and Glendinning's (1989) words rendered
'invisible', the differences between men's and women's experiences of
poverty, and indeed the differences in the extent and depth of poverty
between men and women. The effect of this has most frequently been
seen in the tendency to regard poor women as the wives or partners of
poor (low paid or unemployed) men rather than as the poor (low paid
or unemployed) wives or partners of men who may be in well-paid
employment. And even where women, as heads of households or
breadwinners, are included, the particular problems which may be
associated with their gender, for instance problems of discrimination or
disadvantage within the labour market, are often ignored.

121

In recent years feminist critiques have begun to question and challenge this 'gender blindness' and to argue that a focus upon the differences between men and women in research and policy analysis would reveal that women suffer poverty on a more widespread basis than men, and that their experience of poverty is quite different as a result of expectations about gender roles. Of particular importance here has been the work of Glendinning and Millar, especially the collection of papers published in their reader *Women and Poverty in Britain*, first published in 1987 and updated in 1992.

Recent discussion of gender and poverty has sometimes even talked about a 'feminisation of poverty'. As Millar (1989b) discusses, this phrase was first used in the US, and it is a particularly ambiguous one. It could be taken to refer simply to the fact that as poverty levels increase so more women are likely to experience poverty, or it could refer to a greater risk of poverty for women and thus a change in the balance between the genders, or indeed it could refer merely to an increased emphasis in research and policy on the poverty experienced by women. It is probably used in practice to mean all three, and the evidence is that in societies such as the US and Britain all three are to some extent true.

Certainly if poverty levels generally are increasing, which, as we discussed in Chapter 1, they were in Britain and the US in the 1980s, then this will affect women as well as men. There is also evidence that some of the changes associated with such recent increases have also resulted in a greater proportion of this new poverty being experienced by women. Demographic changes resulting in greater numbers of single elderly, and marital breakdown resulting in single-parent households, have increased the number of households comprised predominantly of women and which are heavily overrepresented amongst the poor. Although there has been a general increase in women's participation in the labour market, which will be discussed shortly, this has not led to equal status with male employees, and the growing impact of part-time and low-paid work, together with the increased levels of unemployment experienced in the 1980s, has affected female workers disproportionately (Glendinning, 1987). Similarly some of the changes introduced into social security policy, for instance the reform of SERPS in 1988, have restricted women's entitlement to benefits, a point to which we shall also return later.

More generally, as Edgell and Duke (1983) discuss, restrictions in public welfare services over the 1970s and 1980s had a disproportionate effect on women as the major beneficiaries of such services. And the increase in private, voluntary and informal welfare has both excluded women from the preferential treatment through the market, because of their position of economic disadvantage within it, and increased the burden on women at home to compensate for the gaps or inadequacies in other services. In terms of broader deprivation, therefore, the position of women has also deteriorated.

The increased focus on the gender dimension of poverty in recent years has directed greater public attention to the poverty experienced by women. But it should not be concluded from this that women's poverty is a recent phenomenon, nor that the disproportionate distribution of the experience of poverty between the genders is a result only of changes introduced in the 1980s. As Lewis and Piachaud (1992) point out, this maldistribution of poverty has been a feature of British society throughout the twentieth century. For instance at the start of the century 61 per cent of adults on poor relief were women and in the 1980s 60 per cent of adult dependants on state benefit were women – as the authors comment, 'plus ça change' (p. 27).

This is partly due to the fact that women-headed households are more likely to be poor because of lower wages or a greater disproportionate dependence upon benefits. But it is also due to the fact that, as we discussed in Chapter 6, even in households comprising men and women with apparently adequate overall incomes, the distribution of resources within the household may leave many, usually women, experiencing poverty. For instance, a study by Graham (1987) of women in families revealed that many experienced poverty, and over a half of those who then separated from their partners felt that they were financially better off on their own, even where their only income was state benefit. One lone mother said:

> I'm much better off. Definitely. I know where I am now, because I get our money each week and I can control what I spend. Oh, he was earning more than I get but I was worse off than I am now. I am not so poor on £43 supplementary benefit a week for everything for me and the two children as I was then. At least I know where the money's being spent and where it's not being spent. It might not last as long but at least it's being put into provisions for the home (Graham, 1987, p. 234).

Studies of women entering refuges to escape domestic violence have revealed similar findings (Binney *et al.*, 1981; Homer *et al.*, 1984), although these were obviously cases where there was severe conflict within the household.

However it is not just the inequitable distribution of resources within households and families which contributes to women's experience of poverty. There is also the issue of who controls resources and directs or determines expenditure, as revealed in the above quote from the lone parent. Where the primary household income is acquired by men, they can then exercise control over how it is spent, and this may enhance the power they already hold within the household. This is part of a broader picture of power and dependency within households to which we shall return later, but one of its effects is to restrict the benefits women can gain even from resources over which they do have ostensible control.

Thus men may give 'housekeeping' money to their wives, but this money is spent on goods and services for all family members, whilst men's surplus income may be reserved for their personal benefit. This is starkly exemplified in the Married Women's Property Act of 1964 which gives legal ownership of all such housekeeping money, and the benefits of it, jointly to husbands and wives. Even where women in paid employment do bring resources under their own control into the household, the value of these is often not recognised because they are used to subsidise shortfalls in the housekeeping budget (Morris, 1989) or are targeted on particular additional goods or services (Piachaud, 1982b).

In addition to lower wages and control over household income there are other factors contributing to women's largely hidden poverty within the home, and these broader aspects of deprivation are very likely to be of iceberg-like proportions. Of particular importance here is the impoverishment which results from women's unpaid caring work within the home, and the dependency and powerlessness which frequently flows from this, as will be discussed later. It also extends to the wide range of means by which women will deny themselves even basic needs in order to cope within inadequate or reduced household budgets.

For instance women may eat smaller portions of food and go without meals, or hot meals, whilst at home alone during the day; or even, as Graham (1987) discovered, they may go without heating, as the following quote from a mother in a low-income household reveals,

I turn it off when I'm on my own and put a blanket on myself. Sometimes we both do in the evening but my husband doesn't like being cold and puts the heating back on (Graham, 1987, p. 238).

As Land and Rose (1985, p. 86) put it, 'self denial is still seen as women's special share of poverty'.

This self-denial includes the time women spend on unpaid work at home, as discussed in Chapter 6. Piachaud (1987) points out that the amount of time spent preparing home-made as opposed to 'oven ready' chips must be accounted for in assessing the real relative costs of each – and this is usually women's unpaid time at home. Much of women's time is expended in such work, and, as Lister (1990) has argued, this can result in a significant experience of 'time poverty' for women who spend large proportions of their lives trapped in unrewarding domestic labour.

The extent of deprivation associated with domestic labour is not only the immediate loss of time and pleasure at home, however. There are also longer term consequences for women's economic and social position which result in particular from the absence from the labour market associated with this, for instance in the loss of career progression and the accumulation of occupational benefits or protections, as will be discussed below.

Thus women's poverty is not only greater and disproportionately more widespread than men's, it is in many ways a quite different experience and thus in a sense a different problem. Poverty, as has been argued, is a political concept; this political context extends to the politics of gender too. The feminist criticism of the gender blindness of much poverty research and analysis is not just that it has failed to measure or has underplayed the poverty experienced by women, but that it has ignored, and in practice concealed, the gendered experience of poverty and the different circumstances in which women are poor and deprived. This point is emphasised by Millar and Glendinning (1989) and is exemplified in much of the more recent research on women's poverty; however it has still to make much headway in the broader policy and political climate of antipoverty strategy. The importance of understanding the different experience of women's poverty, however, cannot be overlooked, and we shall now discuss in more detail four of the major features of this difference.

Employment, Low Pay and Poverty

Paid employment is the major source of income for the majority of people in modern British society, and it has been for well over a century. Thus access to the labour market and the wages received from it are crucial in determining resources for individuals and households, and for providing security and control over those resources. Women's position in the labour market is thus a central determinant of their wealth, or poverty. And research has consistently demonstrated that the position of women is significantly different from that of men (see Dex, 1985; Beechey, 1987).

Although during the early period of industrialisation women were employed alongside men in the rapidly growing factories and workshops, there was a trend away from equal employment during the nineteenth century which involved the direct exclusion, via 'protective' legislation, of women from some forms of employment, such as coalmining, and the indirect discouragement of female labour by discriminatory employment practices, supported by male employees who in return demanded a 'family wage' sufficient to support a dependent wife and children.

The effect of these pressures was to exclude large numbers of, especially married, women from paid employment and force them into dependency upon men. They did not result, however, in the complete removal of women from paid employment. Many women continued to work, and for many families the male 'family wage' was not sufficient to provide for the household without the addition of women's supplementary earnings.

Nevertheless many women did leave the labour market, and by 1891 women's participation rate in paid employment was only 35 per cent compared with men's at 84 per cent (Lewis and Piachaud, 1992, p. 37). Furthermore women's employment came to be seen by employers, male employees and even women themselves as secondary employment operating to supplement male wages or provide minor household luxuries – 'pin money'. Thus women's wages were much lower than men's – for all industries they were 51.5 per cent of average male manual workers' wages in 1886 (Lewis and Piachaud, 1992, p. 39). This created a vicious circle of secondary wage status which indirectly forced women into dependence, at least partially, on men, especially when they had children to support.

By the beginning of the twentieth century, therefore, women's separate and secondary position within the labour market was entrenched, reinforced and recreated by powerful ideological expectations about women's different responsibilities within the presumed family structure (see Gittins, 1985; Donzelot, 1979). During the twentieth century, however, and particularly since the Second World War, women's participation in the labour market has grown. By 1987

51 per cent of women were economically active (in paid employment or self-employment) compared to 75 per cent of men (Lewis and Piachaud, 1992, p. 37).

There have also been some moves towards more equal pay and equal treatment for women at work, although this has been a long, slow and far from complete process. Since 1975 legislation in the form of the Equal Pay Act and the Sex Discrimination Act has required equal pay and treatment for women at work. However despite this women's average hourly earnings have only risen to 77 per cent of their male counterparts' (Lonsdale, 1992, p. 99). The reasons for the failing of the law requiring equal treatment are complex and multifaceted. In part they are a product of the nature of the legislation itself and the mechanisms for enforcing it (see Morris and Nott, 1991), but more generally the failings reflect the fact that the broader structure of women's participation in the labour market, whilst it has grown, has remained quite different from that of men. And this is a major cause of women's greater risk of, and different experience of, poverty.

Even when women do work they tend to work in different jobs and under different conditions from men (see Dex, 1985; Lonsdale, 1992). Thus women are much more likely than men to be working part-time – four out of five part-timers are women – and much of the growth in women's labour market participation can be accounted for by increased part-time working. Yet part-time work generally attracts lower rates of pay and gives rise to fewer contractual and statutory rights and protection. Women's part-time work also includes some of the worst-rewarded and yet most labour-intensive paid work in the form of 'homeworking', for example assembling clothing at home, processing mail orders or undertaking paid child care both on a formal and an informal basis.

In full-time work women are frequently engaged in different work and under different conditions from men. For instance female employees predominate in secretarial and clerical work, in nursing, in residential care and in primary school teaching. Indeed these jobs are sometimes referred to as 'women's work', and they are quite closely related to women's assumed domestic responsibilities. They are also generally low-status and lower-paid employment: and in higher status jobs in the same areas men tend to predominate, for instance as accountants, doctors, managers and lecturers. Within factory production women tend to work in different sectors from men, for example in clothing and hosiery production or food and drink preparation. Even within the same factory they are likely to be placed in different sections of the production process, for instance in the packing department. And again the jobs occupied by women are frequently those with lower status and lower pay.

Of course all labour markets do exhibit significant elements of such segmentation and division. There are better, more secure and better rewarded jobs, and there are low quality, insecure and poorly paid jobs – and there is generally little movement between the different sectors. Barron and Norris (1976) describe this as a dual labour market with two sectors, primary and secondary; and they point out that within such a structure women tend to occupy the jobs in the secondary, poorer sector. In practice segmentation is probably more complex than division into two sectors only; but the overall point is still valid – within a segmented labour market women are generally employed in different, and less desirable, sectors then men.

Thus within the labour market women experience on average less security, worse conditions, lower status and lower pay than men. As Callender (1985) discusses, this is likely to render them more susceptible to unemployment in times of recession, and also to reduce the protection they may receive in such circumstances by way of redundancy pay, protection from unfair dismissal and entitlement to social security benefits (Callender, 1992). Furthermore their less secure and less consistent connection with the labour market is also likely to exclude them from many of the increasingly important occupational protections and benefits such as sickness pay, pensions schemes or share ownership schemes, all of which provide cushions against poverty and deprivation beyond the period of employment itself.

A segmented labour market in which some employees can be kept in insecurity, on lower wages and without occupational protections and benefits is clearly beneficial to employers. Even where there may be no overt sexual discrimination therefore, the advantages of workers whose employment may be perceived by them, as well as by their employers, as secondary are advantages which employers are bound to exploit. Some have argued, using neo-Marxist analysis, that this in effect means that women comprise a 'reserve army of labour' existing on the periphery of the securely employed, largely male, working class (see Beechey, 1978). This may suggest a degree of economic determination of women's position which is rather too narrow as an explanation for women's work-related poverty; but its focus on the broader structure of the labour market certainly challenges the equally narrow view that women's position at work is merely the product of sexual discrimination which could be counteracted by legislative remedies.

Of course women's secondary status within the labour market is inextricably related to ideological expectations about their role in the family. As Morris (1991) points out, the dual labour market is complemented by women's dual roles as worker and housewife. It is because women have to undertake a 'double shift' of paid work and unpaid work that they more frequently work part-time and thus experience worse pay and conditions. And yet it is because they experience worse pay and conditions that there is so much pressure on married women to see their paid work as secondary to that of their husbands. This forces married women indirectly into dependence on their husbands. It is also a source of single women's greater risk of poverty, whether as single young women at work, divorced or separated single parents, or as single or widowed elderly pensioners with no occupational or earnings-related benefits. For many women therefore the experience may be one of being trapped in marriage, or trapped in poverty – or both.

Social Security

Because social security protection has always been based upon support for the wage labour market, as we shall see in Chapter 14, and has acted primarily as a wage substitute linked closely to labour discipline, the treatment of women within social security provision has largely been determined by their treatment within, or outside, the labour market. In the nineteenth century Poor Law 'support' through the workhouse was intended to instil labour discipline, and in the case of women it was also intended to coerce dependency upon a husband. For instance, better treatment was reserved for widows for whom the alternative of family support did not exist.

When insurance-based benefits were developed in the early part of the twentieth century, the fact that they depended upon contributions made whilst in paid employment effectively excluded most married women from protection. However even those women who did paid work were treated differently from men, paying lower contributions and receiving lower benefits – generally around 80 per cent of the full rate. Yet even this reduced protection was challenged during the recession of the 1930s through the introduction of the Anomalies Act to prevent married women who were not 'really unemployed' from claiming unemployment benefit merely to enhance their married lives. The assumption of course was that married women did not need social security support because they could depend upon their husbands. And this assumption was extended in the means-tested Unemployment Assistance schemes of the 1930s to include those presumed to be able to depend upon other close family members too, with the result that single women as well were effectively denied support in most circumstances.

Separate treatment and secondary status for women within social security provision became entrenched with the introduction of the Beveridge reforms after the Second World War. The Beveridge Report made specific reference to the need for separate treatment for married women under the NI scheme on account of their responsibility for 'other duties' (1942, p. 51). Beveridge's assumption was that married women would be engaged in unpaid work at home and thus would not need protection under the scheme other than through a dependents' benefit paid to their husbands. Only when a husband could no longer act as provider for his wife, in widowhood, would payment (Widow's Benefit) be made directly to her. Beveridge had originally also suggested a payment to women after divorce, but this was not taken up by the postwar government when it introduced his proposals for fear of encouraging marital breakdown. Single women at work did pay contributions and could receive benefits in the same way as men. But even when they worked married women could only make a reduced contribution in return for which no benefits were paid.

The means-tested safety net scheme, National Assistance, which accompanied the introduction of NI continued to assume women's dependency upon their husbands through the 'aggregation' of family incomes as the basis for determining entitlement. Thus where husbands had an income their wives could not independently claim benefit. This presumed dependency was extended to single women too, to avoid a situation in which they might be treated more favourably than their married sisters, giving rise to the need for cohabitation tests and intrusive investigation into the lives of all single women claimants. Aggregation and dependence were restricted after the war to spouses or cohabitees, however, and did not extend, as the prewar scheme had, to other close family members.

What this implied was that for the purposes of safety-net support women were presumed to be dependent upon male partners. And through the refusal, or withdrawal, of benefit for women presumed to be cohabiting with a man the scheme operated in practice to enforce a particular model of family or household structure, a point to which we shall return shortly. Beveridge's intention had been that the National Assistance scheme would be of marginal and declining importance compared with the provision of benefit support through NI. As will be discussed in Chapter 14, however, this has not proved to be the case. Dependence upon the means-tested assistance scheme, later retitled Supplementary Benefit (SB) then Income Support (IS), grew inexorably throughout the latter half of the century and was by the 1980s the major feature of benefit provision. Its coercive and intrusive reinforcement of family dependency has had particular consequences for women who, although they constituted the majority of benefit dependants, were until the 1980s excluded from claiming in their own right unless they were single.

In the 1970s and 1980s changes were introduced into social security legislation to remove, at least formally, some of the discriminatory treatment experienced by women. In the 1970s NI was reformed to permit married women to contribute and receive benefits on the same basis as men, although because of their past exclusion many women could still never establish full contribution records for long-term benefits such as pensions. In the 1980s, following a directive on 'equal treatment' for men and women from the EC, means-tested benefits, including SB were reformed to permit either men or women to act as the claimant and receive the family benefit, although aggregation and family dependency remained. Of course in most cases men remained as the nominated claimant, and, as Millar (1989b) has pointed out, such moves towards formal equality of treatment within social security do nothing to address the broader problems of women's assumed dependency which is such a central feature of the gender differences underlying the experience of poverty in Britain.

The expansion of benefit provision, in particular in the 1970s to provide support for some of the additional costs of disability, also initially extended the unequal treatment and exclusion of women within social security. Non-contributory Invalidity Pension, a low-level long-term benefit for people unable to work because of disability but with no entitlement to NI, was not available to married women unless they could also demonstrate that they were unable to perform normal household duties. The assumption behind this was that only in these circumstances would the family be in need, because domestic help would have to be employed rather than being provided by wives. This anomaly was only removed in 1984 following a restructuring of the benefit under threat of the impact of the EC directive on equal treatment.

In the case of Invalid Care Allowance (ICA), however, the government resisted the directive until the eleventh hour. ICA was a low-level

non-contributory benefit paid to those excluded from the labour
market due to their involvement in substantial unpaid caring work
for an adult at home. It was not payable to married or cohabiting
women who were assumed not to be in poverty as a result of such
labour-market exclusion as they could rely for support upon husbands
or partners. With the support of the CPAG this was challenged in the
European Court under the equal treatment directive; and it was only
on the eve of the announcement of the success of the challenge in 1986
that the law was changed to permit all women to claim the benefit
equally.

With the removal of the discriminatory exclusion in ICA, the formal
unequal treatment of men and women was more or less removed from
social security provision. However in practice barriers to benefit
claiming remain for women. They are still less likely than men to
have full NI contribution records, and are thus more likely to be
dependent upon lower, means-tested benefits. Restrictions in NI
entitlement and greater dependency on means testing in the 1980s
have exacerbated these trends (see Glendinning, 1987; Millar, 1989b).
And yet within the means-tested schemes the continued assumptions of
aggregation and dependency within the family unit in effect consign
women to a secondary status.

The 1980s also saw the relatively rapid expansion of private and
occupational provision for social, or individual, security. In particular
this took place through the development of Statutory Sick Pay and
Statutory Maternity Pay, and through the active promotion and
subsidisation of private pensions. Given women's secondary status in
the labour market discussed above, they are consequently disproportionately excluded from participation in, and benefit from, occupational and private provision (see Groves, 1992). Some occupational
and private social security schemes do provide payments for widows
based on their husband's contributions. This is an indirect support,
however, which continues the assumption of women's dependency, and
yet even it can be lost where couples divorce. With rising divorce levels
this can be an unintended, or unforeseen, loss for women which will
further contribute to the increased risk of poverty for single, especially
elderly, women (see Groves, 1992, pp. 203–4).

Social security has been the major antipoverty policy measure in
Britain throughout the last century or longer. However the benefits it
provides, whether through insurance or through means testing within
state provision or through various forms of private protection, have
largely been predicated upon, and structured to support, family units in

which men and women occupy specific and distinct gender roles. The effect of this has been to exclude, either directly or indirectly, many women from receipt of social security benefits, thus increasing their risk of the poverty which may result from benefit exclusion. In particular this exclusion is associated with assumptions about women's caring responsibilities and dependent status, both of which are major sources of women's inequality and poverty.

The Costs of Caring

Women's secondary status within the labour market and the social security scheme is closely related to assumptions about gender roles within families, and in particular women's responsibility for caring work. There is a significant need for care in modern British society. Young children, and adults with illnesses or disabilities, need close and regular personal attention: although there is some limited public and private collective provision for such care, the majority of it is carried out in the private homes where children and adults live, and is carried out by women.

Indeed there is a widespread assumption that women are somehow uniquely equipped to occupy caring roles (see Henwood *et al.*, 1987), and this has largely dominated the development of support for such work. The papers in Finch and Groves' (1983) book, *A Labour of Love*, on caring for adults, discuss this gender stereotyping and point out that the expectation on women to provide care at home is inextricably linked to their emotional ties to their children or other family members. For women therefore caring *about* someone also means being willing to care *for* them, and this is an expectation which many women experience even though they are aware of the heavy costs it involves.

In particular, for our purposes the costs mean greater risk of poverty for women. Those needing care are obviously at risk of poverty, primarily because they are unable to provide for themselves through paid employment or employment-related benefits. This is most clearly the case for children, who in most cases must be supported by their parents. Women who are engaged in providing such caring work, especially where, as with young children or those with severe disabilities, this is effectively a full-time task, are similarly excluded from the labour market and hence at risk of poverty. As Graham (1987, p. 223) says, 'Poverty and caring are for many women two sides of the same coin'.

Caring work at home is unpaid and thus the link with poverty is obvious, unless women can be supported by another wage-earning family member such as a husband, and in the case of child care in particular the predominant assumption is that this will be the case. Even here, however, there is the problem of women's dependency upon their husbands and the problems of inequities in intrahousehold transfers discussed in Chapter 6. And of course there is the problem of the inadequacy of many men's wages to support a dependent family, especially a large one.

It was the potential inadequacy of men's wages to support a large family at home that was the prime economic pressure for the introduction of Family Allowances after the Second World War as a guaranteed form of state support towards the extra costs of child care in all families, although the expectation was that wages should be sufficient to provide for one child and Family Allowances were only paid for second and subsequent children. When Child Benefit was introduced to replace Family Allowances in the 1970s, this was converted into a flat-rate payment for all children paid to the nominated carer, usually the mother. Partly because it is paid directly to the carer, Child Benefit has been regarded as an important contribution towards the costs of caring work. However it is only a partial recognition of the costs of caring for a child which does not even cover the costs of the child itself, for instance as calculated by Piachaud (1979) or as represented by the IS rates for children, let alone the costs of the carer. And during the 1980s the value of the benefit was allowed to fall against inflation to even lower levels. Whatever the merits of Child Benefit in preventing child poverty therefore, and the CPAG have consistently defended it for its important role here, it is not in any sense a recognition of, nor a protection from, poverty amongst carers. This is demonstrably the case for lone parents who cannot rely upon additional support from an employed partner.

For lone parents the costs of caring and the consequent exclusion from a labour market in which collective occupational provision for child care is sparse indeed collide to produce a high risk of, and high levels of, poverty (Millar, 1989a). The vast majority – around 90 per cent – of lone parents are women and for them women's secondary labour market status compounds the more general problem of trying to balance caring responsibilities against paid employment to support a family. Millar argues that gender is the crucial factor in lone parent poverty; 'it is precisely because lone mothers are women that they have a very high risk of poverty' she claims (1992, p. 149), and points out that the relatively small numbers of lone fathers are less likely to be poor.

Exclusion from the labour market is the main problem for most lone mothers: in the late 1980s over 70 per cent were dependent upon IS (Millar, 1992, p. 151). Most lone-parent households are the result of separation or divorce. However continued dependence upon an ex-partner through maintenance payments is not in practice any protection against poverty. As Millar (1989a, pp. 60–1) points out, maintenance is only received by about 30 per cent of lone mothers, and for them the payments are generally insufficient to lift them out of IS dependency and thus in effect are of no value. The changes introduced in 1993 to require the payment of maintenance for single parents, enforceable through the social security system via benefit reductions for mothers who do not provide details of ex-partners, are unlikely to rectify this since most men cannot in any event afford large maintenance payments to children and ex-wives. And as critics have pointed out (Lister, 1991), the operation of the scheme is more likely to add to the pressures and problems experienced by lone mothers than it is to reduce their risk of poverty.

It is not only child care which may trap women in poverty, however. Adults with serious illnesses or disabilities also require care, and, as Parker (1990) has demonstrated, with growing longevity and improved medical standards this demand for care is growing significantly at the end of the twentieth century. Indeed it is somewhat ironic that, as earlier childbearing and smaller families have reduced the scale of the burden of child care for women, the growing demand for adult care has to some extent taken its place, resulting in what Roll (1989, p. 25) has called the development of a 'cycle of caring' for many women.

Adult care too is likely to remove women from the labour market and thus increase their risk of poverty. Since 1986 women engaged in full-time care have been able to claim ICA. But without another source of income or dependency this is no protection against poverty. In the late 1980s and early 1990s the pressure on women to provide care for dependent adults has also been growing because of government policy to use such 'community care' to replace institutional care provided by the state in homes or hospitals. Whatever the theoretical advantages of community-based care, its practical effect, especially if additional resources are not channelled to support it, is likely to be to increase the risk of poverty for the women who are pressured by one means or another into providing it.

It is not just loss of income which contributes to the poverty experienced by carers, however. As discussed in Chapter 5, a wider conceptualisation of poverty as deprivation covers a range of wants and needs which people may lack. Those involved in caring work frequently experience significant deprivation beyond the loss of adequate cash income. In particular they are likely to be trapped within the home for long periods of time and be engaged in monotonous, tiring and emotionally draining work with no obvious reward. This is especially the case for those caring for dependent adults; for whilst children will grow up and leave home hopefully happy and successful, dependent adults are more likely to be in a deteriorating condition which will only be relieved by their death – providing a painful form of relief for their carers. The loss of control over their lives and over their time on a day-to-day basis is thus a significant feature of deprivation for carers. For them the notion of 'time poverty' may be particularly pertinent.

As Joshi (1992) has argued, the costs of caring do not just include those deprivations experienced at the time. Absence from the labour market, for mothers perhaps at a crucial point in their lives, is likely to lead to longer term deprivation resulting from lost occupational benefits, lost training and career opportunities, and perhaps lost opportunities for saving and investment too. These are sometimes described as the 'opportunity costs' of caring work (Joshi, 1988), and they can add up to a significant loss which women in general are likely to experience at some point in their lives. The assumption of course is that such costs can be borne because at such points women will be supported by their husbands. However this assumption of dependency is in reality more of a cause of women's poverty than a solution to it.

Dependency

At the heart of women's social and economic situation, and thus their greater risk of poverty, is their assumed position of dependency upon men within the family. It is because it is assumed that women can depend upon their husbands for material support that they have largely been excluded from full participation in the labour market and social security provision. And indeed in the case of the aggregation rulings within means-tested benefits such dependency has effectively been enforced on women.

As discussed in Chapter 6, however, the allocation of resources within households and families may not be equitable and may leave many women living below the standards enjoyed by their partners. Furthermore the incomes received by men may not be sufficient to provide adequately for a dependent wife (and children) and so in many cases women have to engage in paid work to supplement the family income. However because this is regarded as supplementary income it is frequently seen as less important than that of the male breadwinner and may not even be recognised as part of the family income by men (see Morris and Ruane, 1989). As we have seen, this secondary income status has the effect of reproducing and reinforcing women's lower wage, and secondary employment status within the labour market.

The problem of dependency thus operates as a vicious circle for women who, when young and single, are pressured into marriage, in part at least because of the poor prospects of employment and pay, and once married (and especially after child bearing) are trapped in dependency upon their husbands. Curiously enough there is evidence that this dependent status continues even where husbands are unable to support their wives, for instance because of unemployment. In a study of unemployed men Cooke (1987) found that as men became unemployed their wives too tended to withdraw from paid work, thus continuing their dependency. There were sound financial reasons for this in many cases since, because of the rules which require earnings above £5 a week to be deducted from families' IS entitlement, the wages women would earn for part-time work would not in practice increase the family income. However, Cooke argues that the phenomenon is not purely a financial one, for its persistence appears to outstrip financial logic and to be dependent too upon attitudes and social conventions.

Women's dependence upon their husbands is of course an ideological, and not merely an economic, feature of gender stereotyping. It is closely tied to the broader ideology of family structure and family roles which, as feminists have argued, involve clear differentiation and discrimination between men and women (see Gittins, 1985; Barrett and MacIntosh, 1982). And yet this differentiation, and the inequality and poverty which flow from it, is largely disguised from public view, and therefore from policy response, by the ideological divide between the 'public' and 'private' faces of family life. What goes on inside the private world of the family, it has often been assumed, is of no concern to researchers or policy makers – and therefore, perhaps, is not problematic.

Important research such as Pahl's (1989) on household income distribution has now begun to penetrate this private world of the family. And feminist scholarship has begun to challenge the false nature of the public/private divide, in particular from the position of women at home for whom the private world of the home is also their public world. As Graham's (1987) research has revealed, dependency upon a husband may conceal poverty standards of living for some women, and this is especially so in cases where there is domestic conflict within the family (Binney *et al.*, 1981; Homer *et al.*, 1984).

In cases of domestic violence, of course, the broader aspects of deprivation within a dependency relationship are clearly revealed. Issues of power and control are integral features of dependency and in situations of violence it is clear that the price to be paid by those without power and control can indeed be a high one. There cannot be a much poorer lifestyle that that experienced by a woman constantly in fear of violence from her partner at home.

However even where issues of power and control do not develop into extremes of violence they nevertheless remain important features in structuring the inequality experienced by men and women within the family, and the greater poverty of women within this. The pervading influence of dependency underlines the point discussed earlier about the different experience of poverty for women and men. Even in a household where, because of an inadequate overall income, both partners are poor, for the women the need to be dependent upon, and thus controlled by, her partner provides for her a different and deeper, problem of deprivation. As Lister (1990) has argued, this different experience continues to operate as a denial of 'citizenship' to women, who by and large are relegated to a secondary status within the modern welfare capitalist state. And as she points out, any challenge to this denial would involve 'radical changes' to the personal and domestic life in which it is situated.

9

Racism and Poverty

Racism and Ethnic Minority Inequality in Britain

Any understanding of the distribution of poverty and inequality in society must pay attention to the impact on this of significant social divisions and cultural differences. In modern British society this involves recognising and analysing the impact of racism within the social structure. In broad terms modern Britain is a racist society in that there is significant evidence that black and other minority ethnic communities experience discrimination and disadvantage on a disproportionate basis, which cannot be explained merely as result of chance or misfortune.

This does not make British society unique, nor in a sense is it all that surprising. Discrimination and disadvantage for ethnic minority groups is common in many, if not most, social structures; and certainly there is overt evidence of racism similar to that found in Britain in most other European and western capitalist countries. However, widespread evidence of racism elsewhere should not lead us to overlook the particular features and the particular causes of racism within British society, which have produced a unique pattern of discrimination and disadvantage resulting in significant inequality and levels of poverty for certain groups within society. Nor, of course, should the widespread experience of racism be interpreted as suggesting its consequences are not a problem, or not a problem amenable to analysis and policy response. Indeed it is because 'race' is such an important feature of the structure of poverty and inequality that its impact must be included in understanding, and tackled in policy development.

What is meant by 'race' in this context, however, has been the subject of some debate, both over terminology and the use of terms adopted. It is probably not a debate which can be entirely satisfactorily resolved

139

either because – as to some extent with the debates over the definition of poverty – meaning is inextricably linked to broader theoretical and political questions about the nature of the problem and the appropriate response to it. In the case of modern Britain this debate is founded in the country's imperial past, its subjugation of colonial populations and the assumption of 'white supremacy' which arose from this.

Thus in Britain 'race' is often taken to mean skin colour, and in particular the difference between white and black skins. This has been accentuated by the entry into Britain of a significant number of black ex-colonial residents, in particular after the Second World War. In practice these immigrants, and their offspring, have different cultural backgrounds as well as different skin colours. However they are all potential victims of discrimination or disadvantage based on skin colour, and thus we will distinguish them as 'black', as compared to the indigenous 'white' population.

Within Britain's black population there are a range of different communities with different cultural and religious traditions. When referring to these differing communities we will use the term 'ethnic minority communities', although this also includes non-black communities such as Jews, Arabs, Eastern Europeans and others, all of whom may experience discrimination or disadvantage because of their culture, language or religion. However in modern Britain the racism experienced by the black population overlays their situation as minority ethnic communities. It is this racism of course, and not skin colour or cultural difference, which is the problem for black people in Britain; and it is this problem which is generally the focus of research and analysis of race and inequality in Britain. Thus it is racism and its consequences for poverty and inequality that we will discuss here.

The racism which Britain's black population faces has a history as long as that of the population itself, certainly extending back to the early days of overseas trade and Britain's involvement in the slave trade during the growth of colonisation. Early black immigrants to Britain were generally associated with trading and seafaring activities, and tended to be concentrated in ports such as Cardiff, Liverpool and London. This geographical concentration was a trend which was followed by later groups of black immigrants to Britain, primarily as a result of discrimination in housing and employment markets which forced new residents into poor inner city areas that were less popular amongst the indigenous population. However such concentration may have compounded the problem of racism by appearing to minimise the wider integration of black people into other parts of British society, and, as we shall see, it certainly contributed to the problems of poverty which flowed from this.

In the early part of the twentieth century immigration by Jews and Eastern Europeans introduced new ethnic minority communities into Britain, and many of these faced discrimination and hostility from sections of the indigenous population. After the Second World War, however, and following the conversion of the British Empire into a commonwealth of independant countries with close links with Britain, larger numbers of black immigrants from the former colonies were encouraged to come to Britain, mainly in order to fill menial and poorly paid jobs which an indigenous population enjoying 'full employment' would not find attractive.

It was these immigrants in particular who experienced the discrimination and hostility which forced them into the poorer areas of London and large cities in the Midlands, Lancashire and Yorkshire. It was also they, because of their black skins and former colonial status, who became the focus of a new racism amongst the white community, which began to surface in the form of hostility, abuse, harassment and even violence in the late 1950s. By the 1960s this racism, allied to the weaker economic and geographical situation of the new black populations, was beginning to coalesce into a broader structure of discrimination and disadvantage based on race.

The hostility and racism faced by Britain's ethnic minority communities had not been a feature of the academic and political debate which surrounded the introduction of the welfare state reforms of the postwar period. The welfare state was intended to challenge the 'evils' of prewar Britain identified by Beveridge (see Chapter 16) through the development of state welfare services such as National Insurance. Racism was not recognised as an evil requiring state action, however, and the consequences of this leading to a greater threat that ethnic minority groups would be likely to suffer from the social evils was not addressed.

This absence of a focus upon the particular problems of ethnic minority groups within a supposedly universal welfare state was compounded by the growing black immigration into Britain during the early postwar period and the racism which these black immigrants experienced, not the least from many of the agencies of the welfare state itself. Although black immigrants had often been recruited to work within the state welfare services, working as cleaners and orderlies in the health service for example, they often found themselves excluded from the receipt of such services, for instance by racist practices amongst local authority housing departments who refused to accept new immigrants onto council house waiting lists.

In the 1960s the end of the postwar economic boom, coupled with the growing racist hostility to Britain's new black population, resulted in the introduction of immigration policies to restrict the numbers of those coming into the country from the former commonwealth countries (immigration from non-commonwealth countries was already restricted). These immigration policies have continued in ever tighter controls to restrict the entry into Britain of people from outside the EC, and they have been enforced with particular severity against black migrants (see Moore and Wallace, 1975). The effect of the controls has also been to compound the hostility and racism experienced by Britain's black population, all of whom might thus appear to be potential unwanted or illegal immigrants, and to compound the problems faced by black people in establishing families and communities in Britain and claiming their rights and services from the British state. As we shall see, these problems have significantly increased the risk of poverty for black people and their experience of deprivation.

Their status as recent immigrants, subject to immigration control, has also meant that the black population in Britain exhibits significant differences in structure and distribution than the indigenous population. These differences, and changes within them, have been revealed by a series of surveys of black people in Britain carried out by the Policy Studies Institute (PSI), the most recent being Brown (1984). Perhaps the most significant feature of all here is the fact that almost a half of the black population in Britain were born here and have lived here all their lives. Of course the majority of these are young, and thus the majority of adults amongst the black communities are immigrants.

The surveys also reveal a higher proportion of men to women amongst the black population; this is especially the case amongst Asians from the Indian subcontinent whose wives experience difficulties in joining their spouses here due to the operation of immigration controls, and it is less true of West Indian Afro-Caribbeans. Family size is, however, larger amongst the black population, especially amongst Asians. Numbers of lone parents are greater amongst West Indians, but lower amongst Asians. West Indians are more likely to be renting their housing from a council or a housing association, Asians are more likely to be owner-occupiers; but in either case black people experience worse housing conditions than whites. Many of these features are also associated with greater risk of poverty and deprivation.

As already mentioned, Britain's black population is also not geographically even throughout the country. Access to (largely poorly paid) employment, discrimination in housing and education, and more general racism have all resulted in black people being concentrated in poor inner urban areas in a number of British cities. As discussed in Chapter 5, the geographical concentration of poverty and poor environment within deprived areas can compound the deprivation experienced by those living within them – such areas are sometimes referred to in the US as ghettos. This ghetto existence is a particular feature of the poverty experienced by many black people in Britain, compounded by the racism which may even identify their presence as a 'cause' of local deprivation.

In addition to their geographical isolation, black people in Britain also experience isolation and exclusion as a result of linguistic and cultural differences from the indigenous white population. Communication in Britain, both written and verbal, relies upon the use of English. Those who do not speak or read English fluently are thus unable to communicate adequately, or at all. This is a significant problem for many black people especially within the benefit system, as discussed below. However linguistic exclusion can also be compounded by cultural differences and cultural misunderstandings between black people and British institutions.

Cultural exclusion may take the form of cultural expectations amongst ethnic minority communities that rights and entitlements cannot be claimed from the state (Cohen and Tarpey, 1986), compounded perhaps by fears that this may furthermore threaten their immigrant status. It may also take the form of a stereotyping of the needs and lifestyles of minority groups, for instance the assumption that large Asian families will provide financial support for unemployed elderly or young relatives, or that West Indian families are unstable and prone to separation.

Cultural exclusion, however, also includes the failure to take account of the particular, and different, needs of ethnic minority community members in the provision of universal services geared to an indigenous culture – a problem which is sometimes, unfortunately, referred to as 'colour-blindness'. This would encompass the failure within the health service to cater for conditions to which black people are particularly or exclusively prone, such as the disease sickle cell anaemia. It also includes provision of standard services which do not recognise the religious or cultural preferences of some communities, such as school meals services which do not serve halal meat or school clothing stores which do not provide traditional dress for muslim girls.

Linguistic and cultural exclusion compound the more direct racism which excludes black people from the full benefit of many of Britain's welfare services. Given the important role which welfare services are intended to play, and to some extent do play, in reducing poverty and inequality within the country, then black peoples' exclusion from these is likely to be a significant factor in increasing the risks of poverty for black people. Poverty is therefore likely to be linked to race – or more accurately to racism.

However it is not easy to establish a clear empirical link between poverty and race within Britain because most of the research on poverty and most of the statistical surveys, both government and independant, do not seek to identify the skin colour or ethnic origin of respondents. This is not simply an oversight – a case of colour-blindness; it is in some cases also a response to real, and reasonable, fears amongst the black population that attempts to identify 'race' within official or independant surveys may be a real, or a potential, threat to the immigrant status of respondents or may be used as ammunition for further racism against blacks. It was partly as a result of such fears, for instance, that no questions about ethnic origin were included in the decennial census in 1981 and before. Such a question was included in the 1991 census, but only after considerable debate and disagreement about its form and the uses to which it should be put.

Given their experience of racism it is quite understandable that black people in Britain should be wary about research which attempts to determine their ethnic origin in order to relate this, for instance, to their employment, housing or benefit status. But the result of this, and of a more general failure within poverty research to recognise the importance of racism in structuring the experience of poverty and deprivation, is that empirical evidence, especially statistical evidence, has not always been easy to find. However some of the gaps have been filled by the 1992 CPAG publication, *Poverty in Black and White* (Amin and Oppenheim, 1992), which discusses the greater risk of poverty for ethnic minorities in Britain associated with employment and unemployment, housing and health, social security, and immigration policy. Together with other evidence this provides a consistent picture of inequalities in the experience of poverty between black and white people in Britain.

Racism in Employment

Some employment statistics such as the New Earnings Survey do not contain information on the ethnic origins of employees, but there is sufficient information from the *Labour Force Survey by Ethnic Origin* and the PSI study (Brown, 1984) together with a range of other independant sources to be able to draw some conclusions about the position of black people in the labour market, and the consequences this may have for their risk of poverty.

In a general sense of course for most black immigrants their entry into Britain during the postwar period was in order to occupy particular sections of the labour market which could not be filled by indigenous, white workers. These included low-paid, low-skilled jobs in the growing public services such as transport and health, and low-paid shift work in labour-intensive manufacturing processes such as textiles and hosiery. Within an already segmented labour market this pattern of recruitment placed black workers within disadvantaged segments in a similar way to which women were placed, although for different reasons.

The PSI survey revealed that despite changes in the occupational structure during the postwar period and the introduction of legislation intended to prevent racial discrimination at work, the disadvantaged situation of black workers within the labour market showed little change throughout the 1960s and 1970s. This has been confirmed in other studies (see Robinson, 1990; Amin and Oppenheim, 1992, Ch. 2). Black employees remained in disadvantaged segments of the market, they had fewer qualifications and skills, and they were more likely to be working shifts. Asian men were more likely than others to be self-employed, West Indian women were more likely than white or Asian women to be employed full time and Asian women were more likely than others to be engaged in low-paid 'homeworking'.

The result of this is that average levels of earnings are lower for black people than for white people, with the exception of West Indian women, whose earnings are boosted by their greater likelihood of full-time employment. Although, as Bruegel (1989) discusses, this apparent higher income disguises a generally lower hourly rate of pay and a significantly disadvantaged labour market position compared to white women. Table 9.1 reveals the differences in median weekly earnings in 1982.

Lower wages obviously create a greater risk of poverty for black workers. This is compounded by the larger average family size for,

TABLE 9.1 *Earnings of black and white Britons*

	Median weekly earnings (£)	
	Men	Women
White	129.00	77.50
West Indian	109.20	81.20
Asian	110.70	73.00

Source: Brown, 1984, p. 212.

especially Asian, workers to support, and the likelihood that wages will also be used to support family members outside the household. The PSI survey found that 40 per cent of West Indian households and 30 per cent of Asian households sent money to dependants (Brown, 1984, p. 302). Of course low wages for families may be supplemented by means-tested benefits, but, as will be discussed below, there is evidence that black people are less likely than white people to be claiming these.

Black people's disadvantaged position within the labour market is also mirrored by their position outside it. Many of the low-status, labour-intensive jobs in manufacturing and public services into which black immigrant workers were recruited were those which were disproportionately affected by the impact of recession and public expenditure retrenchment in the 1960s and 1970s. This has led to higher levels of unemployment amongst black people throughout Britain, and this has been accentuated by the discrimination in recruitment experienced by black people seeking jobs, especially young, British-born blacks leaving education and unable to find any employment. 25 per cent of West Indian and 10 per cent of Asian men interviewed in the PSI survey said that they had experienced racial discrimination in job recruitment (Brown, 1984, p. 170).

Thus the unemployment rates are higher for black people in Britain than for whites. Between 1989 and 1991 the difference was 13 per cent for black men compared with 7 per cent for white men, and 12 per cent compared to 7 per cent for women. For young people between 16 and 24 the disparity was greater, 22 per cent for young black men compared with 12 per cent for whites, and 19 per cent compared to 9 per cent for women (Amin and Oppenheim, 1992, p. 3). There is also evidence that black people experience longer durations of unemployment than whites, and again that this is more severe for the young unemployed (Amin and Oppenheim, 1992, p. 4).

Because of the inadequate support for those outside the labour market, unemployment is a major 'cause' of poverty and deprivation. Black people's greater vulnerability to unemployment is thus a major factor in their likely greater vulnerability to poverty. The PSI survey came to a disappointing conclusion on the economic circumstances of black people in Britain,

> The Survey gives us a depressing picture of the economic lives of people of Asian and West Indian origin in Britain today. They are more likely than white people to be unemployed, and those that are in work tend to have jobs with lower pay and lower status (Brown, 1984, p. 293).

Furthermore, evidence suggests that the recession and the restructuring of the 1980s had a disproportionate impact upon black people's disadvantaged position within and outside the labour market. As Arnott (1987) and Ward and Cross (1991) discuss, the decline in manufacturing employment and the cuts and restructuring within public services resulted in more rapid increases in unemployment for black people at a time when unemployment generally was rising. The development of low-wage, low-status jobs within new service industries such as catering and tourism also confirmed trends towards segmentation of the labour market which trap black people in low quality employment.

Thus the labour market position of black people in Britain has remained significantly inferior to that of the indigenous white population, and, as Amin and Oppenheim (1992, p. 41) concluded, the restructuring of employment patterns 'has affected ethnic minority communities particularly harshly'. This is a consequence of both direct discrimination and structural racism, and it has affected British-born black young people as well as their immigrant parents. It has exposed black people to a greater risk of poverty, and it has also resulted in higher levels of benefit dependency amongst black people. As will be discussed below, however, within the benefit system as well black people experience discrimination and disadvantage.

Racism in Benefits

Because of their relative exclusion from the labour market black people in Britain experience disproportionate levels of dependency upon the benefits system; and, because of low levels of benefit, dependency is closely related with poverty and deprivation. Direct evidence of the numbers of black people dependant upon benefits is difficult to obtain, however, because within the social security system records are not kept of the ethnic origin of claimants. Thus conclusions have to be drawn from other sources about black people's experience of benefits.

Higher levels of unemployment amongst black communities are obviously going to lead to benefit dependency, as are the higher proportions of single-parent families amongst West Indians. Although there are still relatively smaller numbers of persons of pension age amongst the black population, as a result of immigration patterns and immigration controls which prevent elderly dependants from coming to Britain, amongst the pensioners who are here there is likely to be a greater dependence upon state benefits because of exclusion from labour-market based occupational pension schemes. Exclusion from private or occupational protection, for instance sickness pay, is also likely to affect unemployed blacks of working age because of their generally less advantaged labour market situation.

Within the state benefit system itself black claimants are likely to be disproportionately dependant upon less generous and lower status means-tested benefits. This is because, as with much of the post-welfare state in Britain, the Beveridge social security system failed to recognise the ways in which its structures could operate to exclude certain groups of people. This is particularly true of NI benefits which are paid in return for contributions made during employment. Black people's relative exclusion from employment is also likely to exclude them from NI benefits. And in the case of pensions, especially earnings-related pensions which are based on contributions made throughout a working life, immigration to Britain as adults or periods of absence abroad can effectively disqualify black people from full entitlement.

Other apparently neutral qualifications for benefit entitlement may also operate against black people because of their immigrant status. This applies in particular to the residence tests applied to some benefits. For instance the major disability benefits, Disability Living Allowance (DLA), Severe Disablement Allowance (SDA) and Invalid Care Allowance (ICA), have a requirement of 26 weeks residence in Britain in the preceding 12 months, and in the past some of these periods were much longer (see Oppenheim, 1990, p. 90). Recent immigrants may be likely to be excluded by these tests, potentially resulting in severe poverty for black people with disabilities.

The effect of their exclusion from NI and noncontributory benefits is likely to force black claimants into greater dependence upon means-tested benefits. However here too exclusionary practices may operate to cause hardship. Means-tested benefits are only available to those ordinarily resident in Britain, and claimants are thus technically required to establish this when they make a claim. Normally speaking this is a formality, but as we shall see, some recent immigrants are excluded from such entitlement and evidence of resident status may be required.

This has resulted in past practices of 'passport checking' for all suspicious black claimants in social security offices. Passport checking operates as an invidious disincentive to any black claimants to seek benefit support, whatever their residence status, and can lead to problems if passports are not readily obtainable. Social security officers are instructed not to request passports routinely as proof of entitlement, but, as Gordon and Newnham (1985) discuss, the practice has become so widespread that 'many black claimants volunteer their passports believing it is only a matter of time before they are asked to produce them' (p. 24). They quote one case where

> L, a 22 year old student, born in Britain, was asked for his passport four times in twelve months when he was claiming benefit in Manchester and Huddersfield (p. 25).

And even where passports are produced social security staff may misunderstand or misinterpret their status and thus refuse benefit or remove passports, causing further hardship.

The requirement to produce passports as evidence of entitlement acts as a particular disincentive for many black claimants because of its apparent link with immigration control. Immigrants who do not have a right to remain in the country may expose their status if they claim benefits in order to relieve poverty, for information provided to social security offices may well be passed on to Home Office immigration control. Much more seriously, however, fear of the Home Office connection may be likely to dissuade many perfectly legitimate black claimants from ever approaching the DSS because of misplaced uncertainty about their status in the country (see Gordon and Newnham, 1985, p. 29).

Even for some of those who do have residence rights in Britain, however, immigration status may affect potential benefit entitlement for a number of reasons. Most important here is the so-called 'no recourse to public funds rule'. Under this provision within the Immigration Rules, all dependants coming to join their families in

Britain are excluded from claiming support from public funds. Public funds includes all the major means-tested benefits, including IS, and housing for homeless families under the Housing Act 1985. The intention of the rule is to prevent immigrants from coming to Britain in order to claim state support; its effect is to exclude from even minimum benefit protection significant numbers of new entrants who may have no other practical source of support if the arrangements made on their entry fall through.

Once again, however, the more disconcerting wider impact of the rule is its role as an indirect disincentive – based on a mistaken belief about exclusion from entitlement – for any black claimants, especially family dependants, to claim benefits, even NI benefits to which they do have independant rights. This is likely to be compounded by the rules about 'sponsorship', which require spouses and children, or elderly dependants, coming to Britain to be sponsored by someone in Britain who gives a written undertaking to provide for them in circumstances of need. This is a particularly draconian requirement, which since the 1980s has been legally enforceable against sponsors through the DSS. It creates particular problems for black people in Britain and is likely to lead to greater risk of poverty.

For a start it means that there must be a sponsor who is able to provide support. This excludes people already on benefits from acting as sponsors and thus prevents their families from joining them. It also contributes to the problem of passport checking in benefit administration to identify potential sponsors for certain claimants, in particular where divorced or separated single parents are seeking support. Furthermore in such cases the need for checking can lead to delays in payment of benefit, and to misunderstandings and misinterpretations by social security staff. Finally the promise of sponsorship is, theoretically at least, a permanent one, and this can lead to the creation of a permanently excluded group of claimants who can only seek state support at the risk of legal action against their sponsor.

There are other groups of claimants who are excluded, in full or in part, from benefit entitlement because of their immigrant status. These include 'overstayers', people whose right to remain in Britain has technically expired and who may be threatened with deportation if they have to recourse to benefit, and those who are appealing against deportation or refusal of entry, who at best can only get urgent payments (see Gordon and Newnham, 1985, Ch. 1). Refugees and asylum seekers are also only entitled to reduced levels of benefit support and are subject to other exclusions from assistance, and yet as

NACAB (1991, pp. 63–4) discuss they are an increasing group of claimants who frequently experience acute deprivation.

All the rules about immigrant status and benefit entitlement apply equally to all immigrants, except those from EC countries who are free to travel within member states and to claim benefit support. However, their effect within a racist social structure in which immigrant status is associated closely with skin colour is to exclude, either directly or indirectly, black people in Britain from free and equal access to the benefit system, and thus to increase significantly their risk of poverty. There are other reasons too, also related to immigration status, which may further disadvantage black claimants.

Those who have dependants or connections abroad may experience difficulty in providing for or maintaining these within the British benefits system, resulting in potential hardship for claimants here and for their relatives overseas. Children or other dependants abroad cannot be classed as part of a family for benefit purposes, thus even if payment is being made to support them in another country no benefit entitlement to cover this accrues. The same is true for absences abroad to visit dependants, as benefits are generally only payable to those resident in Britain. However this exclusion can result in unwarranted hardship for dependants remaining in Britain during a visit abroad by a head of household, for they may fail to recognise the need to claim independently in their own right during the absence, especially where language barriers mean that leaflets and forms on entitlement, even if provided, are not understood. Conversely resources held abroad may be treated as available to claimants in Britain, thus reducing or removing entitlement to support, even where these cannot in practice be realised as assets.

In addition to the formal exclusions of black claimants from full benefit entitlement as a result of rules with discriminatory impact there are a number of informal means by which racist practices may exclude them from receipt of support. A survey of black clients using Citizens' Advice Bureaux revealed many such practices, described by NACAB (1991) as 'barriers to benefit'. These include delays in processing benefit claims while – unnecessary – checks are carried out to determine entitlement, and intrusive questioning to establish certain personal details such as marital status where marriages have been contracted abroad. They can also include direct racist discrimination against black claimants, however, as was revealed in a PSI study of the administration of SB in 1982. Part of the PSI study involved observation of officers in social security offices, and it revealed disturbing examples of racism amongst some officers, one of whom is quoted as saying, 'We get quite a few Pakis like that wandering in like lost sheep' (Cooper, 1985, p. 53). The DSS was initially sufficiently alarmed by this part of the report to prevent its publication along with the other findings (Berthoud, 1984), and it was only released a year later.

Even where treatment is formally equal, however, black people may in practice be denied equal access to support because of the failure of the benefits system to address more generally the particular problems they may experience. Most important here is the language barrier. Social security benefits are administered in English. English is spoken in all offices, all forms are printed in English and must be completed in English, and, with one or two minor exceptions, all leaflets and publicity material on benefit entitlement are also printed in English. For those who do not speak or write English fluently this can be a major barrier to receipt of support, as the NACAB (1991) survey again discusses. Non-fluency in English is a particular problem within Asian communities in Britain: the PSI survey found that less than 50 per cent spoke fluent English, and for Asian women the proportion was much smaller, with 48 per cent having very slight or no understanding of English (Brown, 1984, p. 128). It is very rare for social security offices to be able to provide interpreter services for non-English speakers and thus those making claims may not be able to pursue entitlement adequately. But it is likely that the absence of publicity and other literature in ethnic minority languages means that for many potential claimants even this point of contact is never reached. The link between poverty and language is thus likely to be a strong one for many black people, especially women, in Britain.

It is not just language which may prevent people from identifying and pursuing benefit entitlement. As discussed above, cultural differences stemming from socialisation in different social structures may lead people to fail to identify a right to state benefits as a potential source of support at times of deprivation (Cohen and Tarpey, 1986). And, where such misunderstanding is compounded by lack of publicity material in appropriate languages, exclusion from benefit, and thus risk of severe poverty, is likely to remain a significant, but hidden, problem amongst ethnic minority communities.

Thus although, as will be discussed in Chapter 14, the problem of take-up of benefits is a significant one throughout the social security system, culture and language problems may make it a more serious one for black (non)claimants. For instance a survey in Batley in 1973 revealed that 39 per cent of 'immigrant' households were not claiming benefits to which they were entitled, compared with 23 per cent of indigenous households (Gordon and Newnham, 1985, p. 57), and a more recent survey of FC claimants by National Opinion Polls for the National Audit Office revealed lower levels of take-up of means-tested education and health benefits amongst non-British/Irish respondents (Amin and Oppenheim, 1992, pp. 54–5). These differences are likely to represent a significant accentuation of benefit-related poverty for Britain's black population.

Disadvantage and Deprivation

As discussed in Chapter 5, the problem of poverty is not just a problem of insecure or inadequate cash incomes. Poverty as deprivation includes a broader range of disadvantages, exclusions and power-lessness resulting in a quality of life which is poorer and more restricted. For black people in Britain the existence of racism at all levels within the social structure means that most of these broader features of deprivation are also likely to affect them disproportionately. And in addition racism itself adds a further burden to the problems with which they have to cope.

Housing, as we know, is a significant source of inequality and deprivation; and housing conditions differ widely. After their entry into this country as immigrants in the 1950s and 1960s it was in securing housing where many black people first encountered racism and exclusion. This included both the direct racism of landlords and vendors who refused to rent or to sell to them, and the indirect racism of local authorities who put conditions on the allocation of council houses, such as residence tests, which black immigrants could not meet. One of the early consequences of this was to force black people to live in the poorer inner city areas, where housing was less desirable for the indigenous population and housing conditions were worst.

The PSI survey found that West Indians were more likely to live in low-quality rented accommodation such as high-rise flats, and Asians were more likely to live in old houses with few amenities (Brown, 1984, pp. 71–5). Asians are more likely to own their homes, but they may have experienced difficulty obtaining mortgages. Building societies have been known to exclude certain properties or certain city areas from the granting of mortgages, a practice known as 'red-lining' because it was sometimes represented by a line drawn around a certain area on a map. Houses, and households, excluded in this way were often in the poorer inner city areas where a larger proportion of the black population were seeking to buy. Ethnic minority households are also more likely to be overcrowded, 10 per cent having less than one room per person compared with only 1 per cent of white households – and amongst Pakistani and Bangladeshi households the proportion is one-third (Amin and Oppenheim, 1992, p. 22).

Inequalities in health can also be associated with severe deprivation, and as recognised in the Black Report on health inequalities racial differences can be detected here too (Townsend *et al.*, 1988, p. 58). As Grimsley and Bhat (1988) discuss, there is evidence of higher rates of mortality, and perinatal and infant mortality, amongst sections of the black community, and these are generally associated with poorer health. Black people also suffer from some debilitating diseases which do not affect the indigenous population, such as sickle cell anaemia amongst West Indians. And because of a different, poorer diet other diseases may be more prevalent, for instance rickets (caused by a deficiency of vitamin D) amongst Asians.

Greater incidence of certain forms of ill-health may also be compounded for many black people by relative under-utilisation of health services. As with other forms of welfare service, this may in part be due to language and cultural differences. It may also be a product of the poorer provision of health services in the inner city areas where many black people live. Fears about immigrant status and exclusion from services for illegal immigrants may also discourage many black people from approaching a state service even in situations of ill-health (see Manchester Law Centre, 1984).

Another state service within which black people do not in practice receive equal treatment is education. As well as being a form of deprivation in itself, failure or under-achievement in education is also closely linked with poverty and inequality later in life. Poorer education is initially linked to the generally poorer services to be found in the inner city areas where large numbers of black people live. It is compounded both by direct discrimination within the education system, such as stereotying black pupils as troublemakers or low achievers, and by the indirect exclusion which results from the ethnocentrism of the school curriculum.

The Swann Report on the education of children from ethnic minority groups (Swann, 1985) laid much of the blame for inequalities within education on racism within the wider community. But, as Carr-Hill and Chadha-Boreham (1988) discuss, there is much further evidence to suggest that black people's experience of education is structured by racism within the service and not just outside it. Given the importance that education plays in shaping the attitudes and expectations of future generations, this provides depressing evidence of likely future inequalities.

Deprivation in housing, health and education add significantly to the financial inequality of black people in Britain, and they have remained important despite the introduction in the 1960s of race relations legislation designed to prevent direct and indirect discrimination and promote equality of opportunity. However these indirect consequences may be compounded by some of the more direct scars of racism in ways which may severely deplete the quality of life enjoyed, or endured, by those who suffer under them. Racial harassment is part of a daily burden borne by most, it not all, black people in Britain. It is a burden which white people can never fully understand, and which many do not even recognise, although they may be contributing to it. Harassment ranges from an experience of difference, and distance, to suffering as the victim of violence and disturbance.

All forms of harassment constitute deprivation, but for many black people harassment is a serious problem. The PSI survey found that West Indians were thirty-six times more likely than whites to experience racially motivated offences, and Asians fifty times more likely to. These include abuse and assaults in public, which can discourage black people from sharing public spaces, and threats and attacks in their homes, which can produce enduring fear and insecurity at the heart of black people's daily lives.

The experience of racial harassment is not confined either to the poor inner city areas where large numbers of black people live. Indeed the support and strength of black neighbours and friends in such areas may in part make such deprivation a little easier to bear. But the concentration of disadvantage found in such areas, especially when compounded by the fear and isolation produced by harassment, may contribute to an experience of poverty for black people which is overlain by feelings of exclusion and entrapment.

This has led some commentators, particularly in the US (see Wilson, 1987), to suggest that this separates out sections of the black population as a ghetto-dwelling 'underclass' experiencing a different quality of life from the rest of the population, and increasingly therefore experiencing different expectations and aspirations too. Without the negative, exclusionary overtones this notion has also been raised in some British discussions of the experience of black people (see Rex and Tomlinson, 1979).

Certainly the geographical concentration of disadvantage, overlain with the discrimination of racism, provides a peculiarly acute form of poverty for many black people in Britain, as in the US and many other advanced industrial countries. However, as will be discussed in Chapter 12, there are serious theoretical and political problems associated with the use of the 'underclass' concept to describe or explain localised or racialised deprivation, in particular the implication it can readily carry that poor black inner city residents are in some ways the cause, rather than the victims, of their exclusion from the standards of life enjoyed by the majority of the rest of society. This is a similar tendency to that which identifies 'race' as being linked to poverty or inequality; and, as we have discussed in this chapter, the focus on supposed racial or ethnic differences obscures the racism which is still the real source of black people's greater experience of deprivation and disadvantage.

10

Ageing and Poverty

Poverty and Dependency in Old Age

Most of the studies of poverty which have paid attention to the age of
those who are poor, and those who are not, have revealed that the risk
and extent of poverty varies with age. Indeed a major feature of
Rowntree's (1901, 1941) seminal studies of poverty in York was his
notion of the 'life cycle' changes in the risk of poverty, as discussed in
Chapter 6. Rowntree identified three periods in the life cycle where
there was an increased risk of poverty: childhood, parenthood and old
age; although, as others have argued, changing life chances may in
practice be more complex than this for many. These periods of
increased risk of poverty can be contrasted with periods of relative
plenty where income is higher and/or demands are less. For manual
workers this may be in early adulthood when strength and fitness are at
their peak, and for white-collar workers it may be towards the end of
their careers when incrementally based earnings are highest. In both
cases the effect of distribution of income over lifetime is roughly 'U'
shaped, again as we discussed in Chapter 6.

Rowntree's period of poverty risk associated with parenthood may
mitigate the enjoyment of relatively high earnings in early adulthood,
although this is dependent upon household status and structure and
upon the success, or otherwise, of policies designed to provide support
for children and child rearers. What is consistent about all patterns of
life cycle inequality, however, is the decline in income in old age. And
what many studies of poverty have revealed is that old age is closely
linked to risk of poverty.

As well as Rowntree's early recognition of life cycle poverty in old
age, Booth's (1892, 1894) famous work on poverty in London at the
end of the nineteenth century revealed much higher levels of poverty
amongst the elderly than in the rest of the population. Similar
conclusions about the extent of poverty in old age were reached by

Townsend (1979) in his major 1960s study of poverty in Britain. And more recently Alan Walker (1980; Walker and Phillipson, 1986) has written widely on the link between old age and poverty and the reasons for this.

Townsend (1979, p. 787) found that a much higher proportion of elderly people (64 per cent) than non-elderly people (26 per cent) had income under a figure of 140 per cent of SB entitlement, which was roughly equivalent to his definition of poverty. By the mid 1980s Walker (1990a, p. 230) calculated from DSS statistics that these proportions were around 61 per cent and 19 per cent, suggesting that the risk of poverty in old age was three times greater than that for the rest of society. Furthermore elderly people are likely to spend much longer periods of time living in such poverty, with four times as many spending over five years on SB/IS and seven times as many spending over ten years (Walker, 1986, p. 186).

Evidence of inequality in old age was also revealed in the official findings of the now discontinued Diamond Commission on the Distribution of Income and Wealth (Royal Commission, 1978), who concluded that one in three elderly families had incomes below the poverty line in the mid 1970s and three in four lived in or on the margins of poverty. They also found that the lowest quartile of income distribution was dominated by elderly people, who constituted 48 per cent.

Elderly people's lower incomes and greater risk of poverty are obviously closely linked to their sources of income. Compared with the rest of the population a much higher proportion of elderly people derive the bulk of their income from benefits as opposed to earnings. In the mid 1980s only 9 per cent of pensioners' incomes came from earnings and 60 per cent came from benefits, whereas for the population as a whole the proportions were 69 per cent from earnings and 17 per cent from benefits (Walker, 1986, p. 198). This is a fundamental distinction which results from elderly people's systematic exclusion from the labour market, as we shall discuss below. And as benefits, even pensions, are generally lower than wages, the immediate cause of the general experience of low income in old age is easy to see.

However there are other factors too which may operate to reduce income in old age. Although in theory older people may be able to benefit from savings made over a lifetime, especially in the case of insurance policies or private pensions which mature in later years, in practice, as we shall see, only a few do receive significant resources from such sources. And for the majority with relatively few savings the need to depend upon these can rapidly deplete them, increasing the risk of poverty later on amongst the very elderly. Furthermore savings accrued, and maintained, over long periods of time can be severely affected by inflation, which reduces their real value. Over the last two decades inflation has been a serious problem for those wishing to save or defer income, and despite interest-bearing investment opportunities many, especially smaller, elderly savers have lost out.

Despite the continuing evidence of lower incomes in old age, there have been some improvements in the absolute levels of income for elderly people. State pensions have been increased more than benefits for the working population, notably in 1974, although this difference has remained static since the uprating of pensions was reduced to an annual adjustment in line with rises in prices in 1980, the same basis as other benefits. As will be discussed below, the rising value of earnings-related pensions has also benefited some. These absolute increases have sometimes been combined with the increasing numbers of younger people dependent upon means-tested SB/IS in the 1970s and 1980s, primarily as a result of increased levels of unemployment, to present a confusing picture of an apparent decline in the risk of poverty amongst the elderly.

Certainly the proportion of persons dependent upon SB/IS who are over pension age declined from almost 70 per cent in 1970 to around 36 per cent in 1987–8 (Falkingham and Victor, 1991, p. 6). But this is very largely accounted for by the increasing numbers of those below retirement age claiming SB/IS, and the numbers of pensioner claimants has remained more or less constant. Further, although the value of pensions has increased to some extent compared with benefits for people of working age, thus marginally improving the relative position of older people, this improvement has in no way matched the improvement in earnings for most working people (Falkingham and Victor, 1991, p. 7). And, given that earnings still provide the major source of income for working age people but not for the elderly, as discussed above, this means that the overall relatively poorer position of older people has been maintained and perhaps in the 1980s, with the reduced rise in pensions, even increased.

As discussed in Chapter 5 of course, income is not the only source of poverty, or rather deprivation may result from factors other than low income alone. This broader problem of deprivation may also dispro-portionately be a problem for elderly people for a number of reasons. Because of their generally lower incomes elderly people spend a proportionately greater part of their weekly income on essentials such as food, fuel and clothing (Baldwin and Cooke, 1984, p. 45). This leaves comparatively less to provide for luxury items and in particular for consumer durables such as washing machines or telephones, which significantly enhance quality of life. In addition to this elderly people's physical condition and lifestyle may lead to a greater need for essential items like fuel, and inability to afford such essentials can lead to severe deprivation – and even, as with the now more widely recognised problem of hypothermia in winter, death.

As Wheeler (1986) discusses, there is also evidence of significant inequality and deprivation in housing conditions for the elderly. Elderly people are much more likely to live in privately rented or local authority housing, where conditions are often lower. Even if they are owner-occupiers, however, older people may experience poorer housing conditions, and with lower incomes they may be in less of a position to do much to improve these. Elderly owner-occupiers are more likely than others to live in houses without central heating, and they are much more likely (41 per cent compared with 22 per cent) to live in houses which are unfit or needing over £2500 of repairs (Wheeler, 1986, p. 219).

There is evidence that older people do consume greater proportions of some services, in particular health and social services (see Walker, 1980), but this is most likely to be as a result of their greater need in this area. There are also some concessionary schemes providing free or reduced cost access to some public services, such as transport and leisure facilities. However the apparent benefits of these must be set against older people's generally lower incomes and lesser access to many private services. For instance levels of car ownership are lower amongst the elderly (Falkingham and Victor, 1991, p. 15).

The greater need for health and social services amongst the elderly is obviously related to the greater risk of disability and frailty which is associated with old age. However this association should not be overstated. The vast majority of elderly people (93 per cent) live in homes of their own within the community (Wheeler, 1986, p. 218), and the large majority of these (over 75 per cent) were not functionally impaired and could get around their home and go out on their own without difficulty (Rossiter and Wicks, 1982, p. 21). And of those elderly people who do need care and support the vast majority receive it from members of their family (Qureshi and Walker, 1989, p. 122).

Clearly for those with disabilities or other care needs, the inability to provide for oneself is a severe deprivation, as will be discussed in more detail in Chapter 11. And for those in hospitals or other residential care settings in particular, dependency upon the caring services of others can be a profoundly debilitating experience which substantially undermines their quality of life. For instance in many residential care settings little dignity or respect is accorded to older people who in many cases would still be quite capable of providing many of their own daily needs. However the notion of elderly persons as a burden of dependant people requiring support from the rest of society, as has sometimes been implied in discussion of caring needs, is largely a myth to which we will return at the end of the chapter.

Retirement

In Britain, as in most other advanced industrial countries, earnings from employment are the major source of income for most households, and adequate earnings are the major means of avoiding poverty. For older people, however, earnings are not the major source of income, and risk of poverty in old age is thus considerably greater. And of course the reason why earnings constitute such a smaller proportion of the incomes of elderly people is because beyond certain ages people are systematically excluded from the labour market by the operation of policies designed to encourage, or coerce, retirement from work.

The notion that people should retire from work at a certain age is a relatively recent one – which has only developed in advanced industrial countries over the last century alongside the development of pension payments for the retired. Although it is a notion which many, especially younger, people take for granted, it is in fact an extremely complex issue; and yet it is one which has grown significantly in importance in the latter half of the twentieth century with the extension of longevity due to medical and health advances and at the same time the reduction of the proportion of people, and time, engaged in employment. The growing significance of retirement is also associated with the growth in the availability, and extent, of private pension protection under which workers can effectively save for their future retirement, as will be discussed below.

It was not common earlier in the twentieth century for older workers to retire automatically from employment, and indeed during the immediate postwar period, a time of 'full employment', much store was placed in the value of older, experienced workers (see Dex and Phillipson, 1986). However since that time the numbers of older people in full-time employment has declined significantly, in particular because of the imposition of the age at which state pension entitlement commences (60 for women and 65 for men) as an effective compulsory retirement age for most workers (after this age workers are not protected by law from dismissal). Some people do continue to work after this age, but until 1988 any earnings from such employment could delay their pension entitlement up until 65 for women and 70 for men, and thus many of those who did work did so only part time for relatively low earnings. Although this reduction no longer operates it is unlikely that patterns have changed.

In practice where older people do work they are not, unlike other marginalised groups such as women, black people or those with disabilities, concentrated in particular segments of the labour market, primarily of course because older people in employment did not enter it as older people, but have simply carried on with previous patterns of employment. However the marginalisation of women, black people and others in employment is carried over into old age, and as will be discussed below, these labour market inequalities do also structure inequality and poverty within old age. And there is now evidence emerging that when older workers, even those below pension age, are seeking employment they experience discrimination and marginalisation (Harris, 1991) – a phenomenon that is part of an increasing recognition of the problem of 'ageism' (see Bytheway and Johnson, 1990).

During periods of economic recession, such as that in Britain and much of the industrial world in the 1970s and 1980s, levels of economic activity have decreased, resulting in growing unemployment. In this context the compulsory retirement of older workers has been seen as 'necessary' by many employers, including the state, in order to protect employment levels amongst younger workers. Effectively this means that elderly people, like women, are being used as a reserve army of labour. And although many older workers, in particular those with significant personal pension entitlement, may welcome the opportunity to leave employment, there are many others for whom retirement is a form of redundancy with little prospect of further work (Harris, 1991). During the 1970s and 1980s this redundancy in old age also began to affect workers earlier and earlier in their working lives, with 'early retirement' schemes offering advanced pension entitlement to workers in their 50s and early 60s. Such early retirement was also recognised in the social security scheme in 1977 under the 'job release' scheme designed to encourage older workers to leave employment before pension age, and in 1986 under provisions which allowed unemployed men over 60 to leave the employment register and claim higher SB entitlement. Retirement policies have thus excluded older people from the labour market, and this phenomenon is common in most advanced industrial countries, although it has both positive and negative consequences.

Certainly for those who have accrued significant savings over their lives and are entitled to a relatively substantial retirement pension, leaving work in old age can be an opportunity to enjoy a relaxed and leisurely lifestyle. For those in unrewarding jobs which require strength and stamina rather than experience the opportunity to replace dependency upon wages with dependency upon pensions may also be attractive. And where illness, frailty or disability compound the problem of earning from work this may be particularly important.

However exclusion from the labour market can also have serious deleterious consequences which significantly reduce the quality of life of elderly people. Experience and knowledge are no longer valued, indeed they are usually ignored. Contact with colleagues and friends at work is arbitrarily severed. The status and respect which may go with employment and productivity are taken away. As discussed in Chapter 5, exclusion is a significant feature of deprivation in modern societies, and it is a problem which disproportionately affects older people through retirement.

Most importantly for our purposes, however, for the large numbers of older people who do not have adequate pension entitlements exclusion from the labour market means loss of an adequate income and thus a greatly increased risk of poverty and dependency. For the large numbers of elderly poor therefore, leisure is not a concept they can embrace or enjoy, and retirement becomes a struggle to manage on an income which is below that which they were used to when employed.

The concept of retirement only applies of course to paid employment; unpaid work, especially that done in the home, continues after pension age and job release. In this context therefore retirement is something of a male notion, or perhaps more accurately a male problem. For older women, who are less likely than their younger sisters to be in full-time employment and more likely to be responsible for the bulk of home work, retirement is something which happens to their husbands and is only indirectly a problem for them.

Furthermore unpaid work at home may frequently increase in old age because of increased frailty and disability. Most elderly people needing caring work in their home receive it from family members, and in practice in many cases this work is done by other elderly persons in the family, usually a spouse (Rossiter and Wicks, 1982). Exclusion from the labour market may not therefore mean access to leisure, and it may not mean cessation of work. Rather it may mean a transfer of work and leisure into the home, together with a reduction of income.

Pensions

In the nineteenth century, at a time when life expectancy was much shorter than today, no specific provision was made for income support for people in old age. Although some trade unions and friendly societies, and even some employers, provided some limited pension protection for older members, the majority who reached old age had no rights to financial support. And if such people were unable to support themselves through employment, then the only alternative open to them was dependency upon the Poor Law, and thus the workhouse. It was the poverty amongst older people which resulted from this that was highlighted by Booth (1892, 1894) in his surveys at the end of the century, and it led to some pressure upon government to provide directly for the elderly poor.

Following the example of Germany, therefore, pensions were introduced for certain older people in 1908. This original pension of 5 shillings a week was not based on any prior contributions made during employment; it was paid only to those over 70 and was subject to an income test ('5 shillings a week for cheating death', as one popular song put it). In 1911 a contributory social security scheme was introduced, and in 1925 pensions based on contributions were payable to those over 65.

Following the Beveridge Report (1942) on social security reform the postwar government introduced a supposedly comprehensive National Insurance pensions scheme paying all men over 65 and women over 60 flat-rate pensions, with additions for dependants, based upon their NI contribution records once they had retired. However, because all current pensioners would have been automatically excluded from such a scheme on account of their inability to establish a past contribution record, the contribution conditions were effectively waived and full pensions were paid immediately, with serious consequences for the financial structure of the NI scheme, as will be discussed in Chapter 14.

In order to ensure that pensions were adequate to support the older people depending on them, Beveridge based his recommended rates upon Rowntree's (1901 and 1941) nutrional guidelines for minimum subsistence. However, to avoid a situation in which pensions might exceed earnings and thus discourage employment, and to encourage the development of additional private protection, which Beveridge saw as desirable, they were fixed at only this subsistence level. They were thus barely adequate and provided little protection against poverty. When Abel Smith and Townsend (1965) discovered large numbers of people living below the NA/SB poverty line in the 1950s and 1960s, the majority of these were pensioners living on state pensions which were not adequate to provide them even with the equivalent of the means-tested safety net income, although many of these pensioner claimants were not in receipt of the means-tested supplements to which they might have been entitled

In absolute terms the value of pensions increased in the 1950s and 1960s; and in the 1970s in particular pensions increased in relative terms when compared with benefits for the younger unemployed. In the late 1970s this gap began to grow further because the basic NI pension was increased in line with rises in prices or earnings, whichever was the higher, whilst other benefits were increased in line with prices only. This increase relative to other benefits was obviously of some benefit to pensioners, but it did not alter the relative position of pensions when compared with the earnings upon which the majority of the population depended, and consequently overall the levels of incomes of the elderly remained below those of the rest of the population.

After 1980, however, even the relative position of advantage against other claimants was removed when basic pension increases were restricted, like other benefits, to price inflation only. By the beginning of the 1990s this had lowered the weekly value of basic pensions by around £15 a week for single persons and £25 for couples, and this contributed to a situation which throughout the 1980s saw around three million pensioners receiving incomes on or below SB/IS levels.

Throughout its history the basic pension has thus been kept at a relatively low level. This is in part because, like the benefits for those not in employment, it acts as a wage substitute and is kept below wage levels in order to deter voluntary departure from the labour market. However the link between pension entitlement and retirement, especially after the spread of early and compulsory retirement in the latter part of the twentieth century, has significantly undermined the logic of this unequal treatment. Pensioners who have been required to leave the labour market hardly require financial incentives to seek support through wages, and this may partly explain the relatively advantaged status which pensioners have enjoyed compared with other benefit claimants over this period.

The low level of pension payments was also a product of the basis upon which the postwar NI social security scheme was established, however. By admitting all elderly claimants directly into the NI scheme the financing was effectively based on a 'pay-as-you-go' basis, with current contributions being used to pay for current benefits, as opposed to being saved or invested as a deferred payment to existing contributors. Payment of current pensions out of current contributions thus created an inevitable pressure to keep pension levels down in order to keep the contribution levels for current contributors as low as possible. And as the numbers of pensioners grew throughout the postwar period this pressure became more influential, a point to which we shall return below.

Low levels of basic pension also act as an important incentive to people to seek additional private financial protection in old age. Beveridge (1942) had always hoped that state pensions could be supplemented by voluntary private insurance, and thus provided that basic pension levels were 'adequate' there need be no concern that they were below wage levels, since those in work could use their higher wages to purchase additional pension protection. Taken together with the pay-as-you-go basis of state insurance pensions, this meant that the notion of pensions as deferred earnings, rather than as a wage subsitute for those no longer able to provide for themselves, was restricted to private-sector pension protection. This too has contributed to the 'public burden' myth of pension entitlement to which we shall return shortly.

In practice occupational pensions – additional private protection provided by employers through contributions by employees into a separate pension scheme – did grow rapidly in the 1950s and 1960s as employers sought to attract workers by offering the advantages of pension protection through work. Sometimes referred to as 'super-annuation', these early occupational pensions schemes flourished mainly in private sector employment and the number of workers covered grew from 4.3 million in 1956 to 12.2 million in 1967 (Walker, 1986, p. 202). After this point the numbers covered began to decline, down to 5.5 million by 1983, although the number of public sector employees covered by such schemes was growing at this point, rising from 4.1 million in 1967 to 5.4 million in 1983 (Walker, 1986, p. 203).

Many occupational pension schemes, especially those in the private sector, did not provide very generous protection after retirement. And most could not readily be transferred from one job to another; thus rights accrued could be lost if employment changed. Most pensions payable were not 'index linked', that is they did not rise with subsequent inflation, rendering payments levels increasingly restrictive during the high inflation climate of the late twentieth century. Occupational pension protection also frequently assumed male career patterns of continuous contribution over a working life, with final pension levels based upon earnings at the end of working life. This could seriously disadvantage women workers with career breaks and any employees for whom final earnings were not the highest received.

The limitations on occupational pensions have thus meant that many of those who have been covered by such provision have not eventually received significant financial returns from them. In some cases entitlement can amount to little more than a couple of pounds a week. This limited protection, together with the continued exclusion of many from even limited occupational provision, was one of the major reasons for the introduction of the State Earnings Related Pensions Scheme (SERPS) in 1978. SERPS is a complex extension of NI pensions to provide a measure of additional pension income on top of the basic NI pension based upon contributions made during the working life. This additional protection applies provisionally to all NI contributors, but in order not to undermine the protection provided by some occupational schemes, contributors to approved occupational schemes can 'opt out' of SERPS, paying reduced level contributions and receiving only the basic state pension on retirement (see Atkinson, 1991b).

SERPS was introduced by the Labour government in the 1970s, but it had a measure of cross-party support because of its coalition with occupational protection. The state provision is not due to reach maturity until 1998 because only contributions paid after the starting date of 1978 are eligible for inclusion in the calculation of the earnings-related additional payment. This meant that the scheme was of little or no benefit to existing pensioners, and in the short to medium term it was able to do little to alleviate the risk of poverty in old age. It also contributed significantly to the fears of the potentially high costs of future state pension payments, because like the original NI pension scheme payments were made on a pay-as-you-go basis.

These fears attracted official concern in the mid-1980s and were a major factor in the reviews of social security provision undertaken by the government prior to the reforms introduced in the 1986 Social Security Act. The original proposal in the Green Paper (1985) which preceded the legislation was to remove entirely the additional protection provided by SERPS on the grounds of expected high costs in the early twenty-first century. Opposition to this proposal came from many employers and independent pension administrators as well as from other political parties, and eventually what were introduced were reductions in the amount of additional provision and a change in the basis for determining entitlement, which would have the effect of reducing entitlement for many. The reductions were not to take effect until after 1998, however, once maturity under the original scheme had been achieved.

The cuts in entitlement to SERPS will obviously reduce the protection to be afforded to future pensioners, and may therefore contribute to continuing poverty and inequality in old age into the next century. However they were also linked, in the mid 1980s with government concern to encourage more directly the development of private pension protection to supplement, or replace, protection through the state scheme. Private, as opposed to occupational, pension schemes had not developed much during the early postwar period, although they could have the potential benefit of avoiding the limitations of occupationally specific and employment-related schemes. In the 1980s therefore the government provided significant incentives for those investing in private pensions in the form of tax relief and investment bonuses, and after this private pension protection began to grow rapidly in scope and coverage.

Although still not as widespread as occupational provision, private pensions now provide a third area of pension protection, alongside this and the state scheme. Some private schemes may be more speculative investments than those in the occupational field and, in particular, if some of the tax incentives were to be removed they may not in practice provide any better protection than that enjoyed by beneficiaries of SERPS. However they do contribute to the potential improvement which future pensioners can now look forward to, and such provision may remove their fear of potential poverty in old age.

However the improved prospects of some future pensioners will not remove the risks, and the fears, of poverty in old age for many other current and future pensioners who will not benefit significantly from such additional protection on retirement. Indeed what private and occupational pensions in practice do is to reproduce in old age many of the inequalities and deprivations associated with the inequities of the labour market earlier in life. As early as 1955 Titmuss had referred to the fear that occupational protection could lead to the development of 'two nations' in retirement, one relatively affluent group enjoying the benefits of deferred earnings in the form of insurance payments and private pensions and one generally poor one dependent upon the inadequate basic state pension provision.

This division between rich and poor in retirement has become more accentuated towards the end of the twentieth century, and has even led to the development of new acronyms for the newer, wealthier pensioners, the most widespread being 'Woopies' (Well-Off Older Persons). In practice both the size of this new group of pensioners and the extent of their relative wealth have often been overstated (see Falkingham and Victor, 1991). And certainly their existence has done little or nothing to reduce the risk of poverty which the majority of elderly people still experience.

Nevertheless inequalities in old age have become increasingly important. And these are not only the product of the growing impact of private pension protection. Inequalities also result from the continuation into old age of the inequalities and deprivations experienced earlier in life. This means that class differences of income, housing, health and so on continue to divide people after retirement, so too do gender differences and the dependence which family relationships frequently produce. As Britain's black population grow older differences due to race and racism will also be reproduced amongst the elderly. Thus poverty in old age, like poverty earlier in the life cycle, will reflect broader social divisions.

Inequalities during working lives, and particularly those which affect potential future pension entitlement, are of course more generally very much a product of the overall life cycle experiences of different cohorts of elderly people. As Atkinson and Sutherland (1991) discuss, this means for instance that the generation of elderly people whose working lives were affected by the depression of the 1930s and the Second World War have had very different preretirement opportunities from subsequent generations, who have experienced relatively high levels of unbroken employment since the war. The former group thus experience lower incomes and greater risk of poverty in old age.

As such groups grow older still their circumstances can worsen further as any limited savings made are depleted and possessions grow older and cannot be replaced. This problem is more generally reflected in differences and divisions between the 'young old' and the 'old old', where risk of poverty and experience of deprivation is more acute amongst the latter at a time when their need of support and care may also be at its greatest. Thus class, gender, race and age structure the risk and the experience of poverty in old age. And these divisions have been heightened rather than reduced by developments in pension provision.

The Social Construction of Dependency

As discussed at the beginning of this chapter, the association between ageing, and in particular old age, and poverty is closely linked to the notion of life cycle changes in social status and economic circumstances. However this association is frequently misperceived, or misrepresented, as a kind of 'iron law' of determination, which can also be misunderstood as an assumption that old age is in some way a cause of poverty. As we know, social circumstances cannot be causes of poverty, even though they may be associated with higher risk of it for a range of other reasons. And, as the increasing evidence of relative wealth for some in old age demonstrates, this risk does not apply inevitably or evenly to all.

Nevertheless the link between old age and risk of poverty is well established in Britain, and this pattern is reproduced in most other advanced industrial countries. Of course the motivation, in part at least, for Rowntree's and others' exposure of the phenomenon of life cycle poverty risks was to encourage the development of policies to relieve, or prevent, poverty arising in such circumstances. Family allowances and Child Benefit are examples of such policies designed to prevent poverty associated with child rearing. In the case of old age, however, policy developments have not in general prevented, or even challenged, the risk of poverty – indeed, as A. Walker (1980) argues, in many ways policies towards the elderly operate to both create and to reproduce poverty and dependency.

Walker's argument is that poverty in old age is 'socially constructed'. Of course this is true, as we know, of poverty in all situations. But in the case of poverty amongst the elderly we can identify clear policy assumptions and policy developments which have contributed specifically to the higher risk of poverty faced by many old people. Assumptions are made about the circumstances or the needs of elderly people which are frequently unjustified and inaccurate. And policies are developed to respond to these assumptions, which may compound the problems which some people face or create new problems.

Perhaps the most pervasive, and the most long-standing, assumption about elderly people is that because of their age they are no longer able to contribute to society and may even be unable to care for themselves.

This may be presented sympathetically as justifying support from the rest of society as a 'reward' for previous contribution. But it is a contradictory notion which may also be interpreted as implying that elderly people are a burden on society, which willingly or unwillingly the rest of us have to bear. As we shall discuss shortly this interpretation has achieved more and more prominence in the late twentieth century as the number of elderly people relative to the rest of the population has started gradually to rise, and as life expectancy increases.

In practice only small numbers of elderly people do need care and support in order to remain independent, and many if not most are quite able to contribute to society if they are provided with the opportunity to do this. However some of the policies designed to provide care for the elderly in fact operate to accentuate their dependent status rather than reducing it, in particular the denial of autonomy and control in many residential establishments and the inadequate provision of genuine support services to assist people to survive in the community. Minor disability can thus result in dependency and poverty in old age, when alternative policy initiatives could have prevented it.

What prevents most elderly people from contributing to society, in particular contributing through productive work, are the policies which encourage or coerce retirement from employment at particular ages. Retirement is, as we have discussed, a contradictory notion which is frequently a cover for redundancy. Its effect nevertheless is to deprive most elderly people of access to the major source of income in modern society, and thus to increase significantly their risk of poverty.

The problem of poverty in retirement of course is compounded by the low levels of pension entitlement suffered by many elderly people. This is not a universal problem any more. For some people retirement can be a release from taxing or unrewarding work and a chance to enjoy leisure time on a generous pension supplemented by savings and insurance. But for those excluded from private and occupational pension protection, the policy of keeping state pensions to a minimum level has meant that for many release from work is replaced by a constant struggle to get by on an inadequate income.

As discussed above, one of the major reasons for the low level of the state pension is the desire by government to minimise the cost of pension provision on current NI contributors and taxpayers, which results from the pay-as-you-go nature of state pension funding. This tendency was compounded in the 1980s after the introduction of

SERPS and the recognition of the projected increased numbers of pensioners in the early twenty-first century. It led to the proposal, following the review of pensions in 1985, for the abolition of SERPS, which was rejected in favour of a reduction in entitlement at the beginning of the century. And it was a major factor in the earlier cut in the rates of the basic state pension which resulted from the decision to uprate these annually in line with price inflation only.

These decisions to reduce pension levels were based upon the assumption that the burden of pension payment would become too great for the rest of the population to afford as the numbers of pensioners continued to grow, and as life expectancy increased and people retired earlier. This dependency model has been fuelled by demographic evidence that the 'gerontic ratio', the proportion of elderly persons in the population, has been increasing throughout the twentieth century. It rose from 12 per 1000 in 1901 to 34 per 1000 on 1981, and is projected to reach 38 per 1000 by 2021 (Falkingham, 1989, p. 218).

As Falkingham points out, however, this simplistic link between demography and dependency ignores a wide range of other factors which may or may not result in a need to redistribute resources towards elderly people. These include overall levels of productivity and the ability of older people to provide for themselves, both of which factors changed significantly throughout the early part of the twentieth century whilst the gerontic ratio changed more dramatically than it will over the decades at the turn of the next century. The burden of dependency upon state pensions is also likely to reduce somewhat as entitlement to occupational and private pensions expands. A. Walker (1986, p. 199) notes that state pensions constituted less than a third of retirement income in the mid 1980s. This puts any savings which may be attempted there into a rather broader perspective.

Ironically however, the growing availability of private pensions has led to the development of another equally questionable assumption: that pensioners no longer need state support to avoid poverty. This ignores the 'two nations' problem of inequality in old age and the considerable evidence of continuing risk of poverty for many of the elderly who do not have independant incomes. And as Walker has consistently argued (see 1980 and 1986) reducing the state pension in order to reduce the burden of elderly people on the state is likely to compound this problem rather than resolve it. In practice, by 1980 state pension levels in Britain were much lower than those of other major European countries – 23 per cent of average earnings compared with 36 per cent in West Germany and 32 per cent in France (A. Walker, 1990a, pp. 248–9). The cuts made in the 1980s will have extended this gap even further.

Thus assumptions made about the needs and resources of elderly persons and policies developed to respond to these have operated to create and recreate the problem of greater risk and greater severity of poverty in old age. As Walker (1980, p. 73) puts it,

> So it is not *chronological* age that is significant in causing poverty and dependency ... but the relationship between the *social construction* of age and the social division of labour (emphasis in original).

Dependency and poverty in old age are socially constructed, and the effect of this construction is to make the process of ageing into one which is associated for many with deprivation and exclusion. The risk of such deprivation is also associated with class, race and gender differences earlier in life, and thus its impact is structured by other social divisions. Nevertheless the link between old age and poverty is clearly established in Britain, and in most other advanced industrial countries, providing a curiously ironic example of the short-sightedness of the politics of antipoverty policy.

11

Disability and Poverty

The Costs of Disability

Disability is an umbrella term used to cover a wide range of physical conditions and social circumstances in which people may experience difficulties or problems in providing for themselves or participating in social activity. Of course loss or impairment of physical functions can be problematic: people who cannot see, hear, walk or clothe themselves obviously have to learn to adapt to their limited capabilities. However physical conditions alone need not necessarily lead to social problems. As we shall see, it is because of the need for people with disabilities to survive within social structures which generally assume that people are 'able-bodied' that in practice they frequently do lead to problems in societies such as modern Britain.

Because of this link between physical condition and social context, there is some disagreement, and even controversy, about what is meant by the term 'disability', and more especially by the more pejorative term 'disabled person', which implies that people with disabilities are in some way deficient. For this reason 'disabled person' is not a description approved by organisations representing people with disabilities. Disabilities do vary widely however, including loss or impairment of physical functions such as mobility, sensory deprivation such as blindness or deafness and mental disabilities such as learning difficulties.

In a government-sponsored survey of disability carried out by the OPCS in the 1960s a distinction was made between *impairment*, meaning loss of function; *disability*, meaning restriction of activity, and *handicap*, meaning physical disadvantage limiting individual fulfilment (see Oliver, 1991a). In his major study of poverty in the 1960s Townsend (1979, Ch. 20) went further than this and included chronic sickness in his discussion of the poverty and deprivation associated with disability.

In 1985 and 1986 the OPCS (Martin *et al.*, 1988, 1989; Martin and White, 1988; Bone and Meltzer, 1989; Smyth and Robus, 1989) carried out another survey of disability in which they developed a scale of severity of disability ranging from one, the lowest level of impairment, to ten, the highest level. This is a more sophisticated approach, although it obviously includes in the lower categories people who might not be regarded by some as having disability problems. And this may have had consequences for the links thus established between disability, need and poverty, as the Disablement Income Group (DIG) (Thompson *et al.*, 1988) argued was the case in their assessment of the additional costs associated with disabilities, a point to which we shall return below.

Different studies of the links between poverty and disability therefore may be utilising different definitions of disability, and different definitions of poverty too perhaps, which can make comparisons between findings problematic. The OPCS ten-point scale provides both the broadest and the most sophisticated approach however, and it has been taken up in most of the recent discussions of the issue. We will therefore rely largely upon that here. Using the scale, the OPCS found that there were over 6.5 million people with disabilities in Britain in 1985, ranging from 1.2 million in category one to 240 000 in category ten (see Dalley, 1991, pp. 7–8).

Whatever the extent of disability or impairment, physical conditions such as those covered in the OPCS scale do lead to difficulties for many people who suffer from them in providing for themselves and participating within modern social structures. As mentioned, these individual difficulties need not result in social problems for people with disabilities. However in Britain, and in most other advanced industrial countries, disability is associated with social problems. This is a product of social structures which fail to recognise and make provision for the difficulties which people experience, and of policies towards disability which operate in practice to compound rather than to alleviate the problematic social consequences of impairment. These consequences are wideranging and far-reaching; and they include a significantly greater risk of poverty for people with disabilities, and significant additional deprivation associated with this. As Groves (1988, p. 171) says, 'Poverty is disability's close companion'.

The link between poverty and disability goes back to the nineteenth century and in particular to the growth of urbanisation (see Topliss, 1979). It was recognised by Townsend in his major survey of poverty in the 1960s (1979, Ch. 20). The OPCS survey in the 1980s found that the average income of non-pensioners with disabilities was £98.30 a week compared with £136.50 for the general population (Dalley, 1991, p. 8). Poverty resulting from disability is closely linked to age however – almost a half of those with disabilities are over pension age – and because of the generally lower incomes of older people the differential here is much smaller, £91.90 compared with £93.70.

For pensioners, as we have seen, low income is associated with exclusion from the labour market and access to wages as a source of income. However people with disabilities are also disproportionately excluded from wage labour. The OPCS survey found that only 31 per cent of working-age people with disabilities were in employment compared with 69 per cent of the general population (Martin and White, 1988, p. 13). The effect of these two factors is that 75 per cent of adults with disabilities have to rely on state benefits as their main source of income. And as will be discussed below, the benefit provision for people with disabilities is generally insufficient to prevent significant deprivation for many.

Low income and benefit dependency, are as we know, major causes of poverty. For people with disabilities, however, the receipt of a low income is frequently compounded by the extra costs associated with living with a disability. These include the purchase of physical aids or adaptations to the home, the cost of medicines or creams, the need to consume more fuel in order to heat the home full-time, and perhaps the need to pay for care or support within the home. Without additional income to cover such extra costs they are likely to depress further the standard of living of people with disabilities surviving on low incomes.

In practice there has been something of a debate about the extent of the extra costs associated with disability (see Berthoud, 1991). The OPCS survey included questions about additional needs and concluded from this that the average extra cost was around £6.10 a week. However this figure has been disputed by the DIG, who on the basis of a more in-depth survey of people with more severe disabilities (Thompson *et al.*, 1990), put the figure at £49.86 – a significant difference.

Both these surveys were based on direct questioning of people with disabilities. Berthoud compares these approaches with those which look at what people actually spend in a weekly budget, similar to some of the budget standards studies of poverty discussed in Chapter 4. These demonstrate extra expenditure on some items, such as fuel, durables and tobacco, and reduced expenditure on others, such as transport and clothing. As Berthoud (1991, pp. 77–8) discusses however, these different expenditure patterns conceal overall lower standards of living for people with disabilities because of the impact of extra expenditure on some items leading to overall reductions elsewhere within a generally lower total weekly income. This overall greater risk of deprivation is confirmed by a DSS survey of income and expenditure patterns utilising the FES, which concludes (Matthews and Truscott, 1990, p. ix) 'that at similar income levels disabled people are more constrained and experience a lower standard of living than their able-bodied counterparts'.

As discussed before, of course, poverty is not just a function of low cash income; there are broader and deeper features of deprivation in modern society. In these broader aspects of deprivation people with disabilities also experience greater inequality. Townsend's (1979, Ch. 20) study revealed that people with disabilities experienced poorer housing conditions, possessed fewer consumer goods and were less likely to have regular holidays. Disability is also frequently associated with ill-health, both as cause and as consequence. For many disability may restrict participation in social activities or leisure pursuits by restricting mobility or as a result of sensory deprivation. Overall therefore there is much greater likelihood that the quality of life of people with disabilities will be significantly below that of most able-bodied people.

The poverty and deprivation experienced by people with disabilities is frequently also visited upon other members of their household. As we shall discuss below, this is particularly the case for those who care for such people, including parents caring for children with disabilities. But the lower income and additional expenditure associated with disability mean that in general all household members are subject to a greater risk of poverty (see Glendinning and Baldwin, 1988).

Exclusion from Work

Exclusion from the labour market means exclusion from receipt of wages which, as we know, are the major source of income in modern industrial societies and thus the major means of avoiding poverty. For the near 50 per cent of people with disabilities who are over pension age exclusion from work may be as much a function of age as it is of disability. But for younger people of working age there is considerable evidence that those with disabilities are at greater risk of unemployment than the rest of the population.

The OPCS survey revealed that only 31 per cent of people with disabilities were in work, as opposed to 69 per cent of the general population (Martin and White, 1988), and they calculated that the unemployment rate amongst 'economically active' persons with disabilities was around 27 per cent for men and 20 per cent for women compared with 11 per cent and 9 per cent for the population as a whole (Martin *et al.*, 1989). Figures of this nature have also been reached by the Labour Force Survey and a survey conducted by Social and Community Planning Research (see Floyd, 1991). These overall higher levels of unemployment include particular difficulties for school leavers with disabilities entering the labour market (A. Walker, 1982a) and evidence of older workers being more likely to experience voluntary redundancy or early retirement (Piachaud, 1986).

Disadvantage within the labour market does not only involve exclusion however. There is also evidence that even those who do engage in paid employment receive lower pay, with pay levels falling as the severity of disability increases (Lonsdale and Walker, 1984). Workers with disabilities also have poorer promotion prospects and suffer poorer working environments (Townsend, 1979) and they are more likely to be without formal qualifications at work (Prescott-Clarke, 1990). Ironically poor working conditions and low pay are associated in particular with the sheltered workshops and training centres developed specifically to provide work opportunities for people with disabilities.

Exclusion from the labour market is in part the result of direct discrimination by employers against people with disabilities, who they believe to be unsuitable for many kinds of work and possibly unreliable on health grounds, although it is difficult to measure the extent of the impact of prejudice such as this. However direct discrimination is underlain by other, potentially more important, structural barriers to employment. The failure of the education system to provide equal education for children with disabilities means that many grow up with inadequate qualifications for many jobs. And in many cases this has been compounded by separate educational provision for children defined as requiring special needs (see A. Walker, 1982a). However the major barrier to employment in many workplaces is the failure of employers to adapt workplaces or work practices to permit the utilisation of people with disabilities. People with physical or sensory disabilities are perfectly capable of working within the limitations of their condition, and yet because of the structure of many working environments they are excluded from realising their potential to do this.

In the latter half of the twentieth century a number of initiatives have been developed in attempts to improve the employment opportunities of people with disabilities (see Floyd, 1991). Perhaps the most important of these is the quota scheme introduced by the Disabled Persons Act of 1944. The intention of the scheme is to ensure that organisations with more than twenty employees have at least three per cent of their workforce composed of people registered as disabled. Government departments are excluded from the scheme, as are some other major national employers such as the health service. In any event, however, the scheme has been ineffective in overcoming the exclusion of people with disabilities. Many such people are not registered under the act, the quota system is inadequately enforced, and the average proportion of disabled employees in organisations within the scheme is nearer to one per cent (Floyd, 1991, p. 216).

In the absence of adequate enforcement machinery and the antidiscrimination legislation which provides some protection against unfair treatment for women and black people in Britain, the measures taken to improve the employment prospects of people with disabilities have generally not been successful in overcoming the structural barriers to employment which many face. People with disabilities thus remain in low-status, low-paid employment, or are excluded from the labour market altogether. This exclusion not only prevents them from receiving the financial benefits of reasonable wages, it also effectively excludes them from the increasingly important indirect advantages of employment in the form of fringe benefits, occupational pensions and insurance, and participation in the NI scheme. The result of this exclusion is to carry labour market disadvantage outside the sphere of employment into the area of support available in retirement or other periods of unemployment. Thus here too people with disabilities are likely to receive fewer benefits and thus be at greater risk of poverty.

Benefits and Dependency

Because of their relative exclusion from the labour market, the majority of people with disabilities – 75 per cent – have to rely on benefits as their major source of income. In addition to this greater dependency, people with disabilities are also likely to depend upon benefits for longer periods of time than other claimants, thus compounding the problem of dependency and, because of the low levels of benefits, the experience of deprivation.

Benefit provision for people with disabilities has had a fairly chequered history in Britain. The policy has been one of piecemeal reform and ad hoc adaptation rather than consistent development, and it has resulted in the growth of significant anomalies between the way people with disabilities and others are treated, and even between the different treatment accorded to different groups amongst the disabled themselves (see Walker and Walker, 1991).

People with disabilities who meet the criteria for ordinary benefits can of course claim these in the same way as other people. Indeed such benefits as retirement pension or IS do provide the major benefit provision for large numbers of people with disabilities who are not entitled to any separate or additional provision resulting from their disability. However, following from the Workmen's Compensation Act at the end of the nineteenth century, separate and additional benefits have been provided for some people, depending upon the cause of their disability.

Thus more generous benefit provision has been made for people suffering disability as a result of an industrial accident or an injury sustained in war. In part the logic for such more-generous provision was to provide a measure of compensation for the victims of such unfortunate events. The effect, however, was to secure for such people much higher levels of benefit entitlement than other people with much the same disabilities but which had been acquired in different circumstances. And the differences here could be quite large, ranging in 1990 from £287.55 a week from the war disablement scheme to £63.80 a week for someone not entitled to NI benefit or Severe Disablement Allowance (SDA) (Disability Alliance, 1990).

The postwar Beveridge NI scheme did not make specific provision for people with disabilities. In the 1970s, however, a number of alterations and additions to benefit provision were made to provide some support for some recognised extra needs resulting from disability. These included a higher rate of NI benefit (Invalidity Benefit, or IVB) for those unable to work due to illness or disability for over six months, and a lower flat rate non-contributory benefit (Non-Contributory Invalidity Pension, or NCIP) for those not entitled to NI because of inadequate contribution records. NCIP was below the level of means-tested SB, however, and could not provide an adequate income on its own. Nevertheless it was not paid to married women unless they could demonstrate that they were unable to undertake household duties as well as being excluded from paid work.

In 1984 NCIP was replaced by the Severe Disablement Allowance (SDA), which again was fixed at a lower rate of 60 per cent of IVB. The overt discrimination against married women found in NCIP was removed, but SDA entitlement is dependant upon fairly stringent tests of the severity of disability, unless the condition predated the age of twenty. SDA is still less than weekly entitlement to IS, however, and thus for those who have no independant support receipt of this benefit does not prevent reliance upon the means-tested state benefit scheme.

In the 1970s benefits designed to provide a contribution towards the extra costs of disability were also introduced. Attendance Allowance (AA) was intended as a contribution towards the additional costs incurred by those who needed someone to care for them either during the day or the night, or both. Mobility Allowance (MA) was intended as a contribution towards the costs of basic mobility for those unable or virtually unable to walk. Both benefits were flat rate and were paid in addition to any other income, but neither of them were very generous and were unlikely to meet the full costs of those with severe disabilities.

However stringent medical tests were required to determine entitlement to AA and MA, and certain groups of potential claimants were excluded by age criteria. AA was not payable to children under two, although this was later reduced to six months, and MA was not payable if entitlement arose after sixty-five. The result of this was that large numbers of people with disabilities did not receive these benefits. The OPCS survey discovered that only 9 per cent of disabled pensioners received AA in 1985 (Martin and White, 1988, p. 22) and only 3 per cent received MA (Martin *et al.*, 1988). More worrying perhaps than this was the widespread ignorance of the possibility of entitlement to such vitally important sources of support. The OPCS found that 45 per cent of all adults with disabilities who were not receiving these benefits said that they had not heard of either of them (Martin and White, 1988).

Support for some of the extra costs associated with disability was also at one time provided for claimants of SB by additions, covering special needs, to their weekly benefit entitlement. Although these additions had to be specifically claimed, and thus in many cases were probably not taken up by potential beneficiaries, they could provide a significantly increased weekly income for the many people with disabilities dependant upon the basic means-tested scheme. When SB was converted into IS in 1988, however, these additional payments were abolished and replaced with flat-rate weekly premiums paid on top of basic benefit to certain people with disabilities. Although these premiums were easier to claim they were not as generous as many of the old additional payments and thus large numbers of people with disabilities lost significant benefit entitlement when the reforms were introduced. Transitional protection ensured that this did not result in a real cash loss for any individual claimant, but the overall reduction in entitlement and the general erosion of protection was nevertheless so significant that the government agreed to the establishment of a new discretionary provision, the Independant Living Fund (ILF), to make regular payments to people who had lost out under the reforms and needed to pay for domestic or caring services.

With some trepidation responsibility for administering the ILF was undertaken by the DIG. It was initially assumed that only a few people would be covered, and the budget was originally set at only £5 million a year. However, two years later over 4000 people were receiving payments from the fund and its annual budget had risen to £62 million. It thus became a significant contribution to the benefit provision for people with disabilities. However it was only ever intended as a temporary measure to make up for losses incurred in benefit restructuring, and it was discontinued when full responsibility for all care in the community finally transferred to local authority social service departments as part of the changes in community care following the Griffiths Report of 1988 (see Baldwin *et al.*, 1988).

People with disabilities were therefore some of the main losers in the restructuring of benefit provision in 1988. The replacement of lump sum payments with the Social Fund also meant a potential loss of additional payments, and although the new community care grants available from the fund could have benefited some people seeking care in the community, in practice people with disabilities have benefited little from these, in particular because those on IVB are often just above the IS eligibility level. In theory, however, people with disabilities were not included in the reviews of social security which preceded the 1988 reforms. The intention was that the OPCS survey would pave the way for a separate initiative on the reform of benefits for disability.

In fact reforms to some benefits for people with disabilities were already being introduced before the specific proposals on the restructuring of disability benefits emerged. In particular some of the complex anomalies within the war pension and industrial injuries provisions were simplified, primarily through a levelling down which removed some of the particularly generous provisions which small numbers of claimants had benefited from.

The proposals for general reform following the OPCS survey were eventually published in 1990 in a White Paper called *The Way Ahead* (White Paper, 1990). This proposed some more minor amendments to existing disability benefits and the introduction of two new benefits: the Disability Living Allowance (DLA), to replace the AA and MA, and the Disability Working Allowance (DWA), a new benefit to subsidise low wages for workers with disabilities working 16 hours a week or more (see Hadjipateras, 1992). These new benefits finally came into operation in April 1992.

Although the DLA was really largely a restructuring of existing benefits for disability, it did introduce a new lower rate for those with less serious disabilities; and the DWA was a genuinely new departure, albeit one modelled closely on Family Credit. Together, however they did not amount to the radical simplification and extension of disability benefits propounded by organisations such as the DIG or the Disability Alliance. Both of these organisations have been campaigning for some time for the replacement of all existing disability benefits with a single benefit covering both living costs and costs of disability, with levels being determined in part by the severity of the disability (Disablement Income Group, 1987; Disability Alliance, 1987).

Such a radical reform would certainly overcome some of the problems of complexity and overlap experienced within current provision; and this may therefore help to increase take-up of disability benefits. As already discussed, for many of the benefits specifically targeted at the costs of disability non-take-up is a serious problem, leading to substantial risk of poverty and deprivation. Such a benefit paid on a universal basis would also avoid the 'poverty trap' problem of means-tested benefits, which, as will be discussed in Chapter 14, is an inevitable consequence of tying receipt of benefit to low income, as the DWA does.

However both the existing benefits, including the DWA, and the reforms proposed by critics would continue another form of trap for people with disabilities, which we might call the 'disability trap'. As long as benefits are paid to people because of their disability, then there will remain the perverse 'incentive' to register as disabled in order to receive the benefits, or rather more worryingly to remain disabled in order to continue in receipt when alternative means of overcoming the disability and working 'normally' may be available but appear financially unattractive. The extent of this problem should not be exaggerated however. Although the DWA extends it, it is still a minor issue; and it is not a good reason for failing to pay more generous benefits to people with disabilities.

Nevertheless the problem does highlight a potential contradiction in the position of people with disabilities as benefit recipients. Receipt of benefits as a major source of income is, as we know, closely associated with poverty. Extending benefit provision for such people, rather than providing real opportunities for employment and services at work and at home to permit people to participate more readily in society, may operate to trap people in disability, and thus to trap them in poverty. We shall return to this problem in the final section. However it is a problem which does not just affect people with disabilities, it is also visited upon those who remain at home to care for them and may themselves find that they too are trapped within this role.

The Costs of Caring

As discussed above, disability is a wideranging concept covering a number of serious and not so serious physical or mental debilities. Taking the wider definition employed by the OPCS in the 1980s, many of those who may be classed as having disabilities are quite able to look after themselves, to get about unaided and to work productively. Nevertheless there are a significant number of people for whom their disability means that they need help in performing sometimes quite basic bodily tasks. In order to survive therefore they need, at least for some of the time, the care provided by another person. The dependency which frequently accompanies reliance upon the care of others can severely reduce the quality of life enjoyed by people with disabilities – however it can also have deleterious consequences for those providing the care.

Care can be provided by the state for people with disabilities in residential institutions designed specifically for the purpose, and in severe cases this will mean a hospital bed. However only very few people require such intensive care; and very few get it. The OPCS survey found only 7 per cent of all adults with disabilities lived in residential institutions (Martin *et al.*, 1988). For the vast majority of people requiring care therefore it is provided in the community, or more accurately in the private home where usually both carer and cared for live.

Carers in the home are also usually family members: spouses, daughters or sons; and more often than not they are women (see Parker, 1990). There has been much debate recently over the pressures on women especially to provide unpaid care for other adults in the home (see Finch and Groves, 1983; A. Walker, 1982b). This issue is a controversial one, but there is no doubt that it is also a rapidly growing one. In 1985 the General Household Survey (Green, 1988) revealed that a total of around six million adults were providing care in the home, of which 1.2 million were heavily involved in caring work. The OPCS survey identified around one million 'main carers' within a total of 3.9 million providing help at home.

For those heavily involved in caring work, their responsibilities mean that they generally have to withdraw from the labour market. Even those who are able to remain in employment, however, may find that the work that they can do is limited in terms of time, place, career opportunities and such like. The effect of this is that carers have depressed levels of labour market activity and generally lower levels of income than the population at large (Baldwin and Parker, 1991; Glendinning, 1990). Thus caring for disability, as well as disability itself, is associated with a higher risk of poverty.

The risk of poverty for carers is obviously closely linked to the poverty associated with disability itself. In practice both are likely to live in the same household and experience the harsh consequences of reduced household income. In such situations dependency, of one party on the other, is also likely to accentuate the problems of reduced income. Where the carer is working it is likely to be the person with the disability who is dependant; but where the carer is not in paid employment it is often they who are dependant upon the person for whom they are caring because the household income, probably social security benefits, is likely to be determined primarily by the extent and the source of the disability.

As Glendinning (1990) discusses, the development of benefit support for carers has been based upon criteria for entitlement which depend upon the benefit status of the cared for person. This is particularly the case for the major carers' benefit, Invalid Care Allowance (ICA), which can only be received by those of working age and not in paid employment who are caring for someone in receipt of AA or the care component of DLA. This is also required for receipt of the carer's premium addition to IS and in order to benefit from the home responsibility exemption from NI contributions.

ICA was introduced in the 1970s, although, as discussed in Chapter 8, it was not paid until 1986 to married or cohabiting women providing care. It is fixed at only 60 per cent of the long-term NI benefit rate, however, and is thus below IS entitlement levels and therefore insufficient to provide an adequate income without some other means of support. Nevertheless the extension of entitlement to married women led to a sixfold increase in the receipt of ICA, and in 1988 women constituted 80 per cent of claimants (McLaughlin, 1992), confirming the predominance of women in caring work.

Despite the extension, however, it is likely that many carers are not even receiving the meagre benefits of ICA. For a start it is only payable to those under pension age, and yet a large number of people with disabilities, and their carers, are over pension age. Furthermore its dependence upon receipt of DLA means that the take-up problems associated with this benefit are transferred in addition to ICA, where they are likely to be compounded by ignorance amongst carers of potential entitlement, especially those trying to survive on low part-time wages. Thus there may be many who are potentially entitled to the benefit but are not receiving it. Conversely the requirement that recipients be out of paid employment also constitutes something of a caring trap for those who do benefit from receipt of ICA but would like to enter or return to full-time work but could not afford to lose this benefit.

Whether in receipt of benefits or not therefore, carers' incomes, along with the incomes of those they care for, are likely to be low, resulting in greater risk of poverty and deprivation. It is not only financial deprivation which is associated with caring responsibilities however. There are other costs to caring. Leaving paid employment in order to care does not only result in an immmediate drop in income; it also results in the broader 'opportunity costs' of lost income, promotion prospects and occupational benefits (see Joshi, 1992). Carers may also experience non-income costs of caring resulting from the extra expenditure needed on fuel, laundry or other consequences of sharing a household with a person with a disability (see Glendinning and Baldwin, 1988). In addition to this are the less quantifiable costs of the anxiety of care, worries over the provision of the correct medicines and creams for instance, and the self-sacrifice which home-based caring work inevitably involves.

In general terms the quality of life enjoyed by someone engaged in significant caring responsibilities within the home is likely to be almost as constrained, and constraining, as that of the disabled person. The work is hard, monotonous and demanding. It leads to anxiety, distress and perhaps conflict; and yet it is also frequently bound up with dependency – both financial and emotional. Caring for adults with disabilities can also be profoundly unrewarding; unlike children they will not grow up and become independant; indeed their condition will frequently be more likely to deteriorate than to improve.

It is often only the death of the cared for person which brings caring responsibilities to an end, and then with a depressing tragedy which may deprive the carer of their loved one, their daily work and their only source of income. In circumstances such as these the poverty associated with caring thus continues even after the need for the caring has gone. This is an ironic twist in the interrelationship of dependency between carer and cared for, which because of the lack of other forms of support extends the risk of poverty associated with disability beyond both the disability itself and the person suffering from it.

Reproducing Deprivation

As we have seen, both persons with disabilities and those who provide care and support for them are at greater risk of poverty and are more likely to experience the deprivation and the exclusion associated with a reduced standard of living in our modern society. For persons with disabilities, and for their carers, this may be experienced as a dependency trap, reinforced by exclusion from the labour market, reliance upon inadequate benefits and the additional costs of living with a disability in an able-bodied world.

The existence of disability thus appears to trap those affected by it into dependency and deprivation. The problem of disability consequently becomes the problem of deprivation. But as with age-related poverty there is a danger in perceiving a false causal link here. Disabilities may restrict the capabilities of those who suffer from them and even reduce their potential quality of life because of this, but they are not the cause of poverty. Deprivation and exclusion are socially created problems, and if they are disproportionately associated with the experience of disability it is because the social reaction, or non-reaction, to disability has created this link.

In the case of disability it is very much a case of non-reaction leading to problems for persons with disabilities. Modern industrial societies, and even modern welfare states, have largely been constructed on the basis that the people who inhabit them, who produce and reproduce them and who benefit from them, are able-bodied. This is true of workplaces, public and private buildings, transport systems, information and communication networks, retail outlets – indeed almost all social interaction. In places attempts have sometimes been made to provide for or accommodate some persons with some disabilities, but as is frequently obvious these are generally the exception rather than the rule.

As radical disability campaigners have pointed out therefore, most of the problems associated with disability are created, and recreated, by the failure of social and physical planning to recognise or take account of the needs of persons with disabilities (see Oliver, 1990). As discussed above, one of the more important consequences of this failure has been the exclusion of such people from the major source of adequate income in modern society, the labour market, and the dependence of persons with disabilities and those who care for them on inadequate benefit support. The result of this is that these households disproportionately experience low incomes, and the adequacy of these low incomes is further undermined by the need to meet many of the additional costs of coping with disability in the able-bodied world.

The poverty and dependency associated with disability is thus the consequence, both directly and indirectly, of the failure to provide directly for the needs of disabled people and to ensure that they are as capable as they might be of participating in, and providing for themselves within, the broader social and economic structure.

Benefit provision targeted to meet some of the additional costs of disabilities has not been able to overcome this failure, because it has focused upon the symptom rather than the cause of the problem. It is because of the failure to provide directly for the needs of persons with disabilities that these people experience additional costs, and benefits to meet these will always be inadequate substitutes for more general social and physical restructuring. Their inadequacy is compounded, however, by the low levels at which such cost-related benefits are set, and the inevitable problems of non-take-up associated with them. And in extending dependency upon the benefits system, such targeted benefits can do more in practice to accentuate the problems of poverty and deprivation than to prevent them.

Clearly the restructuring that would be required to redress the social recreation of the problems associated with disability would go much beyond the reduction or prevention of disproportionate levels of poverty amongst persons with disabilities. As disability campaigners recognise, what would be needed to change our able-bodied world would be a radical rethinking of what we are as social beings, and what we should expect of and how we should relate to each other. Without the recognition of the need for such fundamental change, however, it is likely that the disproportionately poorer lives of persons with disabilities will remain an important feature of the distribution of deprivation in modern society.

12

The Underclass

An Emerging Underclass?

Chapter 2 discussed the dynamics of poverty, focusing in particular on the questions of who are the poor and what are the causes of poverty. A range of different explanations of the causes of poverty were discussed, including those which emphasised the individual or community reponsibilities of poor people for their plight, those which directed attention to the role of agencies and politicians, and those which identified social and economic structures as the source of the problems. It was concluded that to an extent all these explanations contained some truth in them, and that the differences of focus were often the function of other disagreements over definitions of poverty, identification of who is poor and, in particular, support for certain policy responses.

This is not to say that in general explanations of poverty cannot be found, nor that some may not be more cogent or comprehensive than others. Rather the point is that there is a relationship between definition of poverty and identification of the poor, and explanation of poverty and the development of policy responses to it. And an understanding of poverty requires an understanding of the importance of this interrelationship. We are returning to this point here, however, to focus on social divisions and the experience of poverty, because in recent years recognition of the social divisions of poverty has been associated with an emphasis upon the social characteristics of those who are poor in a way which has given a new, or a renewed, prominence to particular explanations and understandings of poverty by focusing upon individual and community reponsibility, rather than upon structural context.

In other words research work has demonstrated that particular groups within society are at greater risk of poverty. Part of this demonstration requires a description of the characteristics of these groups and the ways in which these are associated with poverty.

However the description of these characteristics can readily be translated into an identification of them as the reasons why such people are poor. For instance the greater incidence of poverty amongst ethnic minority communities is the result of these communities having different cultures and behaviours. Social divisions thus become social characteristics, and social characteristics then become causes. This trend has become particularly potent in the last two decades of the twentieth century in debates focusing upon the emergence of what is called an 'underclass', although as we shall see this is hardly a new debate, and in practice it is quite a complex one.

In a number of recent studies focusing upon the importance of social divisions and minority groups in understanding the impact of poverty, writers have referred to these groups of poor people as perhaps constituting an underclass at the bottom of, or even below, the rest of society. As early as 1973 Rex talked of black communities in Britain becoming a segregated underclass, which he later (Rex, 1979, p. 86) described as being 'cut off from the main class structures of society'. In his major study of poverty Townsend (1979, p. 819) suggested that the elderly experienced an 'underclass status', a status which he later (p. 920) extended to include the disabled, the chronically sick, the long-term unemployed and single parent families. In a book dealing more generally with the labour market disadvantage of different social groups (Brown and Scase, 1991), Oliver (1991b, p. 133) also argued that disabled people constituted an underclass in modern industrial society.

All of these writers were using the concept of an underclass to describe the particular problems facing particular groups in poverty. Their focus was largely upon the exclusion experienced by such groups, their inability to participate in many social activities and their feelings of being trapped in a position of deprivation. The notion of this as the situation of an underclass is an attempt to demonstrate how traditional class and social stratification approaches, based largely upon labour market division, tend to ignore such social divisions and the circumstances of the poor.

This approach was taken up most prominently by the Labour MP and former director of the CPAG, Frank Field, in a book published in 1989 entitled *Losing Out? The Emergence of Britain's Underclass*. In the book Field argued that in the 1980s the universal values of citizenship which had underlain the postwar welfare state were being abandoned in favour of policies which were leading to social polarisation and the emergence amongst the poor of a new British underclass. He identified the underclass as constituting in particular three groups of people: the long-term unemployed, single parents and the poorer elderly. Field also identified four causes of the emergence of such an underclass: the rise in unemployment, the widening of class divisions, the exclusion of the poor from rising living standards and the change in public attitudes away from altruism and towards self-interest.

Field's account of the emergence of this new British underclass was an outspokenly sympathetic one, and his clear aim in publishing the book was to seek to sway political opinion in favour of shifts in policy which might reverse the trends which he identified. Field was well-known for his views on poverty and social security policy. He was aware, however, that the notion of an underclass had been taken up and used rather differently by other writers, notably Dahrendorf, who in 1987 had talked of high unemployment as being related to the growth of an underclass in Britain, but who associated this also with undesirable characteristics and fatalistic attitudes amongst those affected.

Field was aware that there was 'a danger of these characteristics being interpreted as the "causes" of the problem itself, and from this it is only a short step to falling into the syndrome of "blaming the victim"' (1989, p. 6), although he himself later indulges in such causal association and moral judgement in his discussion of the problems of poor female single parents. In practice the 'danger' of associating description of the characteristics of an underclass with explanation of its causes and moral judgement of the attitudes and behaviour of those within it, is one which is inescapably intertwined within all attempts to categorise those who experience poverty and deprivation in this way, as a review of the history of the underclass concept reveals.

The Legacy of Pathology

The attempt to identify the social characteristics of the poor as the sources of their poverty is usually referred to as a 'pathological approach' to the understanding and explanation of poverty. And the association of such pathological approaches with depictions of the poor as a separate or isolated group in society has been a recurring feature of debates about the problem of poverty in modern industrial society. In Britain this trend can be traced back at least as far as the early studies of poverty of the late nineteenth century.

In his seminal studies of poverty in London, Booth (1889) distinguished a group amongst the ranks of the poor whom he regarded as a 'residuum' of criminal or feckless characters who were a blight on the rest of the poor and lower classes. Stedman Jones (1971), writing about class structure and class struggle in the last two decades of the century, described the fears of both middle-class and 'respectable' working-class commentators that the residuum would constitute a threat to social stability by undermining the work ethic and threatening social order. Part of the characterisation of the residuum, and part of the fears that they supposdly generated, were the assumptions that they did not share the values and aspirations of the rest of society and that this cultural alienation, and the poverty which resulted from it, was transmitted within the underclass from generation to generation.

Macnicol (1987) takes up the development of this notion of intergenerational pathology or inherited deprivation by looking at the investigations by eugenicists during the interwar years into the evidence of genetic transfer of disability or deprivation. In many studies the distinctions between physical disability and social deprivation were confused or overlooked, and it was only with the realisation of the horror that eugenic approaches had led to in Nazi Germany that the prominence of this research began to decline.

In the US in 1960s the pathological tradition was taken up once again in response to the rediscovery of poverty within the affluent postwar American society. One of the significant catalysts for this reemphasis on the categorisation of the poor was the detailed research carried out by Lewis (1965 and 1968) into the lives of poor Puerto Rican families. Lewis described how such families, and the communities in which they lived, had learned to cope with their high levels of poverty and deprivation in part by suppressing expectations of greater wealth, or even secure employment, and developing a culture which focused upon the day-to-day strategies adopted by poor families and individuals to survive without affluence in an affluent society. Lewis referred to this as a 'culture of poverty' and his main concern was merely to identify and describe it as a social phenomenon.

However the idea that poor people in affluent American society might have a separate culture of poverty, which therefore prevented them from ascribing to, or achieving, the wealth which was available to others quickly became adapted as a pathological explanation of the persistence of such poverty. Because poverty in the US is also experienced in much greater proportions by black people, expecially those living in black inner city neighbourhoods, this pathology also acquired a racial, or racist, dimension. For instance Moynihan (1965, p. 5) talked of the 'deterioration of the negro family' as the cause of poverty amongst black Americans; and Wilson (1987) identified poor blacks as belonging to an underclass isolated from other sections of the American community.

As will be discussed in Chapter 15, the reemphasis on pathological explanations of the poverty which was rediscovered within affluent US society in the 1960s was followed by a significant change in emphasis in the policy responses to the problem too, in particular by focusing upon the families and communities of the poor rather then upon the broader social and economic structure of which they were a part. Such a change was also experienced in Britain in the 1960s and 1970s following a renewal here too of pathological approaches to poverty which was based in part on the debates in the US.

Evidence of social pathology could be found in the Plowden Report (1967) on primary schooling, which resulted in the later development of 'education priority areas'. However perhaps the most famous British example of the pathology of poverty during this period were the views of Conservative minister Keith Joseph, expressed in a speech to the Pre-School Playgroups Association in 1972. Joseph referred to poor people as having 'problems of maladjustment' and suggested that such inadequacies might be transmitted intergenerationally via what he described as a 'cycle of deprivation'.

Despite the failures of the policy developments of the 1960s, which will be discussed in Chapter 15, the pathological approach to poverty was returned to again in the US in the 1980s, with direct reference to sections of the poor (black) population as an underclass. This was first identified in the work of Auletta (1982), who talked about nine million people constituting an underclass with undesirable and socially disruptive values. It was taken up particularly however by Murray (1984), a right-wing political scientist, who argued that welfare benefits had helped to create a culture of dependency which attracted some people into underclass status, identifying in particular the supposedly growing numbers of young female single parents who had chosen parenthood and a life on welfare benefits rather then entering the responsibilities of marriage. Murray argued that through such – inadequate – single parenting a culture of deprivation and dependency was transmitted to subsequent generations, thus recreating an isolated and hopeless class of welfare recipients.

In 1989 Murray was invited over to Britain by the *Sunday Times* newspaper in order to investigate the possible development of an underclass in Britain similar to that which he had identified in the US. High levels of poverty and welfare dependency had suggested to some that this might be the case. The problem of a potential underclass had been referred to by Dahrendorf in 1987, and a numer of incidents of social unrest in inner city areas experiencing high levels of deprivation had resulted in press reports suggesting links between hopelessness and lawlessness amongst unemployed benefit dependents.

Murray's findings were published by the right-wing policy group, the Institute of Economic Affairs (IEA), together with commentaries by critics (Murray, 1990). His conclusion was that things were not as serious in Britain in the 1980s as they were in the US, but that a new underclass was emerging as a result of increasing levels of illegitimacy and single parenthood, high levels of criminality and the dropping-out of the labour force by young unemployed male school-leavers who had never developed the habits of employment. His account was both bleak and forthright, identifying the underclass as a 'type of poverty' and suggesting that current policy responses were likely to accentuate rather than relieve the problem. It also contained clear moral overtones disapproving of the characteristics, such as illegitimacy and feckless-ness, which he identified as causing underclass status – in his critical commentary A. Walker referred to this as 'blaming the victims'.

The work of Murray in the 1980s is the clearest, and most recent, example of a long historical tradition of the pathologisation of poverty in academic research and political debate. It focuses upon the culture of poverty as an explanation of the problem of deprivation, and subsequently as a justification for a particular policy response to it. As Ryan (1971, p. 8) put it in a book entitled *Blaming the Victim*:

First, identify a social problem. Second, study those affected by the problem and discover in what ways they are different from the rest of us... Third, define the difference as the cause of the social problem itself. Finally, of course, assign a government bureaucrat to invent a humanitarian action programme to correct the difference.

In blaming the victim therefore, poverty becomes the problem of the poor people themselves, and identifying them as occupying a distinct status as an underclass as a result of this provides a spurious socio-economic justification of this.

Cultural Divisions and the Poor

Murray (1990) and Field (1989) provide quite different usages of the underclass concept in the context of poverty in Britain at the end of the twentieth century. Their political traditions and their political motivations in resurrecting the term and applying it to groups of poor people are very different, and largely conflicting. Murray is a right-wing theorist and wishes to identify poor groups as a separate social category in order to demonstrate that their separation is the cause of their poverty. Field is on the political left and wishes to identify them as separate in order persuade policy makers to develop measures to reintegrate them.

Moreover these different usages are not new or unique to the recent debates on the underclass. Researchers, such as Lewis (1965 and 1968), who have studied the 'culture of poverty' have frequently done so in order to describe rather than to condemn the isolation and separation of the poor. Attempts to identify the social divisions and social characteristics of poverty do not always identify these as causes of deprivation. And even pathological approaches to poverty do not all carry with them adverse moral judgements of the characteristics associated with those found to be poor.

However the 'long and undistinguished pedigree' (Macnicol, 1987, p. 315) of the concept means that its associations with pathological explanations of the problem of poverty are never far below the surface of academic and political debate about the underclass. And thus, as Dean (1991, p. 35) argues, 'It represents, not a useful concept, but a potent symbol'; and in an understanding of poverty this potential symbolism must be recognised and understood. This means that the social divisions and cultural differences that characterise poor groups must be understood within the broader social and economic context in which those groups, and their deprivation, are situated; and that assumptions about the transmission of poverty should be critically examined in the light of empirical evidence. Mann (1992) provides a history of this context and of the role of social divisions within broader welfare policy in Britain.

As discussed in previous chapters, the evidence of greater risk of poverty amongst older people, people with disabilities, black people, single parents and so on does not mean that these characteristics are in some way causally related to their poverty. It is the low wages, labour market exclusion, inadequate benefits and absence of occupational protection which such groups disproportionately experience that are the causes of much of the deprivation they suffer. Discussion of the social divisions of poverty should thus focus upon these exclusions and the structural forces which lay behind them, as well as upon the characteristics of those who are excluded by them.

Research on the transmission of poverty between groups or across generations has cast doubt upon the 'cycles of deprivation' thesis which underlay many pathological approaches towards the poor. Following Keith Joseph's identification of the problem of intergenerational transmission, a major research programme was commissioned by the DHSS and the Social Science Research Council to investigate the evidence on inherited deprivation. The researchers found the problem to be significantly more complex, both theoretically and methodologically, than had been suggested in Joseph's notion of a cycle (Rutter and Madge, 1976), and the overall conclusion which the researchers drew was that there was no evidence to support the thesis of intergenerational transmission of poverty (Brown and Madge, 1982).

Attempts to identify poverty with particular geographical communities, such as inner city areas, are also suspect because even if high levels of poverty do exist there, any conclusions based on this will be ignoring the majority of poverty which is situated outside such areas. Similarly identification of particular groups experiencing greater than average levels of poverty or deprivation, such as single parents or young unemployed, cannot tell us anything about a problem of poverty of which they are only a small part and which includes other groups such as the elderly, people with disabilities, unemployed families and so on.

The assumptions about separate value systems and cultural divisions amongst poor people are also suspect when contrasted with the findings of empirical studies of the lives of poor people. As Townsend's (1979) major study of poverty in Britain revealed, poor people had very similar hopes and values to those who were better off in British society – their problem was that they were frequently prevented from realising these and had learnt, in most cases reluctantly, to cope with this plight. As Bradshaw and Holmes (1989, p. 138) concluded after a study of poor families in north-east England:

> But at a time when British poverty is again being discussed in terms of an underclass, it is of crucial importance to recognise that these families, and probably millions more like them living on social security benefits, are in no sense a detached and isolated group cut off from the rest of society. They are just the same people as the rest of our population, with the same culture and aspirations but with simply too little money to be able to share in the activities and possessions of everyday life with the rest of the population.

In fact studies of attitudes towards poverty which focus not only upon the poor and deprived but upon the whole of the rest of society, reveal that the relationship between the exclusion of the poor and the problem of poverty is rather different to that discussed in pathological approaches to deprivation. Golding and Middleton's (1982) study of press and popular attitudes towards poverty found considerable evidence that those who were not poor, and in particular members of the working class who felt themselves to be struggling hard to avoid poverty, were those who identified poverty as a problem which poor people had brought upon themselves. For instance a forty year-old male teacher provided a classical example of using the cycle of deprivation thesis to blame the victim:

> Poor people often have foolish parents, those who don't encourage industry and thrift, they have confused priorities (p. 197).

What research such as this reveals therefore is that the separation and cultural isolation of the underclass is not the problem of the poor who supposedly inhabit it, but of the rest of society, who see in it some justification for their (slightly) higher social status. There are no cultural differences between the poor and the rest of society; but those who suggest that there are imply that the problems of poverty and deprivation, and therefore inequality, are 'theirs' rather than 'ours'.

Part IV
The Policy Framework

13

The Politics of Poverty

The Arithmetic Tradition

Because, as we have discussed, poverty is a political concept, academic interest in the definition and measurement of poverty, and academic research on the extent of poverty, have always been closely related to attempts to utilise such academic work to influence policy development or reform. And political debate about poverty and antipoverty policy has always been a contested, and even a conflictual, arena. Thus the problem of poverty has produced political activity; and this has been true for at least the last 150 to 200 years of industrial society in Britain. Indeed the political activity generated by the problem of poverty has been growing gradually, although with increasing rapidity, over the last century or two. It has also been becoming both more organised and more varied, and increasingly debate has focused not just on whether to politicise poverty, or what poverty to politicise, but also on how to organise political activity and who should be involved in this. We shall return to look at these issues in a little more detail shortly.

The pioneers of modern poverty research at the end of the nineteenth century, Booth and Rowntree, engaged in quite detailed calculations of the extent and distribution of poverty in the expectation that their evidence of the existence of the problem would create pressure on the government to develop policies to remove it. In the early twentieth century this strategy of using empirical evidence to influence political opinion was developed into a more organised form of political pressure through the work of reformers such as Sydney and Beatrice Webb, who consciously set out to combine academic work with political activity. The Webbs were instrumental in the establishment of the Fabian Society as a political group committed to working for welfare reform through political influence, in particular upon the emerging Labour Party. They were also involved in the founding of the London School of Economics (LSE), an academic institution with a focus upon research and education in social and economic planning.

Through the work of the Webbs and the Fabian Society therefore, the link between academic debate and political activity became established within British institutional structures. Their aim was to use evidence of poverty and social deprivation to expose the failure of the capitalist economic system and to challenge the political domination of the classical liberal tradition of political thought and its emphasis on the non-involvement and non-responsibility of government in economic and social reform. The growth in power of the labour movement and the Labour Party, where Fabian influence was primarily directed, and the gradual expansion of research activity and the numbers of research workers, as a product of the educational influence of the LSE, extended this challenge both quantitatively, in terms of the empirical evidence produced, and qualitatively, in terms of its impact on political, and especially government, thinking. Commentators have come to refer to this development as the 'arithmetic tradition'.

With the introduction of the welfare state reforms of the postwar period by the Labour government of the late 1940s, it appeared that this tradition had finally become the decisive influence on economic and social planning. Beveridge's proposals for insurance benefits to prevent poverty drew heavily on Rowntree's research into the nature and extent of poverty. It also appeared that these reforms were successful in removing poverty, as the Fabians had argued they would be. Further research by Rowntree (Rowntree and Lavers, 1951), carried out after the introduction of the welfare changes, suggested that the people in poverty had been reduced to very small numbers compared with earlier studies.

This belief in the achievements of the postwar welfare reforms was challenged in the 1960s by the evidence that poverty still existed, and had been 'rediscovered', in affluent Britain. The evidence of the continuation of poverty was the product of research work carried out by Abel Smith and Townsend (1965) and other academics at the LSE. It was based on a reassessment of the definition of poverty and a revitalisation of the tradition of empirical research to measure its extent and provide pressure on government to respond to it. It was thus a continuation of the arithmetic tradition of the Fabian Society, albeit with a more sophisticated approach which was directed not so much at the politics of classical liberalism, but rather at the complacency of the postwar 'consensus' that welfare reforms could be, and indeed had been, successful in removing poverty.

The expectation of the postwar Fabians was that governments and opposition parties which supported the role of welfare within industrial capitalist society, would readily respond to evidence that welfare reforms had failed to eliminate poverty and would be prepared to adjust or develop policies in order to achieve greater success. Initially this strategy appeared to be successful, at least in attracting from the Labour opposition of the early 1960s promises to introduce significant policy reforms if they were returned to power.

Labour were returned to power in 1964, but the promised reforms never materialised in the form anticipated by the Fabian protagonists. Whether the failure to make significant changes was primarily the product of changed economic circumstances, or merely lack of political will, will obviously remain a matter of debate. However it led the Fabian academics to continue their efforts to utilise further evidence of continuing poverty to maintain and extend the pressure for reform. This pressure included, as it had in the past, political influence as well as academic research, for instance from Labour cabinet minister Margaret Herbison, who resigned in protest when the promised welfare reforms were abandoned by the government in the mid 1960s. It also included pressure from newly formed campaigning organisations such as the CPAG, discussed below.

It was through the CPAG that the frustration of Abel Smith, Townsend and other Fabian academics increasingly came to be expressed, in particular through the publication in 1970 of a CPAG pamphlet entitled *Poverty and the Labour Government*, which produced evidence that the 'poor had got poorer' under Labour. This was a more outspoken criticism of Labour politics than the Fabians – who had generally regarded the Party as an ally in securing welfare reforms – had previously engaged in. It was received with hostility in some government circles, and was even blamed by some for contributing to the Party's election defeat in 1970.

Following the end of the Labour government of the 1960s the Fabian Society published a critical review edited by Townsend and Bosanquet (1972), of its achievements in the social policy field. The book was written in the spirit of informed academic criticism, but underlying it was a clear frustration at the perceived limitations of Labour's record on social policy reform. Similar frustrations were also felt by many after the end of the Labour administration of 1974-9, and a similar critique was once again published (Bosanquet and Townsend, 1980).

The assumption underlying both critiques, and indeed the assumption underlying the whole arithmetic tradition of Fabian political influence, was a belief that the aim of government within welfare states was to utilise the machinery of the state to resolve, or at least relieve, social problems such as poverty. In other words that there was a political consensus over the role of the state in the prevention of poverty. This was linked to a constitutionalist belief in the strategy of using pressure on Parliament and government departments to persuade them of the need for reform. In the 1980s both of these assumptions came openly into question.

The Thatcher governments of the 1980s were openly critical of the postwar consensus of the role of the state in welfare reform, and in particular of the dangers of continual pressure for extensions of social policy at the expense of support for the private market and the capitalist economy. They challenged the idea that welfare reforms would benefit poorer people, and argued that seeking support for extensions of state expenditure, ostensibly in order to achieve further welfare benefits, was merely an attempt to 'buy votes' (see Green, 1990). In his famous speech on poverty in 1989, the Secretary of state for social services, John Moore, openly attacked the claim that large numbers of people in Britain were still poor. He rejected the relative notion of poverty utilised by Fabian academics and criticised them for their attempts to discredit the achievements of British economic development.

In addition to the changed attitudes of government ministers in the 1980s there was also a change in the climate of political influences on government. The evidence and arguments of Fabian academics and antipoverty organisations such as the CPAG were challenged by academics and organisations seeking to use the same channels of academic debate and political argument to press the case for quite different policy priorities and policy changes. These organisations were arguing for reductions in state welfare and a return to the classical liberal politics of which the old Fabians had been so critical. Although these were not new arguments, they attracted for their protagonists the label of the 'new right'. New right organisations included the Institute of Economic Affairs (IEA), founded in 1957 but revitalised in the 1980s, the Centre for Policy Studies, established by Keith Joseph and Margaret Thatcher, and the Adam Smith Institute (ASI), which produced proposals for radical reform of social security provision (ASI, 1984, 1989).

Faced with such a challenge from the right and with a largely unsympathetic and unyielding government, the Fabian arithmetic tradition experienced a significant setback in the 1980s in their strategy for the prevention of poverty. Their arguments were challenged and their influence severely reduced. As a result of this the politics of poverty in Britain underwent a major transformation during this period. No longer was it possible to assume that poverty and deprivation were problems recognisable by all in British society, and that government was under an obligation to respond to evidence that such problems continued to exist in the midst of growing affluence.

Right-wing proponents inside and outside government argued that such evidence was bogus, and that state obligations extended only to the relief of proven destitution through targeted (means-tested) state benefits fixed at basic minimum levels, whereas left-wing critics continued to claim that poverty had to be understood as a problem of deprivation and inequality, and that only state intervention to redistribute resources across society could do anything to alleviate this. In other words the debate was no longer about what could be done, but rather what should be done. And in this climate detailed empirical research was not such an important factor in the argument.

Thus by the end of the 1980s the arithmetic tradition, which had come to dominate the politics of poverty throughout most of the earlier part of the twentieth century, was under challenge within a changed political climate. However, this did not lead to an abandonment of the Fabian strategy. Academic research into the definition and extent of poverty continued, and indeed continued to grow. And the organisations campaigning to make the problem of poverty a political priority, and to pressure the government into policy reform, increased in size and number, even if their influence was harder to sustain.

The Poverty Lobby

Central to the Fabian strategy of utilising academic argument and academic research to secure change and development in government policy was the attempt to foster close and influential relationships with government ministers and departments. And particularly during the terms of Labour government after the Second World War this was a relatively successful strategy. In the 1970s Abel Smith was an adviser to the secretary of state for social services, and Piachaud was a member of the prime minister's political unit. During this time Donnison was also appointed as chair of the Supplementary Benefits Commission. Fabians have also entered Parliament as elected members, most notably Frank Field – previously director of the CPAG – in 1979, who later became chair of the House of Commons Select Committee on Social Security.

However direct political influence through entry into the corridors, and the committee rooms, of power has been supplemented in the politics of poverty by indirect pressure exerted by campaigning activity outside the exclusive worlds of Westminster and Whitehall. Indeed throughout the twentieth century, in addition to the research and formal political influence of the arithmetic tradition, academics have combined with political activists and members of various organisations representing different special interests and demands to establish independent groups to campaign for a range of policy changes. Such groups have sometimes been referred to by political scientists as 'pressure groups'.

An early example of such pressure group activity was the 1917 Committee, later renamed the Family Endowment Committee, which was established by Eleanor Rathbone and others to campaign for the introduction of family allowances to reduce poverty amongst families and children. The committee was wound up in the 1940s after its eventual success in persuading the government to institute a family allowance scheme, although the scheme was not quite in the form the campaigners had wanted, nor was it entirely the product of their campaigning efforts.

After the 'rediscovery of poverty' in the 1960s, however, and the revitalisation of the arithmetic tradition, Fabian academics began to look again at the possibility of establishing independent campaigning organisations to carry the message of reform outside the narrow confines of academic debate and political influence. Their aim was to establish vehicles outside government and the civil service, and outside academic institutions, which would be free to voice opinions on the need for reform and policy development that were informed by academic argument and research, but not limited by the need to appease narrow political interests. This, it was hoped, would get poverty, and the need for antipoverty policy, onto the political agenda and provide a voice for proposing policy reforms which were not necessarily currently accepted within government or opposition political circles.

Abel Smith and Townsend, the authors of the influential book on the persistence of poverty in affluent Britain (1965), were involved in the aftermath of this rediscovery of poverty in the establishment of a group to campaign for improved support for poor families and children. The group was initially called the Family Poverty Group, but was shortly renamed the Child Poverty Action Group (CPAG) (see McCarthy, 1986). From these modest, but influential, roots the CPAG grew fairly rapidly into a well-informed and well-respected campaigning organisation. It had active and effective leaders in Tony Lynes and then Frank Field and was successful both in attracting the recognition of politicians and civil servants and in helping to put the problem of poverty onto the political agenda (see Whiteley and Winyard, 1983). By 1981 MacGregor (pp. 141–2) was writing that the CPAG had become 'part of the fabric of British politics'.

Getting poverty onto the political agenda was only a part of the aim of the CPAG however, and arguably not the most important part. They were also concerned to bring about genuine policy change to reduce or remove poverty, especially amongst children and families. And this of course was a more difficult task, especially after the mid 1960s when the increasing pressure of economic recession gave little room to governments, they claimed, to increase welfare provision. Nevertheless some important policy changes were introduced, especially during the 1970s, for which the CPAG could claim a fair measure of indirect responsibility. In particular these included the ending of the wage-stop (a means of restricting the benefit entitlement of some unemployed claimants) and the introduction of Child Benefit. The latter was a hard-fought battle indeed, in which cabinet leaks and trade union influence were orchestrated by the CPAG to maintain the pressure for reform on a government which was seriously considering abandoning its promises to implement the scheme (see Field, 1982).

The CPAG is perhaps the most important, and the most widely respected (Whiteley and Winyard, 1983, p. 18), group campaigning for reform in the poverty field. But it is not the only group – there are many others representing different special interests or promoting various policy reforms. These include Age Concern, the Disablement Income Group (DIG), the National Council for One Parent Families (NCOPF), the Low Pay Unit (LPU), Shelter (campaigning against homelessness) and others. In their discussion of these campaign groups Whiteley and Winyard distinguish between promotional groups, comprising professionals or volunteers campaigning for reform on behalf of others, and representational groups, who are representatives of those experiencing poverty or deprivation campaigning to improve provision for all those like them. They point out that both forms of organisation can be found campaigning in the poverty field and that both have their advantages and their disadvantages in the poltical arena. As a whole, however, these groups had by the 1970s begun to develop a collective identity forged out of their shared concern for policy reform, and they had come to be called the 'poverty lobby'

The poverty lobby did not just share a common concern for certain policy reforms however. Where these concerns were sufficiently close various organisations combined to form joint campaigning organisations to publicise particular shared interests or to press for particular policy reforms. Such 'umbrella' organisations included the Child Benefit Now campaign of the 1970s and the 'Social Security Consortium' of the 1980s. In the mid 1980s, when the government's reviews of social security threatened to lead to restructuring and reductions in benefit provision, poverty lobby organisations also combined with trade unions representing employees in the Department of Social Security (described by Whiteley and Winyard, 1983 as 'producer groups') in an organisation called Action for Benefits to campaign against what they regarded as undesirable benefit reforms.

Political activity initiated in response to proposed government changes, as opposed to the promotion of academic arguments or innovative reforms, has also resulted in the formation of new campaigning organisations. These include the Campaign Against the Supplementary Benefit Review (CASBR) in the late 1970s and the National Campaign Against Social Security Cuts (NCASSC) in the 1980s. Not surprisingly, however, these tend to be relatively short-lived groups and consequently they have less political influence or effect. In the case of the two mentioned, they were also largely unsuccessful in preventing governments from pressing ahead with the planned changes.

The campaigning work of the poverty lobby groups includes a wide range of activities aimed at securing maximum publicity and maximum influence for the groups' ideas. The CPAG, for instance, conducts its own research and publishes this together with other research findings in a series of well-regarded policy texts (see Oppenheim, 1990; Becker, 1991). The group also regularly submits evidence and memoranda direct to government departments and ministers, organises meetings and conferences to discuss and publicise proposals at both national and local level, and attempts to utilise the established media – the press, radio and television – to present ideas to a wider audience.

The power of public expression through the media has become of increasing importance to all political campaigners in the latter half of the twentieth century. The media operate both to publicise ideas and to shape them, and their influence in defining the problem, and the politics, of poverty cannot be ignored. Poverty lobby organisations therefore regularly provide press releases to publicise their work and respond to requests for interviews on radio or television. However journalists and broadcasters can themselves initiate influential political debate through reporting evidence of deprivation or even through using the problem of poverty as a theme in fictional dramas. The magazine *New Society* was throughout the 1960s and 1970s an important forum for reporting evidence from poverty research. And during the same period there were a few highly influential television dramas focusing on the problems of poverty in Britain, notably 'Cathy Come Home' and 'The Spongers'.

In their assessment of the influence and achievements of the poverty lobby, Whiteley and Winyard (1983) point out that the success of campaigning work depends upon a number of factors, not all of which are within the control of campaigning groups. They highlight in particular the political environment within which they are operating, the strategies which they choose to promote their ideas, and the resources they have to support their work. These influences vary from group to group and over time. The resources supporting the CPAG have enabled it to survive as an influential campaign group for over twenty-five years, and its broadly based strategies have permitted it to maintain pressure for reform across a range of fronts. However the changed political climate of the 1980s has restricted the influence of the CPAG, as it has the influence of the Fabian academics who have always worked so closely with it. During this decade CPAG achievements in terms of innovative reform were more or less nil, and attempts to prevent unwanted government changes were only rarely successful.

Despite this hostile climate however, the poverty lobby has continued to grow and develop, incorporating an increasingly wide range of specialist groups and umbrella organisations. Most however are mainly composed of professional campaigners employed to carry out the campaigning aims of the various groups. They are campaigners *for* the poor rather than campaigners *from* the poor. The politics of poverty also includes the political activities of those who are poor themselves, and it is to this issue that we shall now turn.

Campaigning by the Poor

Following their distinction between promotional and representational groups, Whiteley and Winyard (1983) conclude that most organisations within the poverty lobby are promotional. That is they are not composed of, or representative of, poor people or benefit claimants. The major poverty campaign group, the CPAG, is a promotional organisation: its National Executive Committee is primarily composed of professionals elected at the open Annual General Meeting, and the daily work of the organisation is carried out by full-time salaried workers.

However the CPAG also has a structure of local branches which meet regularly in many cities and towns up and down the country, and which also meet together annually to elect representatives of branches to the National Executive. Many of these local branches do include claimants and other poor people, which in the 1990s would include higher education students, who are often active participants in local campaigning work. The involvement of such people in the broader activities of the CPAG has posed the question for this organisation of how far such people should be involved and encouraged in policy development within the group. It also raises the more general question of whether the poverty lobby more generally should not be more actively representative of poor people themselves.

This issue of campaigning *by* the poor, as opposed to *for* the poor, is an important one for any discussion of the politics of poverty, and it has been a controversial one in some debates amongst concerned parties, both poor and not poor. One influential protagonist of the case for prioritising campaigning by the poor in the promotion of antipoverty policies has been Holman, one-time professor of social policy and author of an earlier textbook on poverty (Holman, 1978) and later community worker on a large housing estate in Easterhouse Glasgow, who in numerous articles in publications such as the *Guardian* newspaper has argued that poverty campaigning should concentrate on 'letting the poor speak'. His argument is that only those who experience poverty can know what it is like, and tell it like it is; and therefore that their testimony is both the most authentic and the most effective evidence of the problems that need to be addressed. Furthermore if poverty campaigning is seeking to promote the cause of policy reform to address such problems, then the nature of the reforms promoted should be determined not by academics and politicians, even though they may be sympathetic to the poor, but by those who know through experience what they need.

In fact the issue of campaigns by, rather than for, the poor is not a new one. In the nineteenth century part of the fears of government and reformers alike was of the collective action of the disaffected 'residuum' (see Stedman Jones, 1971). In the twentieth century, between the wars unemployed claimants organised themselves into the National Unemployed Workers' Movement and sought to join or to cooperate with the trade unions representing employed workers in the TUC. There was much tension and distrust in this liaison, although it produced some important and influential campaigning activity, most notably the 'hunger marches' and the Jarrow Crusade (see Vincent, 1991, pp. 56ff).

In the 1970s and 1980s unemployed claimants again established membership organisations, now called 'claimants' unions', which attempted to develop political links with other labour movement organisations and with poverty lobby groups. These are sometimes associated with the activities of a Yorkshire ex-miner, Joe Kenyon; but they extended throughout Britain and for a time were co-ordinated by an umbrella organisation called the National Federation of Claimants Unions. The great strengths of the claimants unions, their basis in the spontaneous collective spirit of the unemployed and their exclusive membership from amongst benefit claimants, were also their major weaknesses however, at least in organisational terms. Active membership was difficult to sustain over long periods of time and in the face of little prospect of significant improvement in the circumstances of most unemployed people – unless they became employed and therefore ineligible for membership of course. Individual claimants unions were usually temporary phenomena therefore and the national umbrella organisation was unable to maintain a permanent profile in the political arena.

What the organisational difficulties experienced by the claimants unions reveal are the genuine problems involved in sustained and coordinated campaigning activity by poor people. For a variety of reasons related both to the financial deprivation with which they must constantly struggle and to the social isolation which frequently results from this, poor people do not find it easy to engage in organised political activity, and organised political groups have not found it easy to involve poor people. Some of these problems were discussed at a forum on *Working Together Against Poverty* in York in 1990 (Lister and Beresford, 1991) at which academics and professional poverty campaigners met with representatives of poor people. Financial hardship, limited knowledge, the experience of stigma and lack of energy and confidence were all identified as factors inhibiting poor people from involvement in campaigning activity. As one participant put it:

We may not feel we've got much energy left for anything else. We don't want to speak out when we are unsure of a good response (p. 7).

Ward (1986) discusses more generally the debilitating consequences of poverty and deprivation for participation in political activity. These include the direct costs of participation, such as membership fees, transport, socialising and keeping up to date, and the indirect consequences of poor health, poor environment and lack of time, which inhibit involvement in any organised, active pursuits.

Perhaps most important of all, however, are the political contradictions at the heart of poverty campaigning by the poor. As already discussed, poverty is a political concept. As such it is a problem, an undesirable state of affairs about which something should be, but is not being, done. To identify oneself as poor therefore is to identify oneself as having a problem, and in need of help. This is a negative categorisation, which poor people desperately trying to survive, perhaps with dignity, in a hostile world may not willingly, and openly, wish to adopt. As another participant at the York forum put it:

> Nobody wants to be poor. It's not something we want everyone to know. Some people don't want to tell others they are poor or even admit it to themselves (Lister and Beresford, 1991, p. 10).

In this context therefore it is easy to see how the experience of poverty and the exclusion of the poor operate to reproduce each other in a kind of vicious circle.

Important though the issue of the involvement of poor people in political campaigning is, we must question any implicit assumption that only poor people can act as advocates of the cause of antipoverty. Clearly poverty, and the experience of deprivation, is an issue for poor people; but it is not only an issue for poor people. As we discussed in Chapter 1 there are problems involved in adopting a purely subjective definition of poverty, that is identifying poverty only with the experiences and perceptions of those who are poor. Poverty campaigning which is limited to the experiences and initiatives of poor people runs the risk of being similarly self-defeating, for the reasons just discussed.

Identifying the politics of poverty only with the politics of the poor, however, also ignores the fact that poverty is also a problem for others in society – both in particular, in terms of self interest, because those not poor now may become poor later, and in general because the existence of poverty in society may be unacceptable to many who would wish to be part of a social order in which others did not suffer deprivation. Indeed it is to a shared belief in greater social justice that poverty campaigners must appeal if they are to secure support for policy changes to remove poverty, and this cannot be achieved if poverty is perceived and presented as a problem only for the poor. Thus the involvement of poor people in campaigning against poverty can be a supplement to the more general activities of the academics, politicians and professionals, but it cannot be a substitute for them.

14

Social Security Policy

The Principles of Social Security

The definition and identification of poverty within advanced industrial societies involve an implicit argument that state policy should be developed to remove or prevent this poverty occurring. The politics of poverty is effectively therefore the politics of antipoverty policy. And just as the politics of poverty can be traced back through the development of industrial society, so too can antipoverty policy. What such a historical review reveals is that throughout this period the major focus of antipoverty policy within the state in Britain, and in all other industrial societies, has been social security policy.

The idea behind social security policy is the use of state support, collected in the form of contributions or taxes from those in employment, to provide an income from the state for those who cannot secure an adequate income for themselves and thus are at risk of poverty. Social security is therefore a form of redistribution of resources from those who have more than sufficient to provide for themselves to those who do not have enough. The resources which are distributed are generally cash, in the form of taxes and benefits, but they can, and sometimes do, include state support in kind, for instance the supply of free school meals to the children of poor parents.

The aim of social security payments therefore is the removal of poverty. Implicitly the amount of benefit provided should be sufficient to prevent the benefit claimants from experiencing poverty, as defined by the government. However social security benefits have not always operated as such a simple poverty prevention measure. As Atkinson (1990a) discusses, the fixing of benefit levels is in practice subject to factors other than the determination of a national minimum poverty-prevention income, in particular the concerns to ensure that benefit levels can be afforded in redistributional terms from the taxes which must pay for them, and to ensure that state benefit levels do not interfere with the setting of wage levels within the labour market.

Either explicitly or implicitly therefore benefit support may provide only a contribution towards an income that is sufficient to prevent the experience of poverty. These are problems to which we shall return below.

The assumption that benefit levels represent an income sufficient to prevent poverty has also resulted in conflict and confusion with the definition and measurement of poverty by academics and politicians. As discussed in Part II there is much disagreement about how to define poverty and how to express this in terms of a weekly income. The benefit level is therefore sometimes taken as a proxy definition or measure of poverty approved by the state, and yet this provides a logical contradiction with the role of such benefits in preventing poverty. As government spokespersons have sometimes pointed out, it could result in an increase in antipoverty measures, via a raising of the benefit level, leading to an apparent increase in the numbers in poverty.

Thus although the overall aim of social security policy is the redistribution of resources through state support to tackle the problem of poverty, there is no guarantee that there will be consistency or agreement in how such support should be provided, or in whether in practice it will be effective. Most importantly there is inconsistency and disagreement over whether the aim of social security should be to *prevent* poverty, through the provision of an income sufficient to lift recipients above the poverty level, or merely to *relieve* poverty, through the provision of a contribution towards those falling below a defined poverty level. As we shall see, British social security has at different times fluctuated between the pursuit of these two differing aims, at some times appearing to pursue both simultaneously.

Another major disagreement concerns the issue of horizontal versus vertical redistribution in social security. *Horizontal* redistribution is primarily concerned to tackle 'life-cycle' poverty by the provision of benefits to people at periods of need, such as retirement, which is financed by contributions collected from them at times of relative sufficiency such as employment. Within such a scheme all are potential contributors and potential beneficiaries. *Vertical* redistribution operates according to quite different principles: here the concern is to redirect resources from those with sufficient to those in need without any expectation of a link between payment and receipt. Within such a scheme those in need may never even be in a position to contribute and may require support at any time, and those who pay do not expect themselves to benefit from their contributions. Once again these different structures have at different times been incorporated into British social security provision and for large periods of time have apparently operated in tandem.

In addition to the disagreements over the aims of poverty prevention or poverty relief and the use of horizontal or vertical redistribution, there are some commentators who have called into question the extent to which social security is primarily an antipoverty policy within industrial societies. Novak (1984, 1988) and Squires (1990) have argued that rather then seeking to relieve or prevent poverty, the primary aim of social security policy has been to contain it, or to contain those who suffer from it. Within industrial societies based upon labour markets those outside the labour market will always be at risk of poverty; it is therefore necessary to ensure that they perceive the solution to their deprivation to be an attempt to 'return' to the labour market rather than a rejection or subversion of it. State support through social security therefore operates to provide sufficient support to prevent subversion, but it is coupled with stringent conditions to ensure discipline within and commitment to the labour market. Social security thus controls the poor within the labour market, and since its primary aim is to do this the support it provides will not improve the lot of the unemployed poor beyond the deprivation experienced by those at the very bottom of that labour market. Containment therefore does not prevent poverty, and may do little to relieve it.

Those who see in social security a policy of containment and control often overlook the genuine achievements which social security provisions have made in supporting the most vulnerable people in industrial societies and in redistributing resources within an unequal labour market. Whatever its limitations social security does act as an antipoverty policy. However those who recognise its achievements in reducing poverty can also overlook its constraints and controls. Within a labour market economy social security policy does operate to reinforce labour market discipline and to control the poor. Social security is not redistribution *or* control; it is *both*.

As an antipoverty policy therefore, social security in Britain is more complex and contradictory than one might at first expect. It is the product of conflicting aims and structures and within these policies and priorities have shifted over time. Of course this is because social security policy has been created through political process, not scientific analysis. Changes in political power have resulted in changes in social security policy. Such changes have ebbed and flowed over time, and generally without the products of previous policies being abandoned or overhauled. Like all social phenomena social security policy is a product of history, not logic; and its aims and achievements must be assessed within that historical context.

The Development of State Support

As discussed in Chapter 1, social security policy in modern British society can be traced back to the early seventeenth century and the introduction of the Poor Law in 1601. The Poor Law was a form of locally administered poverty relief providing support, plus discipline, to vagrants and beggars. It was initially a loosely structured system operating within a rural agrarian economy. With the growth of industrialisation it came under increasing pressure, and the 1834 reforms resulted in a tighter national control over Poor Law provision and the introduction of clearer elements of labour market discipline.

The most significant element of this discipline was the principle of 'less eligibility', the requirement that any support provided by the state must be set below the circumstances of the lowest wage labourer in order to ensure that dependence upon state support remained a less eligible status. Linked to the principle of less eligibility was the assumption of family support: husbands, wives, parents and children were expected to provide mutual support at times of need to obviate the need to turn to the state. As we saw earlier, less cligibility and family support were enforced through the 'workhouse test', the grim and rigorous residential regime to which only those with no other potential source of support would wish to subject themselves. Life in the workhouse was unpleasant, and it was intended to be. It also attracted fear and stigma. These elements of control were a central feature of early social security provision and, albeit in a less stringent form, they have remained at the centre of social security policy ever since.

Not surprisingly therefore the Poor Law was not a popular form of state support amongst the rapidly growing nineteenth century working class. In practice too it was unable to provide support for all who might be unable to provide adequately for themselves. In many areas therefore workhouse provision was supplemented by outdoor relief, despite the fact that this was intended to be curtailed after 1834. For more established workers, however, even this form of support was undesirable, or largely unnecessary, and the latter half of the century saw the development of a range of private and voluntary schemes to provide income protection for such workers in times of labour market failure. Most of the schemes were run by friendly societies or trade unions established within the working class. In return for contributions made during periods of unemployment they provided income support in times of sickness or in old age (see Thane, 1982, pp. 28–32). Schemes such as these were limited in scope, however, and generally confined to particular industries or sections of workers.

For the majority of workers, especially low-paid ones, there was no self-protection. By the end of the century, however, additional support was provided for some of the increasing numbers of poor workers and their families by a range of charitable sources organised and controlled by concerned members of the middle class under the general auspices of an umbrella organisation called the Charity Organisation Society. Although partly motivated by a concern for the deprivation experienced by Britain's new urban poor, charitable support was also linked to a concern for the morality of the poor and their attitudes to life and labour. Support was thus often accompanied by moral advice and moral pressure to conform to particular middle-class models of respectable family life.

By the end of the nineteenth century, therefore, state support from the Poor Law was operating alongside privately organised self-help and charitable provision for poor people in Britain. Provision was patchy however, and as the research of Booth and Rowntree revealed it had not removed or prevented poverty. With the growing political and economic strength of the organised working class, and the fear of unrest from the less organised poor, there was increasing pressure on the government to do more to extend and coordinate state support. By the beginning of the twentieth century there was also the example of Bismarck's social reforms in Germany, where work-based insurance protection had been introduced with state coordination and control with the clear intention of relieving working-class pressure for more general social reform – or revolution.

The example of state-based insurance in Germany and the privately organised insurance of the British friendly societies combined in the early twentieth century to create the precedents for the introduction of state-based insurance in Britain too, although in fact the first new state support introduced in 1908, the old age pension, was not a contributory insurance benefit, as we saw in Chapter 10. In 1911, however, insurance-based benefits on the Bismarck model for sickness and unemployment were introduced into some industries, paying benefits for temporary absence from the labour market in return for contributions made whilst in work. The intention was that the state insurance support would be actuarially sound and self-financing; there was thus a lower rate of benefit for women who were assumed to be a greater insurance risk. After the First World War the scheme was extended to include pensions and a wider range of workers and potential beneficiaries, and as unemployment rose dramatically during the depression of the 1920s and 1930s this became more difficult to sustain. There was pressure on the government to restrict entitlement and cut benefits, leading eventually to the defeat of the then Labour government. Restricted entitlement and increasing unemployment also meant that growing numbers of poor people were forced to continue to rely upon the inadequate and unpopular Poor Law.

Despite the critical recommendations of both the Majority and Minority Reports of the Royal Commission on the Poor Law of 1909 (see Thane, 1982, pp. 88–91), no significant changes had been made to the nineteenth century scheme. It remained in local control and thus subject to local variation. Sometimes this led to relatively generous support, as in the controversial case of the Poor Law Guardians in the London Borough of Poplar (see Hill, 1990, p. 23); but in general provision was meagre. In part because of the controversy associated with local variation, the Poor Law was restructured into the new Unemployment Assistance scheme in 1934, and later this was converted into a National Assistance scheme.

Even after these changes, social security provision in Britain at the beginning of the Second World War was a confused structure of partial insurance schemes and means-tested assistance, with the remains of the Poor Law underlying the twentieth century developments. There was need for a radical structural review, and in 1942 this was provided by the *Report on Social Insurance and Allied Services* by Sir William Beveridge. It was a government-commissioned report, but it was largely Beveridge's own work (see Harris, 1977).

Beveridge's report was the first, and so far only, thorough review of state support and the role of social security in the alleviation or prevention of poverty. It was based upon the general argument that state intervention was needed to tackle the major social problems of British society, and it contained in effect a blueprint for the reform of the social security system around the principle that Beveridge called 'social insurance'. The details of his proposals for reform have been discussed elsewhere (see Alcock, 1987, Ch. 4; Hill, 1990, Ch. 3). In essence they involved a full state takeover of the various insurance schemes developed earlier in the century, some aspects of which had remained under the administration of the friendly societies, and the extension of social insurance to provide a comprehensive cover for all circumstances of need arising from non-participation in the labour market.

The intention of the Beveridge plan was that nearly full employment, sustained by government policy, would provide labour-market-based support for most breadwinners. Their contributions into the scheme during their employment could then be used to provide for the payment of benefits during times of sickness, retirement or temporary unemployment. As we saw in Chapter 8, however, Beveridge's plan was based on clear assumptions about family structure and gender roles. Married women, who had 'other duties' than employment, were expected to receive support through their husband's wage or benefit, and thus even when they were in employment they were to be excluded from full participation in the insurance scheme.

Beveridge's aim was that through its link to the labour market and family structure the social insurance scheme would provide comprehensive protection for all. As Atkinson has discussed (1992), this link was central – social insurance was based upon support for the labour market, not upon some attempt to nationalise private self-protection. There was thus the potential problem of some poor people being excluded from both the labour market and the social insurance scheme; and for them Beveridge recommended the retention of a means-tested national assistance scheme, although he expected that this would have a diminishing, safety-net role.

Beveridge's proposals received widespread acclaim, and the report was even a best-seller. The postwar Labour government introduced most of the changes he had recommended, although they retitled the scheme National Insurance (NI) and made some adjustment to the benefit rates. In order to avoid a situation in which currently retiring pensioners would be excluded from protection because of their lack of contribution to the scheme, however, all pensioners were automatically credited with entitlement to insurance pensions. This meant that current contributions had to be used to pay out these benefits, rather than being invested to meet future benefit liabilities in the way a strict insurance scheme would operate. This meant that from the outset the NI scheme was administered on a 'pay-as-you-go' basis with current benefit demand being met from current contribution payments which, as will be discussed, has created problems for the long-term viability of the insurance notion.

The basic structures of the Beveridge plan have dominated postwar British social security provision. There have been reforms within the structure, and in effect a departure from Beveridge's vision of comprehensive insurance protection, but the broad labour-market insurance principle, supplemented by a means-tested safety-net, are still the bases of entitlement to most social security benefits, and the major alleviation of or protection from income poverty. In practice the comprehensiveness of the insurance scheme has never been realised however, and the role of means-tested protection has risen to become in the 1990s the major feature of state support, an issue to which we shall return shortly.

Social Insurance

The Beveridge social insurance plan was in part based upon the Bismarckian tradition of social reform to support existing social structures. As Atkinson discusses (1992) therefore, insurance protection has always been closely tied to support for labour market participation and has operated to provide support only in times of labour-market failure. Beveridge's report was also heavily influenced by Rowntree's research on poverty and in particular his notion of life-cycle poverty within families. If protection could be provided in such periods of high risk of poverty therefore, social security could operate not just to alleviate poverty, as had been the aim of the nineteenth century Poor Law, but to *prevent* it.

The aim of the social insurance scheme therefore was to utilise contributions made through participation in the labour market to build an entitlement to benefit support in times of need. Social security would thus provide for a form of horizontal distribution of resources through the state over the life cycle of its citizens, or rather its workers. This would operate on a collective basis in the NI scheme, but it would be based upon individual contribution and individual entitlement. Indeed it was this individual investment in social security which Beveridge felt was its great popular appeal:

> The capacity and desire of British people to contribute for security are among the most certain and impressive social facts of today (Beveridge, 1942, p. 119).

Despite the appeal of self-protection through contribution into a social insurance scheme however, the British NI scheme has never operated as a form of strict individual insurance protection. As explained above, in order to prevent existing pensioners from being excluded at the start of the scheme contributions were utilised to meet existing benefit entitlement on a pay-as-you-go basis. Thus although all individual contributions are paid into a separate NI fund to meet benefit expenditure, together with a small contribution towards the funding of the National Health Service, the resources in the fund are expended each year in meeting current benefit needs, leaving future contributors to fund future benefit entitlement.

This may in practice, and in principle, be a reasonable way in which to finance benefit expenditure, in effect utilising NI contributions as a form of hypothecated tax for social security. However it is not what is generally understood as an insurance scheme and it does not in practice mean that each individual's contributions will be available to guarantee future benefit entitlement, as many contributors may believe to be the case. Thus those who contribute to NI in the expectation that they are making an investment for their future protection have been seriously misled, although since payment of contributions by employees and employers is compulsory the consequences of this deceit may not be so significant.

Although NI contributions are not invested to meet future benefit entitlement there is nevertheless a link within the scheme between individual contribution and benefit entitlement. In order to sustain the fiction that benefits are paid in return for contributions, and to limit the number of potential claimants on the NI fund, all NI benefits are subject to contribution tests which restrict entitlement to those who have paid the requisite number of contributions during the requisite period of employment. In practice these tests are extremely complex to understand and administer, the best summary being provided in the annual CPAG guide to non-means-tested benefits, and they do include special rules to provide credited contributions during periods of unemployment and to exempt from some contribution conditions people caring for dependent children or adults. However in general the contribution rules make entitlement to NI benefits conditional upon payment into the fund during periods of labour-market participation. They thus retain the logic of the labour-market support discussed by Atkinson (1992) and therefore exclude from NI protection those who have not been able to maintain contributions through paid employment.

Consequently although it is not strictly speaking an insurance scheme, NI entitlement is excluded to those who have not been able to contribute, significantly undermining the comprehensiveness of the scheme. Of course, as was suggested in Part III, this exclusion does not fall equally across social groups because of inequalities in access to the labour market. Thus black people, people with disabilities, the young unemployed and, because entitlement to NI protection during unemployment is in any event restricted to one year only, the long-term unemployed are all excluded. And as levels of unemployment generally have grown in the latter decades of the twentieth century the size of these excluded groups has increased, and the comprehensive appeal of NI has further declined.

As suggested above, Beveridge's insurance plan was also based upon a particular family structure in which married women were dependent upon their husbands' support through wages or benefits. They were thus excluded from entitlement to benefits in their own right. This exclusion was removed by later reform to the scheme, and single or married women in employment are now required to contribute, and are entitled to benefits, in the same way as men. However for some married women who were not contributing fully prior to the reforms the exclusion has been permitted to continue, with the result that some are still excluded. The formal introduction of equal treatment into the NI scheme has not prevented women's unequal position in practice however, because their general exclusion from the labour market and concentration in low-paid jobs which fall below the threshold above which employees and employers are required to make contributions to the fund, mean that many do not meet the conditions for entitlement to benefits (see Alcock, 1987, Ch. 3).

Beveridge's recommendation, incorporated into the original NI scheme, was the payment of flat-rate benefits in return for flat-rate contributions. All would be treated equally within the state scheme, and those who might wish additional protection would have to seek it separately through private insurance. He saw no contradiction between the principle of state protection for all and private protection for some. In order to avoid benefits competing with low wages and thus discouraging labour market participation, benefit rates were also set at a low level, based initially upon Rowntree's calculations of the weekly needs for subsistence living.

Although the benefit rates were later raised, their generally low level resulted in overlap with entitlement to means-tested assistance benefits, which unlike NI included full payment for rent. This meant that many of those receiving NI protection also had to claim means-tested support. It also meant that there was in effect an incentive to seek additional private protection for some, leading to the development of the occupational and private pension protection discussed in Chapter 10. Partly in response to the exclusion from this additional protection of those with only an entitlement to NI benefits, and partly in response to the low levels of benefit payable, NI was therefore extended in the 1960s and 1970s to include earnings-related benefit payments in return for earnings-related contributions.

The earnings-related additions to the so-called 'short-term' benefits such as unemployment and sickness were phased out in the early 1980s as part of a more general reduction in the scope of the NI scheme, to which we shall return shortly. The state earnings-related pension scheme (SERPS), introduced in 1978, has however been retained, despite the proposal in 1985 to abandon it, as was discussed in Chapter 10. SERPS protection is not as generous as that offered by many private or occupational pension schemes however; and entitlement to it was cut in 1988, although only with effect from 1998. Nevertheless it does provide a significant addition to the flat-rate basic pension for some, based upon NI contributions paid after its introduction in 1978.

The proposals to scrap SERPS in 1985 were largely based upon fears that the cost of the earnings-related benefits would place too high a burden on the contributors to the NI scheme in the early twenty-first century, when it is projected that there will be a greater number of pensioners and fewer contributors to provide for their benefits. This is of course one of the ever-present problems of the pay-as-you-go basis of the NI scheme. And although this future funding problem has effectively been postponed, the increased demands on the NI fund in the 1980s which flowed from the rising levels of unemployment, together with a government desire to remove the contribution from general taxation to the NI fund, which Beveridge had included as part of his original plan, meant that contribution levels were increased at the same time as levels of benefit were being cut and the contribution conditions required to establish entitlement to benefit were being tightened (see Hill, 1990, Ch. 5).

The changes to NI in the 1980s have demonstrated most clearly that, whatever may have been Beveridge's intentions or hopes, the insurance scheme has never been independent of more general social security provision or benefit policy. The separate fund is a device for administering the financial management of NI benefits, and the contribution conditions are a – largely arbitrary – means of ensuring that benefit entitlement is restricted to those who have some record of payment into the fund (see Dilnot *et al.*, 1984, pp. 28–34). But NI is in practice simply one part of a complex social security system, providing benefits without means tests for some claimants in some circumstances. For those who do benefit, the avoidance of the means test is a significant advantage; but the generally low level of NI benefit payments means that many who are entitled will still have to claim means-tested benefits in addition to maximise their receipt of state support. And for the increasing numbers who are not entitled, because of exclusion from adequate labour market participation, NI protection is unavailable and full dependence upon means-tested assistance continues to be the major vehicle for income support.

Social Assistance

Beveridge recommended the retention of a social assistance scheme, actually called National Assistance (NA), alongside the new NI scheme because he recognised that there may be some people with no adequate income who would not be entitled to any insurance benefit because they could not meet the contribution conditions. He saw assistance operating as a safety net below the basic state provision, and his expectation was that demand for it would be low and would decline as NI expanded.

The basis for entitlement to assistance was the means test. Only those who could prove that they had no other source of adequate support would be able to receive state support under it. The means test was to be adminstered by the National Assistance Board (NAB) and was based upon the assumption that married or cohabiting men and women and their children would support themselves, although the broader expectation that other family members too could be expected to provide support in times of need, which had operated in the interwar scheme, was dropped (see Deacon and Bradshaw, 1983, Ch. 2).

Unlike the Poor Law Guardians the NAB operated on a national basis; but in many other respects NA was a continuation of the Poor Law, which in effect it replaced. Benefit rates were fixed at a minimum subsistence level to avoid providing an attractive form of support, and receipt was conditional in most cases upon submission to tests of labour market potential – adult claimants of working age were expected to be seeking employment. The principle of less eligibility thus continued into the assistance scheme, and with it went the negative imagery associated with dependence upon state support for those unable to provide for themselves. Beveridge expected that stigma would accompany dependence upon means testing; indeed this was indirectly a desirable feature for it would underline the attractions of the non-stigmatising NI scheme under which claimants had provided, through the state, for their support and thus had a *right* to claim benefit.

Assistance benefits were financed out of direct taxation rather than through individual contribution. In social policy terms therefore they were redistributive on a vertical equity basis, transferring resources from (relatively) rich to poor. It was because of this however that stringent eligibility criteria had to be included to ensure that only the real (and the deserving) poor were able to benefit from them. The process of claiming means-tested benefits thus involved intrusive questioning into the circumstances, and the opportunities, of potential claimants in a climate of suspicion that not all who presented themselves for support might necessarily be in need. This is a legacy which, as we shall see, has come to create serious problems for assistance claimants as the number of these has grown and grown over the last four decades.

The stigma associated with dependency upon means-tested benefits might have been a more manageable problem had such dependency remained, as Beveridge predicted, at a minor and declining level. This has not been the case however; although the NA benefits were initially fixed at a minimum subsistence level, below NI benefits, they included separate provision for the cost of rent, which NI did not. This was because rent levels fluctuated widely and yet were an unavoidable cost for those with no adequate support; but it meant that even those who were entitled to NI benefits might also be able to claim NA to pay for their rent. There was thus an inevitable overlap built into the two schemes.

In addition to the overlap between NI and NA was the problem of those who could not establish an entitlement to NI benefits. For such people dependence upon assistance was the only means of surviving in poverty, despite the unattractiveness of the means-tested scheme. Contrary to Beveridge's expectations therefore the numbers of claimants needing such means-tested support, either because of the inadequacy of or exclusion from the NI scheme, grew rather than declined in the 1950s. And in their famous study of poverty in the welfare state in the early 1960s (Abel Smith and Townsend, 1965) found over one million people with incomes on or below the NA scale.

In the 1960s many of those depending on NA were pensioners. Both Conservative and Labour governments during this period promised to improve pension provision to prevent the problem of such high levels of means-test dependence in old age. For different reasons, however, neither succeeded in doing this. Instead in 1966 Labour decided to reform the still relatively unpopular NA scheme. It was retitled Supplementary Benefit (SB), and put under the administration of a new government body the Supplementary Benefit Commission (SBC). In practice not much else changed, although the SB scheme included a fixed basic weekly rate which those with an income below this level would now have a right to claim, and in addition to which – on a discretionary basis – extra payments might be made for extra needs.

The idea of the right to benefit was an attempt to overcome one of the major problems identified with means-tested benefits as a source of state support. Payment of them is not automatic, they must be claimed; and the claiming of means-tested support involves an intrusive and uncomfortable process of questioning. Many therefore may be put off from claiming because of fear of the process, thus reducing the take-up of such benefits by those who need them. The idea was that creating a right to the basic weekly rate would help to overcome this. After some initial improvement, however, there is little evidence that this was a successful move (see Deacon and Bradshaw, 1983, p. 107).

In the 1960s and 1970s dependence upon the reformed SB scheme continued to grow, in particular as levels of unemployment grew and those unemployed for long periods of time exhausted their entitlement to NI support. Between 1966 and 1975 there was a 12 per cent increase in claimants (Deacon and Bradshaw, 1983, p. 107). In addition to the dependence upon SB there was also an extension in the scope of means-tested benefits to provide other forms of state support. These included the introduction of Family Income Supplement (FIS), rent and rate rebates, and a range of other specific benefits in areas such as health and education, for instance free school meals for the children of low income parents.

The reasoning behind the extension of means-tested assistance was the twin desire to tackle a problem which had come to be referred to as the 'unemployment trap' and to focus, or target, the limited funds presumed to be available for additional state support on those who could prove poverty or low income. The unemployment trap was the presumed effect of a potentially significant entitlement to SB – for a large family with a high rent – on the employment opportunities, or motivation, of an a unemployed man (women were assumed to be dependent partners in SB) who might only command a low wage in employment. Because a low wage may not be sufficient to substitute for SB entitlement, sometimes referred to as an insufficient 'replacement ratio' of wages to benefits, such a man was therefore financially 'trapped' in unemployment.

In the 1960s one means of dealing with such a problem was the use of the 'wage stop', under which benefit entitlement was reduced to below the expected wage level. This was an extremely harsh and ineffective measure. In the 1970s it gave way to the use of means-tested support to boost low wages for families with high rents through FIS (paid to low-income workers with dependent children) and rent rebates. This extension of means-testing may have been preferable to the punitive wage-stop, but it resulted in a significant increase in the scope of such social security provision. In 1976 the National Consumer Council counted forty-five different means-tested benefits operating in Britain.

The development of new means-tested benefits involved in effect a shift in government policy on social security away from the *universal* principles of the NI scheme, under which all who had paid into it were automatically entitled to claim benefit, towards the notion of *selectivity*, under which state suppport was targeted only on those in proven need (see MacGregor, 1981, Ch. 5). In the 1980s this trend was taken much further by the Thatcher governments, who were quite outspoken in their support for selectivism and means testing in social security provision.

In 1980 SB was again reformed to introduce rights to weekly and lump-sum additions to the weekly rate. But in a climate of growing unemployment and reductions in NI benefits, this only led to ever greater levels of dependency, and consequently escalating costs of benefits and administration. By the mid 1980s there were over eight million people dependent upon SB assistance and it was occupying a significant proportion of social security expenditure. It was at this time that the government instituted its review of social security policy, which focused in particular on the role of means-tested provision.

The Green Papers in 1985 which followed the reviews and the 1986 Social Security Act which implemented the proposed changes, comprised a thorough reform and restructuring of means-tested support (see Alcock, 1985; Deakin, 1987, Ch. 5). The aim of the reforms was to simplify the structure and the administration of all the major means-tested benefits in order to encourage take-up and reduce administrative costs. As in the 1960s this involved some changing of names. SB was retitled Income Support (IS), FIS became Family Credit (FC) and rent rebates, which had been renamed Housing Benefit (HB) a few years earlier, kept this new title. Critics argued that the restructuring led to significant losses in entitlement for many claimants when the changes were introduced in 1988 because of the overall aim to reduce or contain expenditure on the benefit programme (see Berthoud 1985, 1986; CPAG, 1985), although transitional relief cushioned against a cash loss for any individual claimant.

The main aim of the 1988 changes, however, was to confirm the central role which means-tested support now had within the benefit system and to ensure that consequently its entitlement and administrative structure were as simple and effective as possible. Whatever their consequences in terms of levels of entitlement for individual claimants, these were undoubtedly laudable aims. But they signified a final departure from the principles of the Beveridge plan and the comprehensive role for social insurance in providing social security support. In the 1990s British social security provision is a mixture of insurance and assistance protection, and as will be discussed shortly this has resulted in major problems in its effectiveness in combating or relieving poverty. The benefit picture is even more complicated than this however, for there are other forms of state support that derive from neither the insurance nor the assistance traditions.

Universal Benefits

Although the NI benefit scheme is informed by universal principles, insurance benefits are not really universal. Despite the lack of a means test, receipt of benefits is dependent upon meeting the conditions for contribution into the NI fund. Genuine universal benefits should be payable without any qualifying conditions. Beveridge was aware of this principle, and although he rejected it in favour of social insurance for his major benefit proposals, he did propose universal support towards the costs of child care for all families in his support of the introduction of Family Allowances (FA).

The idea behind FA was for the state to provide a contribution towards the costs of rearing all children, in part as a recognition of their role as future citizens and workers and to encourage couples to have children, and in part to raise the overall income of families with children and thus reduce the hardship which might otherwise result in households with low incomes or dependent upon benefits. Because all children had no income and all families experienced similar needs, allowances were paid universally to all. However the FA scheme introduced after the Second World War was only a partial support for these needs; allowances were only paid for second and subsequent children and the rate payable was only a contribution towards the weekly needs of a child.

Despite its shortcomings the FA scheme did introduce a universal benefit into the British social security system. Unfortunately the level of the benefit fluctuated and was allowed to fall below its original postwar levels. It was also not the only state support for children; relief against income tax was also provided for tax-paying parents. As discussed in Chapter 13, one of the major focuses of CPAG campaigning in the 1960s and 1970s was the growing problem of child poverty in low-paid and claimant families. They proposed a reform of the FA to tackle this, and after turbulent political debate (Field, 1982) changes were made with the introduction of of Child Benefit (CB) in 1978.

CB is a universal benefit paid to the parents, or in practice the nominated carer – usually the mother, of all children. It was based upon an amalgamation of FA and tax relief, with the latter disappearing; but it remained only a contribution towards the costs of rearing a child. It has remained significantly below the costs of a child as calculated by research such as Piachaud (1979); but more significantly it is below the weekly rate provided for children in the means-tested SB/IS schemes. Thus, for those in receipt of means-tested benefits therefore, CB is effectively discounted from their benefit entitlement and they receive the higher means-tested support.

In the 1980s government preference for means-tested benefit support meant that SB/IS and FIS/FC were seen as more desirable means of providing for the children of poor parents, and the value of CB was permitted to fall in real terms as inflation rose. By the end of the decade therefore it had become something of a token contribution towards child care costs. But after the replacement of Thatcher with Major as prime minister it was once again increased, initially with extra for the first child; and in the early 1990s it has remained as a major universal benefit covering a significant proportion of the population.

There are, however, now other universal benefits within British social security provision. These are the benefits for attendance and mobility for people with disabilities, and thus they affect only a relatively small proportion of the population. As discussed in Chapter 11, Attendance Allowance and Mobility Allowance were introduced as universal benefits for people with serious disabilities in the 1970s. In 1992 they were amalgamated into the single Disability Living Allowance, paid at different levels according to the nature of the disabled person's needs. There are problems with both the scope and the operation of these universal disability benefits. Even for those with disabilities they occupy only a relatively minor role within the overall provision of state support, and they add further complication to the overlapping range of benefit provisions.

Problems with Benefits

Social security is the major antipoverty measure within British social policy. In providing state support as either a substitute for or a supplement to income from the labour market, its aim is to either relieve or prevent poverty by ensuring that the claimant, and their family, have what the government regards as an adequate income. Clearly there is much debate amongst politicians and academics about what constitutes an adequate income and thus how benefit levels should be fixed. The theoretical issues involved here were discussed in Part II, and Atkinson (1990a) discusses the background to the fixing of benefit levels. Leaving this aside, however, there are serious problems within the current benefit system which lead to many people not receiving even the minimum levels that the system appears to provide, or even if they are receiving them not in practice benefiting significantly from this.

As suggested above there is a potential problem of non-take-up within any means-tested benefit system. Only those who identify themselves as poor enough to qualify for benefit, who recognise the potential of benefit entitlement, and who are prepared to undergo the rigorous process of submitting and defending a claim will be assessed for entitlement and receive benefits. Given the complexity of the benefit system and the range of means-tested, and other, benefits available, many may fail to recognise potential entitlement; and, given the claiming process and the stigma associated with dependence upon means-tested benefits, many may choose not to claim even where they suspect that they might benefit.

The problem of non-take-up can of course exist with any form of benefit. There is evidence that not all people with disabilities receive the universal disability benefits to which they might be entitled (Martin and White, 1988). However in general take-up of universal and insurance benefits is high, with CB achieving nearly 100 per cent take-up. Most of the problems of take-up are associated with means-tested benefits, because of the complexity of entitlement and the stigma of dependency. Bradshaw (1985) demonstrates that on the government's own calculations the levels of take-up of the major means-tested benefits varies between 50 and 75 per cent. Obviously, as Craig (1991) discusses, there are difficulties involved in measuring what is essentially a negative phenomenon; but independent research using FES data seems to confirm government estimates of high levels of non-receipt of benefits (Fry and Stark, 1992).

The problems of non-take-up reveals a major failing in social security as an antipoverty measure. If benefit levels can be taken as a proxy for a government-approved poverty line, despite all the problems associated with this that were discussed above, then low levels of take-up are evidence that many are still living in poverty despite the extensive benefit provision available. And in terms of scale the problem is far more serious than its converse of benefit abuse. Despite all the fears of 'scrounging' on state benefits discussed in Chapter 2, official estimates of the cost of social security abuse are much lower than the estimates of unclaimed benefits (Smith, 1985; Cook, 1989).

The problem of non-take-up is primarily associated with means-tested benefits, and the other major failure of social security as an antipoverty measure is also associated with the use of selectivity in determining benefit entitlement, but in this case the problem is both inevitable and, ultimately, unavoidable. It is the problem of the poverty trap.

The poverty trap is a consequence of the use of means-tested benefits to tackle poverty, especially in larger households, by supplementing low wages. As discussed above the potential of significant means-tested benefit entitlement for large households in periods of unemployment gave rise to the problem of the unemployment trap, the lack of incentive for a breadwinner to take paid employment because of the low replacement ratio of wages to benefits. Supplementation of wages by means-tested benefits such as FC and HB is a means of relieving this problem by making low-paid work more attractive. However the effect of these benefits, together with the impact of taxation liabilities on low-paid workers inevitably creates another, arguably more serious, problem in the poverty trap.

The poverty trap was first 'discovered' in the early 1970s (Field and Piachaud, 1971) at the time when means-tested benefits for those on low wages were being rapidly extended, and it is discussed in some detail by Deacon and Bradshaw (1983, Ch. 8). In simple terms the problem arises because of the loss of entitlement to means-tested benefit additions for low-paid workers if their wages rise. Means-tested additions generally provide a fraction of the difference between low wages and an income level fixed in the scheme; in the case of FIS 50 per cent of the difference was paid and in the case of rent rebates up to 29 per cent. If wages rose therefore these additions were progressively lost, although in the case of FIS the effect was delayed because it was paid for periods of twelve months at a time. In the early 1980s this could mean that the combined effect of losing 50p in the pound of FIS for each extra pound earned, plus 29p of rent rebate together with an income tax rate of 30p and NI contributions at 8p, plus the potential loss of free school meals for children and other benefits, meant that people on low wages faced a 'marginal tax rate' (the amount of income forgone for each extra pound carned) of over 100 per cent. In other words even if they were able to secure a rise in wages they would actually see their overall income reduce.

As Deacon and Bradshaw (1983, Ch. 8) discussed, the effect of this high marginal tax rate was to nullify the effect of any change in earnings in increasing family income over a wide range of low wages from around £70 to £120 a week. Thus those on these low wages were trapped in poverty. The receipt of benefits ensured that they had an income just above SB/IS level, but the consequences of the criteria for entitlement kept them continually on this low income unless they could make a spectacular leap in their labour market situation.

The reforms to means-tested benefits in 1988 were in part designed to remove some of the worst aspects of this poverty trap for those on low wages. Certainly the alignment of means-tested benefit entitlement across the different benefits and the changes made in the means of calculating this did remove the problem of marginal tax rates of over 100 per cent. But rates of over 90 per cent still remain for some, and the consequence of removing the worst effects for some has spread the experience of relatively high rates of tax and benefit withdrawal from income over an even wider range of low wages.

The problem of non-take-up and the poverty trap both seriously undermine the effectiveness of social security provision in alleviating the experience of poverty within a wage-labour economy. They are also a direct consequence of the expanding role of means-testing within the benefits system over the last two decades. The apparent attractiveness of linking receipt of benefits to proof of poverty or low income is not effective in practice because of the failure of many people in need of benefits to recognise or pursue their entitlement to them, and because of the disincentive effects which flow from targeting state support only upon the poor. These practical problems, and the confusion over the policy framework for social security from which they result, have led increasing numbers of commentators to argue that social security provision in Britain is in need of radical reform if it is to continue to play an effective part in antipoverty strategy. We shall now look briefly at whether there are alternatives to the current social security structure that might better perform this task.

Alternative Models for Social Security

The debate over alternative structures for social security provision is not a new one. The Beveridge social insurance plan was itself presented as an alternative to the previous Poor Law and social assistance approaches to state support; and after the 'rediscovery of poverty' and the criticism of the postwar scheme in the 1960s, further discussion about potential structural reform of the benefits system began to reemerge in academic and political debate (see Atkinson, 1969). The extension of means testing within social security in the early 1970s reopened the debate between the social assistance and social insurance approaches to benefit provision, and the Conservative government of 1970–4 seriously considered far-reaching reform to restructure benefit and taxation policy into a combined, means-tested, tax/benefit system (see Sandford, 1980), though in the end the plans were not realised.

In the 1980s the growing problems with means-tested benefits and the increasing failure of social insurance to provide comprehensive protection for all in Britain, and in other Western European countries, prompted further discussion of the need for an alternative to both insurance and assistance approaches in the form of a basic income paid to all citizens as a means of preventing poverty and creating incentives to take paid employment. Campaign and research networks were set up in Britain (Basic Income Research Group, or BIRG) and Europe (Basic Income European Network, or BIEN) to promote further exploration of this as an alternative to current social security systems.

By the end of the 1980s debates about social security reform had crystallised into three broad approaches to the role of the state in providing income support, which can be summarised as the Tax Credit approach, the Basic Income approach and the Social Insurance approach (see Alcock, 1987, Ch. 11; Hill, 1990, Ch. 9). We will consider each of these and briefly outline their advantages and disadvantages.

The *Tax Credit* approach is that considered by the Conservative government of the early 1970s and since promoted by the Institute for

Fiscal Studies (Dilnot *et al.*, 1984) and the Adam Smith Insitute (ASI, 1984, 1989). It is based upon an attempt to rationalise the relationship between current means-tested benefits and income taxation to create a single basis for state income support, thus replacing all current insurance and universal benefits with a new unified tax/benefit scheme. The basic aim is to target state support upon the poor – those with no income or inadequate incomes – and to use the taxation system, which already contains records of income received, to do this.

The advantage of scrapping the current confusing and overlapping benefit system and replacing it with a unified means of income redistribution organised through the Inland Revenue is clearly an attractive one, at least in organisational terms. Benefit administration would be simplified, and perhaps therefore take-up improved. All income assessments would be made by one body and then either tax would be collected from households above a fixed income threshhold or benefits (or tax credits) paid to those below it. By this means poverty could be alleviated and income redistributed, without state interference in wage levels or employment policy, and without the imposition of compulsory insurance. Income assessments and entitlement calculations could be made annually, or adjusted weekly if circumstances changed.

The superficial organisational attractions are substantial in Tax Credit proposals, but as Collard (1980) and Sandford (1980) discuss, they disguise serious practical and policy problems. Because they are based squarely upon the principle of means testing, Tax Credit proposals are likely to run the risk of reproducing in any reformed scheme the operational problems associated with existing means-tested provision. Even with a simplified administrative structure take-up could continue to be a problem, especially if stigma were to continue to be associated with receipt of credits. The rapidly changing circumstances of those at the bottom of the income scale and thus likely to be entitled to credits may also result in errors and underclaiming. Even with a simplified entitlement criteria, means testing requires complex and intrusive questioning to determine the right to benefit, together with the constant suspicion that some may be unjustly receiving state support.

The adminstrative and attitudinal problems of means-testing are therefore likely to be reproduced in any Tax Credit scheme, as are the contradictory and perverse incentives of the poverty trap. If Tax Credits raise the income of those below the threshhold up to a fixed income level, then the incentive for those below the level to improve their circumstances through their own efforts is entirely removed. Thus most Tax Credit proposals involve crediting only a proportion of income below the fixed level, thus leaving those in receipt of benefit still technically with an inadequate income. Nevertheless even such partial credits must be withdrawn if initial income rises, thus maintaining the poverty trap. As we have seen the poverty trap is an inevitable consequence of means-tested benefit support. Since Tax Credit proposals in effect institutionalise means testing they also institutionalise the poverty trap; and so as a radical alternative to current social security provision they still leave a lot to be desired.

Basic Income proposals flow from attempts to get around the problem of the perverse incentives created by the poverty trap and to appeal to the collective ethos of social insurance at the same time as avoiding the exclusive tendencies of the insurance contribution principle. In other words Basic Income is an alternative to both means testing and insurance provision. The idea is that a standard benefit is paid by the state to all individuals, irrespective of employment status, to provide for or contribute to a modest but adequate income on top of which all wages from part-time or full-time work would be additional income. It is a universal scheme, like Child Benefit, only for adults. Basic Income would avoid the poverty trap since all income would be additional to state benefit, although obviously such income would have to be subject to relatively high levels of income taxation in order to fund the payment of basic benefit to all.

Supporters of Basic Income range from those on the left (Jordan, 1987; Purdy 1988) who propose high levels in income sufficient to provide for subsistence at least, to those towards the centre and right (Ashby, 1984; Parker, 1989; Rhys Williams, 1989) who recommend partial basic income to replace current tax allowances for those in employment and to contribute towards benefit entitlement for those outside the labour market. They have also attracted an increasingly wide range of supporters throughout Europe (see Van Parijs, 1992). Partial Basic Income could be introduced at relatively low levels of payment without significant additions to current income tax rates; but it would not remove the need for additional means-tested benefits for those out of work or contribute towards housing costs. Full Basic Income would presumably replace all existing benefit entitlement, but it would require tax rates on any additional earned income of sixty per cent or more, which may be a severe disincentive to employment. Full Basic Income would also replace, both in practice and in principle, wages as the major source of income support for the majority of the population. Radical proponents such as Gorz (1982) argue that this is an inevitable step as we head towards a post-industrial world order; but it may be difficult for such radical reform to attract much widespread support within existing political and economic circumstances (see Alcock, 1989).

The problem with Basic Income proposals therefore is that they are either so radical that they could only be introduced after a fundamental restructuring of the socio-economic order, or they are so limited in scope that they do not replace existing means-tested benefit provisions and thus do not avoid all the difficulties experienced with these. As an alternative to current social security provision they are either unachievable or largely irrelevant. And although their supporters in the BIRG and BIEN have in recent years grown in prominence, they remain on the margins of mainstream antipoverty policy debate.

The undesirability or unachievability of Tax Credits and Basic Income have thus left many academics and politicians seeking a revitalisation of *Social Insurance* in order to overcome the contradictions and complexities of current benefit provision. Atkinson (1969 and 1989) has been perhaps the most consistent proponent of a return to Social Insurance principles, although this has also been the path largely supported by the major antipoverty campaign group the CPAG (see Lister, 1975). In the 1960s and 1970s, as the scope of means-tested benefits began to undermine the comprehensive aspirations of the NI scheme, proponents of Social Insurance largely based their proposals on a call to return to the proposals initially contained in the Beveridge plan for insurance, sometimes referred to as a 'Back-to-Beveridge' strategy.

However most social policy academics are now aware of some of the serious limitations of the Beveridge insurance plan due to its reliance on contributions made during participation in the labour market as a condition of benefit entitlement, thus excluding from insurance protection many of those who may experience poverty. In the 1980s proponents thus began to address the possibility of retaining a scheme of state support for those unable to provide for themselves through wages in the labour market without their having to be submitted to contribution tests as a condition of entitlement (Lister and Fimister, 1980). Such provision would not be insurance-based in the strict, self-protection, sense of the term, but then as we have seen above the 'pay-as-you-go' British NI scheme has never in practice operated on such a basis in any case.

The idea of Social Insurance in the 1980s and 1990s is therefore being presented not so much in order to make the case for a return to the Beveridge notion of benefits in return for contributions made, but rather to appeal to a revitalisation of a collectivist notion of Social Insurance in which all who can contribute in order that all who need can benefit (see Alcock, 1992). In practice this could take the form of a hypothecated social insurance tax, such as NI contributions, which is utilised to pay benefits to all who are not in full-time paid employment (perhaps with partial benefits for part-time employees). Proponents argue that this should replace – gradually – existing means-tested benefit provision as all those who are out of work would be entitled to it. For those in employment it is argued that a statutory minimum wage should be introduced to ensure that low wages do not continue to be a cause of poverty. A statutory minimum wage, which would not need to be subsidised by benefit support, would also remove the problem of the poverty trap.

Proponents of Social Insurance reforms generally argue that these could be achieved gradually from within current benefit provision by building on the progressive elements of a reformed NI scheme and reducing and marginalising the scope of means testing. They argue therefore that such proposals are a more viable alternative than the radical Tax Credit and Basic Income approaches (Lister, 1987). However it is just this gradualist appeal that also may be the major cause of the downfall of such proposals in practice. For, as most of the history of social security policy has so emphatically demonstrated, gradualist changes can be rapidly sidetracked or overturned as political or economic circumstances change and antipoverty policy becomes subject to the whims or the vagaries of political fortune.

Whatever the desirability of a fundamental reform of social security policy in one form or another, unfortunately it is likely that for the foreseeable future changes will be minor and largely contained within the existing confused and complicated benefit system. They are thus unlikely to do much to alter the limited success which social security has had in tackling poverty in an affluent welfare society. This limited success has led some to suggest that antipoverty policy might therefore be better concentrated on initiatives outside the social security system, and it is to some of these other initiatives that we will now turn.

15
Targeted Antipoverty Strategies

Pockets of Poverty

Since the nineteenth century or earlier social security provision has been the major plank of antipoverty policy in Britain. State support through social security is a response to an identification of the structural relationship between poverty, income and the labour market. And via a range of different benefit measures it has sought to redistribute resources either horizontally or vertically in order to substitute or supplement income from the labour market. Receipt of benefits is therefore intended to prevent or relieve poverty. However social security is an extensive, and expensive, antipoverty strategy. In the early 1990s social security expenditure in Britain was running at over £50 billion a year, by far the largest item of public expenditure. Without this expenditure it is certain that many people would, at least in the immediate term, experience significantly increased deprivation. However, as critics have for some time been pointing out, it is debatable whether social security provision has succeeded to any large measure in either preventing or relieving poverty in modern British society.

Critics on the right, such as Murray (1984), have argued that social security policy has not prevented poverty because, by providing state support, it has encouraged dependency upon the limited benefit system rather than self-support within the labour market, whereas critics on the left, such as the CPAG (Oppenheim, 1990), argue that benefit provision has not prevented poverty because benefit levels are too low, and through means testing, trap people in poverty. Whilst there is little shared ground between such disparate approaches, both do focus on failings or limitations within social security provision and its impact on those who are still poor in affluent society.

The failure of social security provision within affluent society was very much the central theme of the 'rediscovery of poverty' in Britain in the 1960s. The research evidence and the political campaigning pointed to the continued experience of deprivation for large numbers of people despite the achievements of the welfare state, and suggested that further government action was needed to address this. As we have seen in Chapter 14, however, major expansion of social security protection was not perceived as a viable strategy in the 1960s, in particular because at a time of developing economic concern the costs of such expansion were politically unpalatable. Alternative means of responding to the continuing problem of poverty in the midst of affluence were thus likely to be attractive to government.

As discussed in Chapter 12, the 'rediscovery of poverty' was also associated with a renewed emphasis upon poverty as a pathological phenomenon within advanced industrial societies. Drawing upon the 'culture of poverty' thesis advanced by Lewis (1965 and 1968), politicians such as Joseph (1972) argued that poverty might be a product of individual apathy and inadequate upbringing, a 'cycle of deprivation', rather than policy failure. This blaming the victim approach to poverty amongst affluence, as we have seen, has serious shortcomings; but it provided a framework for the development of a rather different approach towards state policy to combat poverty which began to become prominent in a number of advanced industrial societies in the latter part of the twentieth century. As the quote from Ryan that was mentioned in Chapter 12 put it:

> define the difference [of the poor] as the cause of the problem. Finally, of course, assign a government bureaucrat to invent a humanitarian action programme to correct the difference (Ryan, 1971, p. 8).

Implicit in this framework is a perception of poverty as caused not so much by the failings of social and economic policy planning, but rather by the inability of poor people to take advantage of the opportunities which such planning already offers. And the action programme that is required is therefore not the extension of social security support and the further redistribution of resources to the poor, but rather the identification of poor people within affluent society and the use of state support to employ humanitarian professionals to work with them to encourage them to overcome the cultural barriers between them and the rest of the society in which they are unable to participate. Resources should thus be focused on the poor, not to relieve their poverty but to help them to escape from it.

This new approach to the focusing of resources was also a response to another feature of the research and campaigning thrown up by the 'rediscovery of poverty'. The research of Townsend (1979) and others on the experience of deprivation within affluent society revealed that income poverty was only a partial feature of the deprived environment in which many poor people found themselves, including poor housing, inadequate services, pollution and so on. These deprived environments were identified in particular with run-down inner city areas in many of Britain's decaying industrial conurbations. In inner cities therefore poverty and deprivation were concentrated in what commentators began to refer to as 'pockets of poverty'.

If limited state resources were to be focused on poor people to help them overcome their deprivation and take advantage of the opportunities of modern society therefore, then the rundown inner city areas identified by the poverty researchers provided the obvious foci for the channelling of these resources. In pockets of urban poverty the cultural problems of transmitted deprivation were likely to be greatest, and at the same time the opportunities for escape would be close at hand. Professionals working in such concentrations of deprivation could thus influence relatively large numbers of poor people within relatively limited overall costs, and so provide a model for self help and upward mobility which could then be applied to other poor areas. Geographical targeting thus coincided with pathological perceptions of the problem of poverty to create a climate for a new approach to antipoverty policy in advanced industrial societies, which was taken up by government in Britain and elsewhere from the 1960s onwards.

The War on Poverty

Targeted antipoverty strategies in Britain were influenced significantly by the development of such approaches in the US in the early 1960s. As we shall see, in many respects British initiatives were modelled on the programmes introduced in the US a few years earlier. Perhaps typically, however, the initiatives in the US were rather grander than their later British counterparts, and they were presented as part of an apparently more substantial government commitment to eliminate poverty. At more or less the same time as the US was beginning to escalate its involvement in the war in Vietnam, President Johnson announced in 1964 a 'national war on poverty', with the objective of 'total victory' in ensuring that every citizen shared 'all the opportunities of society' (James, 1970, p. 65).

What the war on poverty represented in practice was federal government funding for locally targeted initiatives in which professionals would work in deprived areas to help poor people to take advantage of the opportunites of affluent American society. The money was channelled through a new government agency called, appropriately, the Office of Economic Opportunity (OEO). And to use the jargon of the scheme the money was intended to provide 'doors, not floors' – an emphasis on education and job programmes to encourage mobility through self help (doors out of the cellar of poverty) rather than the provision of additional resources for poor people themselves (a raising of the floor on which the poor stood) (see Higgins, 1978, pp. 108 *et seq*).

The notion of self-help, helping the poor to help themselves, was closely linked to pathological explanations of the causes of a transmitted culture of poverty and to the geographical targeting of resources on poor urban areas. In the US this was furthermore overlain with perceptions of the racial dimension of the problem of urban poverty, which was at its worst in inner city areas with large black populations and high levels of urban unrest. Part of the not-so-hidden agenda of the OEO programme of antipoverty work, therefore, was the avoidance, or control, of racial violence and urban protest, although this was a strategy with rather mixed achievements in the real world of black urban politics (see Wolfe, 1971).

Most of the resources of the OEO therefore went on a range of community action programmes in poor urban areas. They were designed to improve educational provision and job opportunities and to encourage local poor people to take advantage of these. Many of them, such as 'Head Start' and the 'Neighbourhood Youth Corps', focused particularly upon children and youth as the logical point at which to seek to break the chain of transmitted deprivation.

There is little doubt that many youngsters in poor American inner city areas did benefit from some of the community action programme initiatives. However there is also not much doubt that overall the initiatives did not succeed in providing total victory over urban poverty. As Marris and Rein (1974) pointed out, the community agencies had little power to challenge the local and central power structures within which urban poverty was located. Identifying the problems of urban poverty therefore often brought the agencies into conflict with entrenched social and economic interests. This conflict was inevitable, but it was one which they could not hope to win.

Piven and Cloward's (1972) analysis was perhaps even more critical. In channelling antipoverty activity into limited initiatives to provide for the urban poor within existing welfare programmes, they pointed out, the war on poverty diverted attention away from any broader structural approaches to welfare problems and thus acted as a diversion from social and economic reform. In the 1970s the war on poverty in the US was brought to an end without achieving the total victory which had been sought at its outset. In reality of course this victory was no less elusive than the victory in Vietnam had been. But in abandoning the war the lessons of the limitations of targeted antipoverty strategies were only partially recognised; and yet in Britain the focus on community action to combat urban poverty drew heavily on these American ideals of upward mobility.

Government Initiatives

In Britain in the 1960s debate on antipoverty strategy and fears of economic constraint provided a climate in which government initiatives to combat the growing recognition of continuing poverty began to follow closely the targeting policies of the American war on poverty. The first example of such an approach emerged from the recommendations of the Plowden Report on the transition to secondary education which proposed the targeting of additional resources to improve schooling in a number of identified priority areas (see Halsey, 1972).

As a result of these proposals the first government initiative on targeting was introduced in the form of the Educational Priority Area (EPA) programme in 1968. Drawing on the Head Start programme in the US, the EPA scheme involved the provision of extra resources for primary schools in a small number of poor areas to ensure that educational disadvantage did not provide a reinforcement of cyclical poverty for children in these areas. The scheme was only on a small scale in a small number of areas, and it lasted only for a few years; but it was subject to high profile research analysis (Halsey, 1972) and it provided a model of targeted government support that was to be taken much further in a range of later initiatives with much wider horizons.

The most extensive and long lasting of these broader initiatives was the Urban Aid programme, which was also launched in 1968. This too involved extra government resources being channelled into poor urban areas in order to help break the cycle of transmitted deprivation. However Urban Aid money was not restricted to resources for schools – grants could be obtained for any appropriate local scheme aimed at neighbourhood-based action to work with local people to combat poverty. The idea was that local authorities and voluntary agencies would propose projects such as community centres, play schemes or remedial education, which would then receive Urban Aid funding and be run on a partnership basis by the authority and representatives of the local community. Some local authorities were understandably sceptical of the political motivation behind tying additional local funding to designated action programmes. It suggested to the authorities that they were not trusted to use rates and block grants to support such community initiatives. But the attraction of extra cash for projects in run-down areas was more than most could resist and Urban Aid grew rapidly over the ensuing decades to become a major source of support for a range of community-based activities in urban areas.

In the mid 1970s the idea of additional local resources for designated partnership schemes between central and local government and the voluntary sector was extended with the inner cities partnership programme. This was a more comprehensive attempt at harnessing neighbourhood-based activities within a selected number of city areas (see Berthoud *et al.*, 1981, pp. 273–4). However, both politically and symbolically, the most important of the government antipoverty initiatives of the 1960s and 1970s was the Community Development Project (CDP), which was based very closely on the American community action programme and which ran for ten years from 1968 to 1978. The CDPs were something of an experiment in the utilisation of government funding for community-based action, and although they were fairly limited in scope and number they received a great deal of attention from academics and politicians (see Lees and Smith, 1975; Loney, 1983).

The CDPs were in large part the brainchild of a senior civil servant in the Home Office, Derek Morrell. They were a response to a range of overlapping pressures: arguments for a more community-based focus in social work, pressure on government to act on the problem of urban poverty, fears of racial violence and unrest stemming from immigration law changes and Enoch Powell's well-publicised attacks on Britain's black population, and a resignation that any new government measures must contain only minimal public spending commitments. Over their ten-year life the CDPs cost little more than £5 million. They consisted of twelve projects in small areas of high unemployment, the largest being Canning Town in London with a population of 42 400, and they were administered directly by the Home Office. Each project comprised of professionals recruited to engage in community development work in the area and a research team, linked to a higher education establishment, to assess and analyse the success of the project. The research focus emphasised the experimental nature of the projects and they were given a budget to publish their findings. This helped to raise the profile of the CDPs; it also contributed to their downfall.

As in the American community action programme the thinking that informed the CDPs was a pathological conception of transmitted poverty. As one of the senior researchers put it:

> poverty and deprivation and consequent multi-problem families and individuals were conceptualised as the problems of a marginal minority who had slipped through the net of welfare, whether through personal or cultural inadequacy or through the services' own lack of co-ordination or administrative failures (Mayo, quoted in Loney, 1983, p. 49).

The idea was that highly specialised and focused community development could help to overcome this marginalisation and restore the residents of the deprived areas involved to active social and economic citizenship. But the idea backfired.

The newly recruited action and research teams in the CDPs were quickly made aware of the poverty and deprivation in the areas in which they were based. At the same time, however, they also quickly realised that much of this was the product not of individual inadequacy or service malfunctioning, but of wider social and economic policies leading to industrial decline, unemployment and deprived local environment. A few professionals with few resources to support local activities could do little or nothing to counteract these wider forces. Indeed, as one of the most famous of the CDPs numerous published reports – Coventry CDP's aptly titled *Gilding the Ghetto* (CDP, 1977) – pointed out, the mere existence of the project in the area could even make things worse by confirming its reputation with potential investors as a neighbourhood in serious economic decline.

With their research back-up and high profile publishing strategy the CDPs became a focus of debate about the theoretical and practical contradictions of utilising small-scale targeted resources to challenge large-scale urban poverty. The workers knew that the experiments were doomed to fail, and they said so. After ten years, in which economic recession had meant that in most of the areas the problem had become worse rather than better, an embarrassed government accepted the inevitable and closed the last ones down.

As with the American war on poverty, the CDPs were bound to be a temporary experiment – high profile, targeted activity cannot be sustained for long. And, as with the American experiment, they were bound to fail to eliminate poverty and deprivation, for as we know these are not the product of pathological inadequacy concentrated into a few run-down neighbourhoods. As will be discussed shortly, there are inescapable contradictions in utilising targeted initiatives in order to combat poverty. However it would be shortsighted and unjust to conclude from this that the CDPs, and other targeted initiatives, achieved nothing in the struggle against poverty.

The CDP action teams included some highly motivated and innovative community development workers. During the ten years of the projects they developed some interesting and innovative community actions, some of which went a significant way towards tackling some of the problems of deprivation faced by local residents. For instance CDP workers collaborated in the establishment of pressure groups of local residents, such as tenants associations which could challenge local housing departments to improve council housing and other amenities in the area. And, perhaps most interestingly, CDP workers in Batley, Coventry and elsewhere worked to develop a welfare rights service with local residents, providing advice and advocacy to ensure that poor people were at least getting the basic state benefits to which they were entitled (Bradshaw, 1975). The welfare rights approach begun in some CDPs survived their demise and has developed to become a major feature of targeted antipoverty activity.

Welfare Rights

Welfare rights work started as something of an experiment in some of the CDPs as a way of working with local people within existing social and economic policy constraints to minimise their deprivation by ensuring that at least residents were getting the basic state benefits to which they entitled. Although with limited benefit provision this was not a transformatory achievement, it did lead to significant gains in the weekly income of some local people. Furthermore it was providing an advice and advocacy service which neither the DHSS nor local legal services had been willing or able to offer.

Thus when the CDPs were closed down in the mid to late 1970s some of the workers carried on this local advisory service from within revamped community-based agencies. Some of these agencies attracted funding from the local authority, who recognised the value of the service provided, and following this new advice and advocacy agencies began to grow, in places building upon the national Citizens' Advice Bureau (CAB) network which had provided local information and advice on a voluntary basis since the Second World War. As well as local authority funding local advice centres were also able to exploit the funding provided for local job-creation projects by the rapidly expanding Manpower Services Commission (MSC). This meant that the voluntary workers who had always constituted the backbone of local advice and information work could be supplemented by some people on temporary employment contracts supported by the MSC, perhaps under the overall coordination of a supervisor paid by the local authority or the national CAB funding body, NACAB.

On this basis local advice agencies providing welfare rights advice on social security, housing, homelessness and other areas of state welfare affecting poor people began to grow rapidly during the late 1970s and early 1980s. In Sheffield, for instance, the number of agencies grew from 5 to 34 between 1975 and 1985. Such generalist community based agencies were also supplemented in many places by the development of specialist agencies concentrating on particular aspects of welfare rights work, such as tribunal appeals, housing cases or immigration law, sometimes on referral from local centres. These included housing aid centres (McDonnell, 1982) and especially law centres (Stephens, 1990).

Of course one of the reasons for the rapid growth of community-based welfare rights work was the rapidly growing problem of the low take-up of means-tested benefits in the 1970s and 1980s, resulting from the growth in the number of claimants and the expansion of means-tested benefits. Wherever agencies were set up they quickly attracted large numbers of local enquiries about benefit rights, and they were often able to secure improved take-up, and thus additional resources, for local people. As a form of antipoverty activity welfare rights work was thus flushed with early success, albeit that this was the result of the twin failures of economic policy and social security delivery.

The growing numbers of poor people, and the growing dependency upon means-tested benefits during this period, also began to be recognised as a contributory factor to the problems experienced by many clients of social service departments (see Hill and Laing, 1979). Recognition that social services too may have a role to play in combating poverty through improving benefit take-up began in 1972 when Manchester City Council appointed a welfare rights worker within their social services department. The idea was that such workers could provide specialist advice and support in helping social workers to maximise their clients' incomes through improving benefit take-up. The appointment in Manchester was quickly followed by other welfare rights workers being recruited to other social service departments, and by the development of welfare rights work as a part of the repertoire of social work tasks (see Cohen and Rushton, 1982; Fimister, 1986; CCETSW, 1989).

The number of welfare rights workers employed in local government grew rapidly in the early 1980s, and although most were placed in social service departments, some were given broader strategic responsibility for non-take-up and antipoverty work within the local area and extended their work beyond social service clientele. A study carried out by the PSI revealed a rapid growth in welfare rights work and a wide range of activities developed by workers (Berthoud *et al.*, 1986).

In addition to the increasing numbers of locally based welfare rights workers, there was also a growth at this time of national organisations providing support for local workers and a central focus for the development and dissemination of welfare rights initiatives. These included the NACAB, which rapidly expanded its role in servicing local advice agencies with information and training, and the Citizens' Rights Office of the CPAG, which provided specialist support for welfare rights work and published annually comprehensive guides to benefit rights which were used by all welfare rights workers. There were also specialist bodies providing support for work with particular groups of claimants, such as the Disability Alliance and the Campaign for the Homeless and Rootless (CHAR).

Because of the complexity of, in particular, the SB scheme of the 1980s, welfare rights workers were able to secure significant increases in benefit for many claimants by encouraging them to make claims for all the items of need specified in the regulations. However providing such advice and encouragement to claimants on an individual basis was time-consuming and costly, and welfare rights workers began to experiment with ways of providing such information on a broader and more cost effective basis. The first attempt to do this was carried out by Strathclyde Regional Council, the largest local authority in

Britain, who mailed to all local residents a card advising them of benefit entitlements under the regulations and inviting them to make a claim by returning the card to the local social security office. The idea was that large numbers of claimants would thus make claims that they would not otherwise have made, which the DHSS would then be required to process and – where appropriate – meet, thus massively increasing local take-up.

The idea of such blanket rights advice came to be called 'take-up campaigning'. In Strathclyde the organisers claimed that £1.3 million in additional benefits had been claimed locally as a result of the campaign; and following this lead other local authorities soon engaged in similar exercises. As local take-up campaigns expanded they also became more and more sophisticated in the methods used to encourage claims and in the groups of potential claimants at whom information was targeted. The Greater London Council spent £2 million on a campaign which included television advertising and computer-based back-up advice; others used a variety of means of conveying information to groups known to be likely to be underclaiming particular benefits (see Alcock and Shepherd, 1987).

Take-up campaigns, like the welfare rights work from which they sprang, were relatively successful in increasing local benefit take-up, and thus combating local poverty. However they were of course only securing for people the relatively limited state benefits which in practice the DHSS/DSS was failing to deliver to them. This was an important gain for those who benefited from it, but it was also in one sense merely a transfer of benefit delivery work from central to local government. This transfer was also extremely patchy in its operation since, although many local authorities did develop benefit take-up initiatives during the 1980s, many did not, and in such areas many claimants no doubt remained in more serious deprivation.

By increasing take-up, campaigning also revealed quite starkly the failings of the operation of the state benefit system itself. Many of the more radical welfare rights workers saw in this a direct challenge to the social security policy and practice of the government. Unfortunately the challenge to some extent backfired. Part of the reason for the reform of means-tested benefits in 1986 was a response to the increase in additional payments under the scheme which had been generated by take-up campaigning. And the effect of the reforms was to undermine the success of such work by removing the entitlement to such additional payments, leading in many cases to overall reductions in levels of benefit entitlement. Perhaps this was an inevitable response from central government to the contradictions in benefit policy revealed by welfare rights work; but it was something of a setback for a welfare rights movement which was by then a major feature of focused antipoverty work (Alcock *et al.*, 1991).

Local Antipoverty Strategies

Local authority support for welfare rights work was based in large part on the view of many, especially Labour-controlled, authorities that it would lead to significant increases in resources for local people. The GLC take-up campaign of the mid 1980s claimed to generate £10 million of additional income for Londoners (GLC, 1986). This was, of course, potential additional revenue for local businesses, but it was also a significant contribution towards reducing the deprivation experienced by local poor people. As with the government initiatives of the 1960s and 1970s therefore, it was in effect a form of antipoverty strategy; and local authorities who were engaged in supporting welfare rights work began to recognise that they might also be able to use other aspects of local services to combat local poverty.

In 1984 the CPAG devoted a special issue of their journal *Poverty* to the role that local authorities might play in combating local poverty (CPAG, 1984). A range of local welfare rights and take-up initiatives were summarised, and in a more general discussion of a possible role for local authorities, Hume argued that there were a number of other areas of local services, such as housing, education and transport, where a focus on antipoverty initiatives might lead to new means of maximising income and services for the poor.

In the early 1980s the transfer of control of many of the larger urban authorities to more active, and more left-wing, Labour councillors created a climate in which such initiatives might also receive direct political support. What some of these new councillors wanted to do was to use local Labour councils to provide an example to the Thatcher government that public services were popular and defensible. Some, such as the GLC, Sheffield and South Yorkshire, even presented this as an experiment in 'local socialism' (see Boddy and Fudge, 1984; Stoker, 1988). Whatever the political motivation, however, many of the initiatives that were undertaken by local authorities during this period did have as a major aim the prevention or alleviation of local poverty.

These initiatives included the transport policies of South Yorkshire and the GLC which involved freezing or reducing the fares for local transport by the use of subsidies from rates revenue to provide a cheap and accessible transport system for all, benefiting those who had most difficulty in affording private cars. The GLC called it their 'Fares Fair' scheme. The GLC and other urban councils also appointed new policy officers to act as advisors and initiators for local antipoverty strategies. These officers were often based outside of traditional service departments and had a brief to coordinate activities across a range of local activities.

Of course just as the CDPs had recognised that the roots of local poverty lay in broader economic trends, so too did many of the new Labour councillors. Thus a number of authorities established employment or economic development departments to try to protect local employment and promote economic activity which would lead to increased job prospects for local people. Some of the officers in these new departments, and in other antipoverty initiatives, had also in the past been workers in the CDPs, continuing a commitment to local development work within a broader economic framework which had begun in the ill-fated government schemes (see Benington, 1987).

That these new local antipoverty initiatives were part of a broader political strategy by the new urban left was one of their early strengths, providing cooperation between authorities and officers. It was also, however, one of their greatest weaknesses, for the challenge to government that they represented was unlikely to go unnoticed. At a time when government was endeavouring to curb state welfare expenditure both locally and nationally, and to question the role of the state as the primary focus of antipoverty activity, the political and economic challenge of local antipoverty initiatives was, to say the least, embarrassing.

The Thatcher governments of the 1980s therefore acted to reduce the scope of local authority activity, and in particular the high profile challenges to government priorities. In the case of the GLC and the other metropolitan authorities this meant outright abolition. The other urban authorities could not all be abolished, but their activities were restricted by outlawing initiatives such as the 'Fares Fair' scheme and by squeezing local expenditure through rate control, and later by the imposition of the Poll Tax. The aim was to press local authorities into the restricted role of carrying out only direct statutory responsibilities for such things as education and social services.

As a result of such pressures the attack on local government in the 1980s was to a large extent successful in restricting the scope of local antipoverty initiatives. Many of these were abandoned or severely depleted; but they were not entirely wiped out. Indeed, despite the government challenge, the success of some urban authorities in developing strategies for challenging local poverty had provided a model, or a series of models, which other authorities, equally concerned about levels of deprivation within their area, later sought to follow. At the end of the decade Balloch and Jones (1990) conducted a review of local authority antipoverty initiatives for the Association of Metropolitan Authorities and found a range of different activities being undertaken by a large number of authorities.

The initiatives discussed by Balloch and Jones included welfare rights work to improve benefit take-up, policies to minimise fees and charges for services for the poor, support for voluntary services for local poor people such as credit unions lending money at low interest, moves to decentralise and democratise services into poor areas, and economic development work to increase local job opportunities. They provided examples of good practice within the various initiatives and suggested ways in which further development may take place. What the survey revealed was that focused antipoverty work was now a widespread feature of local authority and voluntary sector activity. The experiment in targeted antipoverty work which began in the 1960s had thus now become entrenched in social policy practice. However many of the fundamental problems revealed by the early projects, such as the CDPs, still remained.

Missing Targets

The main aim of targeted antipoverty strategies has been to expose and challenge the limitations and failings of existing state provision in preventing or relieving poverty, by channelling limited resources into work in local areas to improve the delivery and receipt of existing services. Important though these initiatives have been in revealing problems in providing protection for the poor and in securing much-needed extra support for those generally experiencing extreme deprivation within modern society, there are nevertheless serious problems, and contradictions, in the role of targeted initiatives in challenging poverty.

For a start, in overall terms the amount of resources which have gone into targeted initiatives have, relatively speaking, been very small. It was the low cost of a small number of targeted projects which first attracted the governments of the 1960s and 1970s to such initiatives, at a time when pressure to curb the overall growth in state welfare expenditure was growing. The infamous CDP programme for instance only cost a total of around £5 million, a small fraction of the annual social security budget. Targeted strategies are cheap because they are small scale. This is in effect a structural feature, and a structural problem. If the strategies were to be extended into a wide scale they would no longer be targeted; they would also no longer be cheap, and questions would have to be asked about whether such large amounts of money might not be better spent in other ways, such as on improved social security benefits.

What is more, most of the limited resources involved in targeted initiatives have gone not to local poor people, but to the employment of professionals such as welfare rights workers to work with them. No doubt welfare rights workers would justify the money spent on their salaries by pointing to the additional resources in extra benefits that they have been able to generate for local clients. But these extra benefits have come from the social security system, not from the antipoverty initiative funding. If such funding can 'lever out' extra resources from other sources, then perhaps the expenditure on professionals is justified; but if it can not, then some might sceptically ask why the money could not be given straight to those who need it most.

As discussed above, the assumption behind the use of targeted resources to employ professionals to 'help the poor to help themselves' is inevitably based, in part at least, upon a pathological model of the causes of urban poverty in affluent society, stemming from the culture of poverty and cycle of deprivation theses discussed in Chapter 12. The CDP workers were generally well aware of the shortcomings of such approaches to the dymanics of poverty, and no doubt most other antipoverty workers are too. Nevertheless the focus of targeted initiatives upon poor people and poor communities is inevitably a focus upon the symptoms rather than the causes of continuing poverty. The workers may argue, as they did in the CDPs, that what is really needed is a change in broader economic and social policy; but then this is not what targeted initiatives are intended to achieve, as the CDPs discovered.

Finally, and perhaps most importantly, the most fundamental problem with targeted antipoverty initiatives is the fact that they are targeted on particular – usually urban – areas. Of course large numbers of poor people do live in run down inner city areas; but many, indeed most, do not. For those outside the target area, or the particular local authority, the resources going to help people in one area are of no benefit to them. This is especially the case for the rural poor, who tend to live in small isolated communities, often with less active Conservative local authorities who do not pursue antipoverty strategies. These people are probably also poorly provided for by local services such as education and transport. Their deprivation is likely to be acute; but they are unlikely to be the beneficiaries of targeted antipoverty initiatives.

Thus targeted antipoverty strategies in hitting one target inevitably miss many others. Of course this is not a reason for not undertaking them; but it is a reason for recognising their intrinsic limitations. Furthermore it must also be recognised that the existence of some targeted strategies might even be counter-productive for those outside the target areas. For instance the widespread development of advice agencies and welfare rights work has created expectations, amongst DSS officials in particular, that such independent advice and advocacy work is available to all claimants, and in response the DSS has to some extent withdrawn from extending its take-up initiatives. For those who do not benefit from such local services there is here a double deprivation.

Against the significant gains achieved by some targeted antipoverty initiatives therefore, must be balanced the structural limitations upon their role and thus their overall impact in challenging poverty. They must now be recognised as a part of the policy framework within which antipoverty policy is understood and assessed. However this policy framework must also include the whole range of social and economic policy initiatives which operate to create and recreate poverty in affluent society. As discussed in Part I, poverty is ultimately the product of this overall socio-economic order, and of the distribution of power and resources within it. Any assessment of the prospects of antipoverty policy must therefore consciously address this broader context, and it is to this which we finally now turn.

16

Poverty, Inequality and the Welfare State

The Problem of Poverty

Poverty, as we saw in Chapter 1, is a problem; and an academic and political concern with poverty is based upon the assumption that something should be done in response to the problem. Poverty is identified and measured in order to provide a basis for antipoverty policy; and, as we have seen, the disagreements over definition and measurement are inextricably intertwined with disagreements over the policies which should, or should not, flow from them. Understanding poverty involves recognising this political context and the links within this between definition and policy. Understanding poverty also involves understanding the broader context of the inequality within which it is situated. Poverty is the unacceptable face of inequality; and although they may not be aimed at producing equality, policies to combat poverty must also seek to change patterns of inequality, even if only minimally. Fundamentally therefore understanding the problem of poverty requires a focus on the relationship between poverty and antipoverty policies, and the impact which these have on broader patterns of inequality.

For those who argue in favour of a largely absolute measure of poverty, the problem is restricted to the extremes of inequality which leave some without the resources to survive, and antipoverty policy is limited to the redistribution of just enough resources to provide for some measure of basic subsistence. Such policies also usually seek to restrict the redistribution of resources to those in proven circumstances of need through the use of means tests, and to ensure that those who do receive support are encouraged by a variety of means to seek self-support rather than continued dependence.

For those who argue in favour of a more relative measure of poverty, or deprivation, the problem of poverty is an exaggerated aspect of an unequal distribution of resources in which some are so far below the rest that they are excluded from many important aspects of current living standards, and antipoverty policy is extended to include the redistribution of a range of resources to assist those who cannot participate fully to become more integrated into society. Such policies usually seek to extend redistribution to reduce more general inequalities in society and provide guaranteed support for a range of people who may be in circumstances that are likely to place them at the bottom in the distribution of resources.

There are differences within these two broad approaches of course, and some protagonists at the extremes who may not fit readily into either. And there is conflict between the two at the level of both theory and practice. Nevertheless they have dominated the debate about poverty and the development of antipoverty policy in Britain and most other advanced industrial countries over recent times. And they have resulted in the range of antipoverty measures discussed in Part IV, in particular social security provision and targeted support for poor communities. By and large these are measures which have been developed by the state, and most debate and policy development has been directed at and through state organs. Not all measures directed at combating poverty are the result of state-based initiatives however – private sector protection and voluntary activity are also important. But even these are generally controlled and regulated by the state, and debate about their impact and development is largely bound up with debate about the wider role of the state in responding to the problem of poverty.

Thus debate about the problem of poverty, and its solution, is largely a debate about identifying and measuring inequality and deprivation to provide a basis for state policy to intervene, directly or indirectly, in order to redistribute the resources to alleviate this. And if much of the current debate is to be believed, then state policy has not thus far been very successful in achieving this. As discussed in Chapter 1, poverty continues to exist despite state policies for redistribution, and indeed it seems to be getting worse. In part this may be because the policies are not working as intended or that they do not go quite far enough; but it may also, and more importantly, be because, as discussed in Chapter 2, they do not take account of the broader dynamics of the problem of poverty.

Antipoverty policies focus upon poor people and the provision of support or the redistribution of resources to those who are poor. However, as Ferge and Millar (1987, p. 298) have cogently stressed,

'Who becomes or stays poor is a *structural social consequence*' (emphasis in original). What causes poverty is not individual action, or inaction, although this may be a contributory factor at times. The causes of poverty are the dynamics of social and economic forces within societies which structure the production and distribution of resources. Poverty is the unacceptable consequence of these social forces, and antipoverty policies which focus on this consequence are concentrating on the symptoms of the problem of poverty, not the causes.

Certainly policies concentrating on the redistribution of resources to the poor can, and do, mitigate the problems resulting from the harsh inequalities of the initial distribution of resources in society. But such policies can only play a mitigating role if their focus is on poverty and redistribution. Once the broader structural forces that produce the inequalities of which poverty is a part are recognised, then these need to become the targets of policy initiatives which seek to prevent, rather than to mitigate, the problem of poverty.

Marxists, such as Novak (1988), argue that these forces are the product of the capitalist economic system which predominates within a society such as Britain, and that only when that economic system is overthrown and replaced with an egalitarian system of production and distribution will poverty disappear. This is a rather Utopian perspective, however, and it generally tells us little about how such revolutionary change might be achieved. Further, although capitalist investment and profit does exercise a predominant influence over the British economy and its consequent labour market, capital is not the only structuring feature of what is in practice a complex social and economic order, and its removal is neither a precondition for combating poverty nor a guarantee of it, as the different levels of poverty in both capitalist and non-capitalist societies demonstrate.

Where the Marxists are partially correct, however, is in their focus upon the need for broader structural change to prevent poverty. And structural inequalities must be tackled if poverty is to be prevented. This requires a broader strategic approach to policy development than measures focusing only on redistribution to the poor. An attempt to challenge the structural dymanics of poverty requires attention to the broader context of inequality within which poverty is produced, and an attempt to develop a 'strategy of equality' to combat these structural forces at a number of levels. The case for such a strategy of equality has been argued by a number of academics and politicians concerned with the problem of poverty throughout the last century, and it has formed the basis of some of the most important aspects of social and economic policy development pursued by governments in Britain and elsewhere.

The Strategy of Equality

The Fabian campaigners, such as Sydney and Beatrice Webb, who sought to promote the politics of poverty in the early twentieth century were aware that the prevention of poverty and the achievement of socialist reform required a concerted strategy by government to secure greater equality within British society. As discussed in Chapter 13, evidence of the problem of poverty was used by Fabians to persuade governments to act to prevent it; but the actions the Fabians championed were intended to produce wideranging reform through the extension of state provision for welfare to improve the overall standards for all in society. Their aim was not just the elimination of poverty, but the greater efficiency of the whole social order through the enhancement of state intervention and control – the development, in other words, of a *welfare state*.

The pursuit of state welfare as part of a broader strategy to remove poverty through structural reform was also promoted by academics and politicians outside the fairly narrow utilitarian perspective of Fabian politics. These included in particular influential writers such as Tawney (1931) and Marshall (1950).

Tawney was a Christian socialist who saw the struggle against poverty in moral as well as practical terms. He believed that greater equality could be achieved by state action to extend welfare in order to minimise the privileges enjoyed exclusively by the rich and raise the standards of the bulk of the population. He did not think that absolute equality was either achievable or necessarily desirable; but his belief in common values and common standards for all people led him to argue for state welfare as a means of reducing differentials and eliminating deprivation. And though not intended to produce an egalitarian social order, Tawney referred to the development of such welfare policies through the state as a 'strategy of equality'.

The major focus of Marshall's work was on the development of citizenship within society. He argued that as industrial society developed then rights of citizens within it became more extensive, thus creating greater social cohesion. He argued that *civil* rights of freedom of speech and of property had developed in the eighteenth century, and that *political* rights in the democratisation of public power had developed in the nineteenth century. In the twentieth century, he argued, citizenship should be extended to include *social* rights to welfare, security and economic participation, and that this would be achieved by the development of a welfare state granting rights to welfare to all citizens, and by reducing social divisions. Marshall saw this as leading to

> an equalisation between the more and the less fortunate at all levels –
> between the healthy and the sick, the employed and the unemployed,
> the old and the active, the bachelor and the large family (1950, p. 56).

Thus like Tawney he saw in the achievement of social citizenship a strategy to reduce inequality by guaranteeing minimum standards through state welfare.

Both Tawney and Marshall were writing at the time when the role of state welfare was being reconsidered at government level during and after the Second World War. Beveridge's (1942) report on social security reform, commissioned by the wartime coalition government, shared their support for the extension of state welfare to remove all social ills. Beveridge referred to these as the 'Five Giants' of Disease, Idleness, Ignorance, Squalor and Want, and he expected the state to ensure that after the war all would be the objects of welfare reforms, including the social security proposals which he himself was recommending.

The postwar Labour government did introduce Beveridge's social security reforms in large part. They also tackled the other giants with the development of the National Health Service, free state education, a public housing programme and a commitment to full employment. Together these policies have generally been referred to as the 'welfare state'. They did much to achieve Marshall's hopes of social citizenship, although in practice many citizens did not benefit fully from all the welfare reforms; and they did much to translate Tawney's strategy of equality into a wideranging reform of the whole social and economic order. Despite the change to conservative Governments in the 1950s the basic structure of the welfare state was maintained throughout the decades following the war, and politicians from both major parties pledged support for its aims and achievements.

However the welfare state and its strategy of equality were not without their critics. As we have seen, by the 1960s Fabian academics were once again arguing that poverty was a serious problem within

British society and that state welfare reform was needed to eliminate it (Abel Smith and Townsend, 1965; Townsend, 1979). This suggested that the strategy of equality had failed because state welfare reforms had not sufficiently raised the standards of all. Other critics of the strategy went further, arguing that, worse than that, state welfare reforms had actually operated to benefit the better off.

This criticism of the perverse achievements of state welfare in promoting inequality has been argued most influentially by Le Grand (1982). Le Grand claims that the strategy of equality was never properly developed within state welfare to ensure equality of outcome, as opposed to equality of opportunity, and that when the evidence is examined it reveals that much of the growth of public expenditure on state welfare services, such as health and education, has not gone to raise standards for all but to benefit the more active and articulate middle classes who are most able to benefit from these services. He concludes that public expenditure on welfare has therefore not reduced differences flowing from inequalities in monetary income, but has tended to multiply them, and that consequently the strategy of equality has failed.

The tendency of welfare expenditure to promote inequality was also identified, as early as 1958, by one of the most famous of the postwar Fabians, Titmuss. He argued that there were in effect divisions within state welfare between expenditure on state services for all, which benefited the poor, and expenditure in the form of tax reliefs to support individual services for the few, which benefited those wealthy enough to purchase such services in the first place. This 'fiscal welfare' has grown in significance throughout the postwar period, providing a major counterbalancing influence to the equalising impact of direct welfare spending. Taylor Gooby (1991, p. 26) estimated the extent of the major tax reliefs on an annual basis at the end of the 1980s as £10.9 billion on mortgage interest relief to owner-occupiers, £12.9 billion on occupational and personal pensions, £300 million on support for private schools and £100 million on support for private medical insurance.

These tax reliefs all benefit the better off disproportionately, and they constitute government support for welfare services which seem to be in direct contradiction to the supposed aims of the strategy of equality in utilising state welfare expenditure to reduce differentials by raising common standards for all. Thus Le Grand's conclusion that the strategy of equality had failed seems to be vindicated; and the evidence of continued and growing problems of poverty and deprivation suggests that expectations of Tawney, Marshall, Beveridge and the early Fabians that state welfare would prevent want were misplaced. However much of the increased poverty experienced in Britain in the 1970s and 1980s was associated not so much with the failings of postwar welfare services, but with the onset of economic recession and the adaptation of welfare provision to meet changed social and economic priorities. By the 1980s it was not at all clear that a strategy of equality was underpinning state welfare policy, indeed some critics were arguing that a 'strategy of inequality' had come to dominate social and economic policy in Britain.

A Strategy of Inequality

Criticism of the failure of the postwar welfare state to combat the problem of poverty did not only come from Fabian and other left-wing critics. There have also been critics on the right who, following on from the early arguments of Hayek (1944) that state welfare would inevitably conflict with economic freedom, have maintained that welfare reforms could not succeed in removing poverty by raising the living standards of all in society. These criticisms have been articulated in Britain by the Institute of Economic Affairs in particular, most recently by Green (1990), but they have also been voiced by some prominent Conservative Party politicians, such as Keith Joseph (Joseph and Sumption, 1979) and Rhodes Boyson (1971).

In general terms right-wing critics argue that state welfare has an inevitable tendency to push the overall cost of public expenditure beyond the limits which a market economy can afford. This is because a wide range of state welfare activity providing services for large sections of the population naturally becomes expensive when seeking to meet more and more needs; and, in the absence of any overall assessment of the broader impact of this, it receives popular support for such expansion. The problem is that such activity cannot continually expand without endangering overall economic growth, as was revealed in the economic recession in Britain and other advanced industrial countries in the 1970s, as a result of which public welfare expenditure had to be curtailed.

Some critics, such as Murray (1984) in the US, have gone further than this, however, and have argued that redistributive welfare spending also destroys the incentives that individuals would otherwise have to provide for themselves and their families, and that it instead provides 'perverse incentives' for them to remain dependent upon further state support. This notion of the creation through state welfare of a 'dependency culture' was central to Rhodes Boyson's earlier criticisms of a welfare state which, 'saps the collective moral fibre of our people as a nation' (1971, p. 385), and to Secretary of State John Moore's speech attacking the poverty lobby and the notion of relative poverty in 1989. And, as we saw in Chapter 12, it also informs some of the pathological approaches to the problem of poverty which have underlain recent debates about the problem of a growing underclass in affluent welfare capitalist societies.

The conclusions which the right-wing academics and politicians draw from these failings within state welfare are not just that public welfare expenditure will need to be curtailed in times of recession in order to support economic growth, but also that redistributive policies which result in increased welfare dependency should be withdrawn, or redrawn, in order to reduce, or at least minimise, the extent of the dependency culture. This leads to an increased unwillingness to support state welfare expenditure and the transfer to the private or voluntary sectors of welfare services, leaving only a residuum of those who could not afford self-protection to depend upon a reduced, and targeted, state suport. The consequence of these conclusions in policy terms is an attempt to reverse the strategy of equality and the growth of state welfare expenditure in order to support market-led economic growth and to provide incentives for self-protection, which will itself encourage further growth.

In Britain in the 1980s the Thatcher governments did attempt such a strategy, at least to some extent. Their aim was to reduce state expenditure by reducing state dependency and encouraging private protection through the market. Of course the cuts in state expenditure which resulted from this and the reduction in tax rates, aimed especially at creating incentives for the rich, resulted in the increased inequality discussed in Chapter 1. But the government believed that this would lead to greater overall economic growth, as a result of which some of the greater overall wealth would 'trickle down' to the poor at the bottom.

How much of the economic growth did trickle down to the poor in the 1980s is of course a matter of some debate, although the government's own figures on the changes in the real value of incomes over the decade from 1979 to 1989, released in 1992 (DSS, 1992), revealed that although average incomes had risen by 30 per cent, the incomes of the bottom decile of the population had *declined* by 6 per cent. Furthermore it is impossible to know whether the economic growth which was achieved in the 1980s could have been matched, or bettered, had redistributive welfare policies continued to be actively followed, although other Western European countries achieved growth rates equal to or better than Britain's during the same period without equivalent retrenchment of welfare policy. Nevertheless it is arguable that right-wing critics were successful in Britain in the 1980s in persuading the Thatcher governments to attempt such a policy reversal, or as A. Walker (1990b) called it, a 'strategy of inequality'. The aim of the strategy was to use economic growth supported by free market policies, rather than redistributive welfare spending, to raise overall standards – neatly encapsulated by Joseph and Sumption's (1979, p. 22) assertion that, 'You cannot make the poor richer by making the rich poorer'.

In one sense of course Joseph and Sumption are clearly wrong; in the short run at least redistribution would raise the living standards of the poor, whereas the trickle down policies of the 1980s appear to have reduced them. The argument behind the right-wing support for a growth-led rise in overall standards, however, rests on the assumption that in the longer run only free markets and non-interventionist states can produce sustained economic growth. The record of the British economy over the latter half of the twentieth century however, and that of most other major industrial societies, does not lend much credence to such beliefs. Growth has been sustained in economies with high welfare spending, such as Sweden, and recession has been experienced in those with minimal state welfare, such as the US. Indeed the improved growth which Britain experienced in the 1980s was followed in the early 1990s with a severe recession, which the Conservative government themselves attributed to international economic trends rather than public expenditure patterns in Britain.

Furthermore although, as A. Walker (1990b), Millar (1991) and others have argued, the strategy of inequality has led to increased inequality and increased deprivation in Britain in the late twentieth century, the attempt to reverse the expansionary tendencies of state welfare could hardly be counted as successful. State expenditure on the major welfare services such as social security, health and education has continued to grow, and, despite the minor growth of private protection in some areas, no alternative to state welfare as a means of meeting these major welfare needs has emerged. As Taylor Gooby (1991) argued therefore, support for the welfare state has not been undermined, indeed attitude survey evidence suggested growing support for expanding welfare expenditure towards the end of the 1980s and, in spite of the fears of a dependency culture, attitudes towards poor benefit claimants began to become more rather than less sympathetic. Thus Taylor Gooby concluded that the loss of support for state welfare and the transfer to the private sector did not take place, and although inequalities were exaggerated this did not lead to social polarisation.

Thus the strategy of inequality in Britain in the 1980s also failed. It did not produce sustained growth. It did not raise the living standards of all. It did not remove either the need for or support for increased state welfare. And by the beginning of the 1990s it is arguable that, with the replacement of Thatcher by Major as prime minister, it had been effectively abandoned. As with the failings of the strategy of equality recognised in the 1970s, it appears that welfare policy in the 1980s was unable to escape from the broader context, and conse-quences, of the changing balance of economic forces. This is because, just as with the creation and recreation of poverty, the welfare state is shaped by these economic forces.

At the same time, however, once introduced, state welfare itself also begins to shape economic forces. It is in this interrelationship between welfare and economic policy that strategic planning for equality or inequality must take place; and if in the past strategies appear to have failed, it may be because they have failed to appreciate the importance of this broader canvas of social relations.

The Welfare State

Once we recognise that poverty is the product of the operation of social and economic forces, in which individual choices or individual responsibility may be important but can never generally be decisive, then we must look for the solutions to poverty in antipoverty policies which take account of and seek to influence these major social and economic forces. Both the strategy of equality and the strategy of inequality were attempts to engineer such changes, but both failed because they did not extend far enough in tackling the relationship between social and economic forces in a complex industrial society, and because in practice therefore they were never really fully explored.

Curiously enough both the strategy of equality and the strategy of inequality saw the introduction of state welfare as the focus of antipoverty policy, either as the means of engineering greater equality or as the cause of lower overall standards. State welfare was seen as the use of social policy to adjust the consequences of economic forces within a capitalist economy. What this overlooked, however, is the fact that the welfare state is *not* merely the product of benevolent, or misguided, social policy. As Gough (1979) has argued, the introduction of state welfare is the product of a process of economic adjustment within capitalist society in which state intervention in the reproduction and maintenance of a range of major services, such as health and education, has become a necessary means of ensuring the continuation of existing economic forces, just as much as a means of redistributing resources to the poor.

Thus the introduction of state welfare results in a transformation of economic forces, indeed in a transformation of social and economic structure itself, into what Therborn (1984) has called 'welfare state capitalism'. The major extension of state intervention into the reproduction of social forces, and in many countries into production too through the nationalisation of major industries such as energy, steel and transport, transforms capitalist economies into some form of mixed market economy in which state policies become a major determinant of economic as well as social trends. And whether this is the product of government intention – or government conspiracy as some critics on the far left might imply – is not really all that important; although as Therborn demonstrates, despite some variations in the forms of state welfare its extension has been a consistent trend throughout all major advanced industrial economies in the latter half of the twentieth century. What is important, for our purposes at least, is that it means that antipoverty policy must recognise the structural role that state welfare now plays in shaping social and economic forces.

This casts a new light on the criticisms of Le Grand (1982) and others of the failure of the strategy of equality. As Hindess (1987) has pointed out, Le Grand's criticisms are really misplaced since their assumption that state welfare was introduced as the vehicle for a strategy of equality cannot be justified. Tawney and the Fabians may have wished state welfare to play such an equalising role in the combating of poverty; but this has only ever been one part of what state welfare has been designed and developed to accomplish. Indeed, as Hindess suggests, the fact that so little was done to monitor the impact of state welfare in achieving equalisation is evidence not so much of failure, but of a lack of attention to this as a relevant goal for services such as education, health and even social security. Thus the strategy of equality has not really failed, because it has not really been attempted.

The failure of the strategy of inequality too is based upon a misconception of the role, and the extent, of state welfare. The welfare state is not, as right-wing critics such as Rhodes Boyson (1971) have argued, merely a means of taking resources from the rich and successful and transferring them to the poor and dependent. It is a part of the broader structure of production and reproduction in advanced industrial societies, upon which the rich and successful are equally dependent for providing the social and economic environment in which their industries and investments can flourish. Economic forces depend upon state welfare, and political forces reflect this reality. As Therborn and Roebroek (1986) have argued, state welfare services have become 'irreversible' features of advanced industrial societies not just because of their economic role but also because the services they provide secure political support across a wide range of the social structure, and too many people know that they would lose too much if these were to be withdrawn completely.

It is not surprising therefore that the attitude survey evidence discussed by Taylor Gooby (1991) reveals continued high levels of support in Britain for state welfare services and for the use of these to combat poverty in the late 1980s, despite almost a decade of a supposed strategy of inequality. Nor is it surprising therefore that most critics argue that despite significant cuts and privatisations, Thatcherism was unable to remove, or even reverse, the growth of state welfare in Britain in the late twentieth century (see Johnson, 1990). Indeed, as with the strategy of equality, it could be argued that in the extreme form promoted by critics such as Green (1990) or Murray (1984) a strategy of inequality aimed at removing the major features of state welfare in favour of entirely market-based or voluntary provision has not thus far been attempted in Britain.

The British welfare state thus is, in part, an antipoverty policy; and it has, as Taylor Gooby (1991, Ch. 2) points out, done much through redistribution to reduce some of the harshest aspects of initial inequalities. However it is also much else; and if it is to achieve the broader antipoverty aims of the strategy of equality outlined by Tawney and the Fabians it will have to be significantly transformed. Indeed a broader antipoverty strategy would require not just a transformation of state welfare but also a transformation of the social and economic forces of which it has become a significant part.

As Hindess (1987) and others (see Townsend, 1984) have argued, in its response to the problem of poverty the British welfare state has largely adopted a 'casualty approach' to service development. This is particularly true of social security policy that has sought to identify and compensate the victims of harsh inequalities within the wage labour market and the broader distribution of wealth via the redistribution of cash through benefits, rather than seeking to alter or influence the initial distribution of wealth or the labour market which has largely produced it. Means testing, or selectivity, reveals most starkly this casualty approach which requires proof of need, with its stigmatising undertone of social and economic failure, before resources can be claimed.

An antipoverty policy which seeks to transcend such a casualty approach to welfare would have to develop, jointly, policies on wealth and incomes as well as on benefits. An income and wealth policy would require intervention into the labour market to influence both availability of employment as a source of income and the level of wages which employment might provide. It would also require policies of taxation and investment to direct wealth into productive industries or social services, rather than it being squandered on private affluence. An income and wealth policy would therefore, require intervention in economic forces as well as social structures; it would require the welfare state planning directly for production and distribution, and not only for redistribution. Only thus might such a welfare state be able to achieve economic as well as social change, and to advance a strategy of equality as a means of challenging the problem of poverty.

Such a welfare state appears to imply, however, a significant shift from the casualty-based policy developments of twentieth century welfare, even perhaps a revolutionary change. But in practice moves towards a more interventionist social *and economic* strategy for welfare are neither revolutionary nor untried. British governments have variously tried to influence investment policies and practices throughout most of the postwar period, albeit often without any clear overall strategic objectives. British governments have also tried to influence wealth and income distribution, for instance through legislating for minimum wage levels in certain industries and in seeking to control prices and wage rises. In other welfare-state capitalist countries similar policies have been developed, and often taken further. For instance many Western European countries impose statutory minimum wages and control overall wage levels; and many use government investment in industries and services to shape and direct economic growth and development. Indeed such strategies are commonplace within the EC and are now promoted by the European Commission as part of a wider European programme for social and economic development.

In the future it is likely that the further integration of Britain within the EC will require the greater development of such social and economic strategies within this country too. After 1992 Britain will be a member of the single European market; it will be likely to participate in, and benefit from, EC investment strategies both nationally and on a regional basis; and, as discussed in Chapter 3, despite securing the right to opt out of the Social Charter it is likely to come under increasing pressure to guarantee a range of social rights in common with other member states. The further integration and development of social and economic policies within the welfare state are not revolutionary therefore, rather they are inevitable.

Of course greater social and economic policy integration within Europe will not immediately remove the problem of poverty from Britain, nor from the other states in Europe. But it is to such a future integration that those who wish to see the removal of poverty must look, rather than to the poor themselves. Once we recognise that those approaches which seek to identify an 'underclass' of poor individuals – who are the willing or unwilling victims of dependency – in order to focus antipoverty policies onto them only are ignoring the structural context in which people become or remain poor, then our understanding of poverty will draw our attention to the broader social and economic forces which shape the social structure for all. Only by changing those forces which affect *all* people will we be able to change the position of the poor too. As Tawney's famous statement, quoted in the Preface, succinctly put it in 1913, the problem of poverty is a 'problem of riches' too.

References

ABEL SMITH, B. and TOWNSEND, P. (1965) *The Poor and the Poorest* (G. Bell and Sons).

ADAM SMITH INSTITUTE. (ASI). (1984) *Omega Report: Social Security Policy* (ASI).

ADAM SMITH INSTITUTE. (ASI). (1989) *Needs Reform: The Overhaul of Social Security* (ASI).

ALCOCK, P. (1985) 'The Fowler Reviews: Social Policy on the Political Agenda', *Critical Social Policy*, issue 14, Winter.

ALCOCK, P. (1987) *Poverty and State Support* (Longman).

ALCOCK, P. (1989) 'Unconditional Benefits: Misplaced Optimism in Income Maintenance', *Capital and Class*, no.37, Spring.

ALCOCK, P. (1992) 'Social Insurance in Crisis?', *Benefits*, issue 5.

ALCOCK, P. and SHEPHERD, J. (1987) 'Take–up Campaigns: Fighting Poverty Through the Post', *Critical Social Policy*, issue 19, Summer.

ALCOCK, P., SHEPHERD, J., STEWART, G. and STEWART, J. (1991) 'Welfare Rights Work into the 1990s – a Changing Agenda', *Journal of Social Policy*, 20.1.

AMIN, K. and OPPENHEIM, C. (1992) *Poverty in Black and White: Deprivation and Ethnic Minorities* (CPAG/Runnymede Trust).

ANDERSON, D. (1991) Paper to Social Policy Association Annual Conference, Nottingham University, July.

ARNOTT, H. (1987) 'Second class citizens', in Walker, A. and Walker, C. (eds), *The Growing Divide: A Social Audit 1979–1987* (CPAG).

ASHBY, P. (1984) *Social Security After Beveridge – What Next?* (Bedford Square Press/NCVO).

ATKINSON, A. B. (1969) *Poverty in Britain and the Reform of Social Security* (Cambridge UP).

ATKINSON, A. B. (1983) *The Economics of Inequality, Second Edition* (Oxford UP).

ATKINSON, A. B. (1989) *Poverty and Social Security* (Harvester Wheatsheaf).

ATKINSON, A. B. (1990a) A. *National Minimum? A. History of Ambiguity in the Determination of Benefit Scales in Britain* (LSE/STICERD, WSP/47).

ATKINSON, A. B. (1990b) *Comparing Poverty Rates Internationally: Lessons from Recent Studies in OECD Countries* (LSE/STICERD, WSP/53).

ATKINSON, A. B. (1991a) *Poverty, Statistics, and Progress in Europe* (LSE/STICERD, WSP/60).

ATKINSON, A. B. (1991b) *The Development of State Pensions in the United Kingdom* (LSE/STICERD, WSP/58).

ATKINSON, A. B. (1992) *Social Insurance* (LSE/STICERD, WSP/65).

ATKINSON, A. B., MAYNARD, A. K., and TRINDER, C. G. (1983) *Parents and Children: Incomes in Two Generations* (Heinemann).

ATKINSON, A. B. and SUTHERLAND, H. (1984) 'TAXMOD: User Manual' (LSE).

ATKINSON, A. B. and SUTHERLAND, H. (1991) *Two Nations in Early Retirement?: The Case of Britain* (LSE/STICERD, WSP/56).

AULETTA, K. (1982) *The Underclass* (New York: Random House).

BALDWIN, S. and COOKE, K. (1984) *How Much is Enough?* (Family Policy Studies Centre).

BALDWIN, S, PARKER, G. and WALKER, R. (eds). (1988) *Social Security and Community Care* (Avebury).

BALDWIN, S. and PARKER, G. (1991) 'Support for informal carers – the role of social security', in Dalley, G. (ed.), *Disability and Social Policy* (PSI).

BALLOCH, S. and JONES, B. (1990) *Poverty and Anti–Poverty Strategy: the Local Government Response* (Association of Metropolitan Authorities).

BARRETT, M. and MCINTOSH, M. (1982) *The Anti–Social Family* (Verso).

BARRON, R. G. and NORRIS, G. M. (1976) 'Sexual Divisions and the Dual Labour Market', in Barker, D. L. and Allen, S. (eds), *Dependence and Exploitation in Work and Marriage* (Longman).

BECKER, S. (ed.). (1991) *Windows of Opportunity: Public Policy and the Poor* (CPAG).

BECKERMAN, W. (1980) *National Income Analysis, Third Edition* (Weidenfeld and Nicolson).

BECKERMAN, W. and CLARK, S. (1982) *Poverty and Social Security in Britain Since 1961* (Oxford UP).

BEECHEY, V. (1978) 'Women and production: a critical analysis of some sociological theories of women's work', in Kuhn, A. and Wolpe, A. (eds), *Feminism and Materialism: Women and Modes of Production* (Routledge and Kegan Paul).

BEECHEY, V. (1987) *Unequal Work* (Verso).

BENINGTON, J. (1987) 'Local economic strategies: paradigms for a planned economy', *Local Economy*, no. 1.

BENINGTON, J. (1991) 'Local Strategies to Combat Poverty: Lessons from the European Programmes', *Critical Public Health*, no. 1.

BERTHOUD, R. (1984) *The PSI Study: the Reform of Social Security – Working Papers* (PSI).

BERTHOUD, R. (1985) *The Examination of Social Security* (PSI).

BERTHOUD, R. (1986) *Selective Social Security: an Analysis of the Government's Plan* (PSI).

BERTHOUD, R. (1991) 'Meeting the costs of disability', in Dalley, G. (ed.), *Disability and Social Policy* (PSI).

BERTHOUD, R., BENSON, S. and WILLIAMS, S. (1986) *Standing up for Claimants: Welfare Rights Work in Local Authorities* (PSI).

BERTHOUD, R., BROWN, J. and COOPER, S. (1981) *Poverty and the Development of Anti–Poverty Policy in the UK* (Heinemann EB).

BERTHOUD, R. and KEMPSON, E. (1992) *Credit and Debt: The PSI Report* (PSI).

BEVERIDGE, SIR W. (1942) *Report on Social Insurance and Allied Services*, Cmd 6404 (HMSO).

BINNEY, V., HARKELL, G. and NIXON, J. (1981) *Leaving Violent Men: a Study of Refuges and Housing for Battered Women* (Women's Aid Federation).

BLACKBURN, C. (1991) *Poverty and Health: Working with Families* (Open University P).

BODDY, M. and FUDGE, C. (eds). (1984) *Local Socialism? Labour Councils and New Left Alternatives* (Macmillan).

BONE, N. and MELTZER, H. (1989) *OPCS Report 3: the Prevalence of Disability among Children* (HMSO).

BOOTH, C. (1889) *The Life and Labour of the People* (Williams and Northgate).

BOOTH, C. (1892) *Pauperism: a Picture of the Endowment of Old Age: an Argument* (Macmillan).

BOOTH, C. (1894) *The Aged Poor: Condition* (Macmillan).

BOSANQUET, N. and TOWNSEND, P. (1980) *Labour and Equality* (Heinemann EB).

BOWLEY, A. L. and BURNETT–HURST, A. R. (1915) *Livelihood and Poverty* (G. Bell and Sons).

BOYSON, R. (1971) *Down with the Poor* (Churchill).

BRADSHAW, J. (1975) 'Welfare rights: an experimental approach', in Lees, R. and Smith, G. (eds) *Action Research in Community Development* (Routledge and Kegan Paul).

BRADSHAW, J. (1985) 'Tried and found wanting: the take–up of means-tested benefits', in Ward, S. (ed.), *DHSS in Crisis: Social Security – Under Pressure and Under Review* (CPAG).

BRADSHAW, J. and ERNST, J. (1990) *Establishing a Modest but Adequate Budget for a British Family* (Family Budget Unit).

BRADSHAW, J. and HOLMES, H. (1989) *Living on the Edge: a Study of the Living Standards of Families on Benefit in Tyne and Wear* (Tyneside CPAG).

BRADSHAW, J., MITCHELL, D. and MORGAN, J. (1987) 'Evaluating Adequacy: the Potential of Budget Standards', *Journal of Social Policy*, 16.2.

BRADSHAW, J. and MORGAN, J. (1987) *Budgeting on Benefit: the Consumption of Families on Social Security* (Family Policy Studies Centre).

BREWSTER, I. and TEAGUE, P. (1989) *European Community Social Policy – Its Impact on the United Kingdom* (Institute of Personnel Management).

BROWN, C. (1984) *Black and White Britain: the Third PSI Survey* (Heinemann EB).

BROWN, J. (1988) *Child Benefit: Investing in the Future* (CPAG).

BROWN, M. and MADGE, N. (1982) *Despite the Welfare State* (Heinemann EB).

BROWN, P. and SCASE, R. (eds). (1991) *Poor Work: Disadvantage and the Division of Labour* (Open University P).

BRUEGEL, E. (1989) 'Sex and Race in the Labour Market', *Feminist Review*, no. 32.

BYTHEWAY, B. and JOHNSON J. (1990) 'On defining ageism', *Critical Social Policy*, issue 29, Autumn.

CALLENDER, C. (1985) 'Unemployment: the Case for Women', in Brenton, M. and Jones, C. (eds), *Yearbook of Social Policy 1984–5* (Routledge and Kegan Paul).

CALLENDER, C. (1992) 'Redundancy, Unemployment and Poverty', in Glendinning C. and Millar J. (eds), *Women and Poverty in Britain: the 1990s* (Harvester/Wheatsheaf).

CARR–HILL, R. and CHADHA–BOREHAM, H. (1988) 'Education', in Bhat, A., Carr–Hill, R. and Ohri, S. (eds), *Britain's Black Population: a New Perspective, Second Edition* (Gower).

CCETSW (1989) *Welfare rights in Social Work Education: Report by a Curriculum Development Group*, Central Council for Education and Training in Social Work, paper 28.1.

CHILD POVERTY ACTION GROUP (CPAG) (Annual) *National Welfare Benefits Handbook* (CPAG).

CHILD POVERTY ACTION GROUP (CPAG) (Annual) *Rights Guide to Non–Means-tested Benefits* (CPAG).

CHILD POVERTY ACTION GROUP (CPAG) (1984) *Poverty*, no. 57 (CPAG).

CHILD POVERTY ACTION GROUP (CPAG) (1985) *Burying Beveridge: a Detailed Response to the Green Paper – Reform of Social Security* (CPAG).

CLAPHAM, D., KEMP, P. and SMITH, S.J. (1990) *Housing and Social Policy* (Macmillan).

COATES, D. and SILBURN, R. (1970) *Poverty: the Forgotten Englishmen* (Penguin).

COHEN, R., COXALL, J., CRAIG, G. and SADIQ-SANGSTER, A. (1992) *Hardship Britain: Being Poor in the 1990s* (CPAG).

COHEN, R. and RUSHTON, A. (1982) *Welfare Rights* (Heinemann EB).

COHEN, R. and TARPEY, M. (1986) 'Are We up on Take-up?', *Poverty*, no. 63.

COLLARD, D. (1980) 'Social dividend and negative income tax', in Sandford, C., Pond, C., and Walker, R. (eds), *Taxation and Social Policy* (Heinemann EB).

COMMUNITY DEVELOPMENT PROJECT (CDP) (1977) *Gilding the Ghetto: the State and the Poverty Experiments* (CDP).

COOK, D. (1989) *Rich Law, Poor Law: Different Responses to Tax and Supplementary Fraud* (Open University P).

COOKE, K. (1987) 'The Withdrawal from Paid Work of the Wives of Unemployed Men: a Review of Research', *Journal of Social Policy*, 16.3.

COOPER, S. (1985) *Observations in Supplementary Offices: the Reform of Supplementary Benefit Working Paper C* (PSI).

COWAN, R. (1988) 'Blaming the Buildings', *Roof*, March/April.

CRAIG, P. (1991) 'Costs and Benefits: a Review of Research on Take-up of Income-Related Benefits', *Journal of Social Policy*, 20.4.

DAHRENDORF, R. (1987) 'The erosion of citizenship and its consequences for us all', *New Statesman*, 12 June.

DALLEY, G. (ed.) (1991) *Disability and Social Policy* (PSI).

DEACON, A. and BRADSHAW, J. (1983) *Reserved for the Poor: the Means-test in British Social Policy* (Basil Blackwell and Martin Robertson).

DEAKIN, N. (1987) *The Politics of Welfare* (Methuen).

DEAN, H. (1991) 'In search of the underclass', in Brown, P. and Scase, R. (eds), *Poor Work: Disadvantage and the Division of Labour* (Open University P).

DEPARTMENT OF SOCIAL SECURITY (DSS) (1988) *Low Income Statistics: Report of a Technical Review* (HMSO).

DEPARTMENT OF SOCIAL SECURITY (DSS) (1992) *Households below Average Income: a Statistical Analysis* (HMSO).

DESAI, M. (1986) 'Drawing the line: on defining the poverty threshold', in Golding P. (ed.), *Excluding the Poor* (CPAG).

DEX, S. (1985) *The Sexual Division of Work* (Wheatsheaf).

DEX, S. and PHILLIPSON, C. (1986) 'Social Policy and the Older Worker', in Phillipson, C. and Walker, A. (eds), *Ageing and Social Policy: a Critical Assessment* (Gower).

DILNOT, A., KAY, J. and MORRIS, C. (1984) *The Reform of Social Security* (Oxford UP).

DISABILITY ALLIANCE (1987) *Poverty and Disability: Breaking the Link* (Disability Alliance).

DISABILITY ALLIANCE (1990) *Disability Rights Handbook* (Disability Alliance).

DISABLEMENT INCOME GROUP (1987) *DIG's National Disability Income* (DIG).

DONNISON, D. (1982) *The Politics of Poverty* (Martin Robertson).

DONNISON, D. (1988) 'Defining and Measuring Poverty: a Reply to Stein Ringen', *Journal of Social Policy*, 17.3.

DONZELOT, S. (1979) *The Policing of Families: Welfare versus the State* (Hutchinson).

EDGELL, S. and DUKE, V. (1983) 'Gender and Social Policy: the impact of the public expenditure cuts and reactions to them', *Journal of Social Policy*, 12.3

ESPING ANDERSEN, G. (1990) *The Three Worlds of Welfare Capitalism* (Polity).

EUROPEAN COMMUNITY (EC) (1977) *The Perception of Poverty in Europe* (EC Commission).

EUROPEAN COMMUNITY (EC) (1989) *Medium-term community action programme to foster the economic and social integration of the least privileged groups*, EC Commission Bulletin, Supplement 4/89.

EUROPEAN COMMUNITY (EC) (1990) *The Perception of Poverty in Europe*, Poverty 3, EC Commission.

EUROPEAN COMMUNITY (EC) (1991) *Final Report on the Second European Poverty Programme 1985–89* (EC Commission).

EVASON, E. (1980) *Ends That Won't Meet* (CPAG).

FALKINGHAM, J. (1989) 'Dependency and Ageing in Britain: a Re-Examination of the Evidence', *Journal of Social Policy*, 18.2.

FALKINGHAM, J. and VICTOR, C. (1991) *The Myth of the Woopie?: Incomes, the Elderly, and Targeting Welfare* (LSE/STICERD, WSP/55).

FERGE, Z. and MILLAR, S.M. (eds) (1987) *Dynamics of Deprivation* (Gower).

FIEGEHEN, G.C., LANSLEY, P.S. and SMITH, A.D. (1977) *Poverty and Progress in Britain 1953–73* (Cambridge UP).

FIELD, F. (1982) *Poverty and Politics: the Inside Story of the CPAG's Campaigns in the 1970s* (Heinemann EB).

FIELD, F. (1989) *Losing Out: the Emergence of Britain's Underclass* (Blackwell).

FIELD, F. and PIACHAUD, D. (1971), 'The Poverty Trap', *New Statesman*, 3 December.

FIMISTER, G. (1986) *Welfare Rights Work in Social Services* (Macmillan).

FINCH, J. and GROVES, D. (eds) (1983) *A Labour of Love: Women, Work and Caring* (Routledge and Kegan Paul).

FISHER COMMITTEE (1973) *Report of the Committee on Abuse of Social Security Benefits*, Cmnd 5228 (HMSO).

FLOYD, M. (1991) 'Overcoming barriers to employment', in Dalley, G. (ed.), *Disability and Social Policy* (PSI).

FORD, J. (1991) *Consuming Credit: Debt and Poverty in the UK* (CPAG).

FRY, V. and STARK, G. (1992) 'Modelling the Take-up of Means-tested Benefits', *Benefits*, issue 3.

GAMBLE, A. (1989) *The Free Economy and the Strong State: the Politics of Thatcherism* (Macmillan).

GEORGE, V. (1988) *Wealth, Poverty and Starvation: an International Perspective* (Harvester Wheatsheaf).

GEORGE, V. and HOWARDS, I. (1991) *Poverty Amidst Affluence: Britain and the United States* (Edward Elgar).

GEORGE, V. and LAWSON, R. (1980) *Poverty and Inequality in Common Market Countries* (Routledge and Kegan Paul).

GITTINS, D. (1985) *The Family in Question: Changing Households and Familiar Ideologies* (Macmillan).

GLENDINNING, C. (1987) 'Impoverishing Women', in Walker A. and Walker, C. (eds), *The Growing Divide: a Social Audit 1979–87* (CPAG).

GLENDINNING, C. (1990) 'Dependency and Interdependency: the Incomes of Informal Carers and the Impact of Social Security', *Journal of Social Policy*, 19.4.

GLENDINNING, C. and BALDWIN, S. (1988) 'The Costs of Disability', in Walker, R. and Parker, G. (eds), *Money Matters: Income, Wealth and Financial Welfare* (Sage).

GLENDINNING, C. and MILLAR, J. (eds) (1987) *Women and Poverty in Britain* (Wheatsheaf).

GLENDINNING, C. and MILLAR, J. (eds) (1992) *Women and Poverty in Britain: the 1990s* (Harvester/Wheatsheaf).

GOLDING, P. (ed.) (1986) *Excluding the Poor* (CPAG).

GOLDING, P. and MIDDLETON, S. (1982) *Images of Welfare: Press and Public Attitudes to Welfare* (Basil Blackwell and Martin Robertson).

GORDON, P. and NEWNHAM, A. (1985) *Passport to Benefits: Racism in Social Security* (CPAG/Runnymede Trust).

GORZ, A. (1982) *Farewell to the Working Class* (Pluto P).

GORZ, A. (1991) 'The New Agenda', *New Left Review*, no. 184, January.

GOUGH, I. (1979) *The Political Economy of the Welfare State* (Macmillan).

GOUGH, I. and DOYAL, L. (1991) *A Theory of Human Need* (Macmillan).

GRAHAM, H. (1987) 'Women's Poverty and Caring', in Glendinning, C. and Millar, J. (eds), *Women and Poverty in Britain* (Wheatsheaf).

GRAHL, J. and TEAGUE, P. (1990) *1992 – The Big Market: the Future of the European Community* (Lawrence and Wishart).

GREATER LONDON COUNCIL (GLC) (1986) The Work of the GLC Welfare Benefits Project (GLC).

GREEN, D. G. (1990) *Equalizing People: Why Social Justice Threatens Liberty* (IEA).

GREEN, E., HEBRON, S. and WOODWARD, D. (1990) *Women's Leisure, What Leisure? The Sociology of Women's Leisure* (Macmillan).

GREEN, H. (1988) *Informal Carers*, General Household Survey 1985 (HMSO).

GREEN PAPER (1985) *Reform of Social Security, Volumes 1, 2 and 3*, Cmnd 9517, 9518, 9519 (HMSO).

GRIMSLEY, M. and BHAT, A. (1988) 'Health', in Bhat, A., Carr–Hill, R. and Ohri, S. (eds), *Britain's Black Population: a New Perspective*, Second Edition (Gower).

GROVES, D. (1988) 'Poverty, disability and social services', in Becker, S. and MacPherson, S. (eds), *Public issues and Private Pain: Poverty, Social Work and Social Policy* (Insight).

GROVES, D. (1992) 'Occupational Pension Provision and Women's Poverty in Old Age', in Glendinning, C. and Millar, J. (eds), *Women and Poverty in Britain: the 1990s* (Harvester/Wheatsheaf).

HADJIPATERAS, A. (1992) 'Reforming Social Security Provision for People with Disabilities: Ways to Move Beyond Mere Tinkering', *Benefits*, issue 3.

HALSEY, A. H. (ed.) (1972) *Educational Priority: EPA Problems and Policies* (HMSO).

HARRIS, J. (1977) *William Beveridge: a Biography* (Oxford UP).

HARRIS, C. C. (1991) 'Recession, Redundancy and Age', in Brown, P. and Scase, R. (eds), *Poor Work: Disadvantage and the Division of Labour* (Open University P).

HARRISON, P. (1983) *Inside the Inner City* (Penguin).

HAYEK, F. A. (1944) *The Road to Serfdom* (Routledge and Kegan Paul).

HENWOOD, M., RIMMER L. and WICKS M. (1987) *Inside the Family: Changing Roles of Men and Women* (Family Policy Studies Centre).

HENWOOD, M. and WICKS, M. (1986) *Benefit or Burden? The Objectives and Impact of Child Support* (Family Policy Studies Centre).

HIGGINS, J. (1978) *The Poverty Business: Britain and America* (Basil Blackwell and Martin Robertson).

HILL, M. (1990) *Social Security Policy in Britain* (Edward Elgar).

HILL, M. and LAING, P. (1979) *Social Work and Money* (George Allen and Unwin).

HILLS, J. (1989) *Distributional Effects of Housing Subsidies in the United Kingdom* (LSE/STICERD, WSP/44).

HILLS, J. (1990) 'Conditional Response', *Roof*, September/October.

HINDESS, B. (1987) *Freedom, Equality and the Market: Arguments on Social Policy* (Tavistock).

HOLMAN, R. (1978) *Poverty: Explanations of Social Deprivation* (Martin Robertson).

HOMER, M., LEONARD, A. E. and TAYLOR, M. P. (1984) *Private Violence: Public Shame* (Cleveland Refuge and Aid for Women and Children).

JAMES, E. (1970) *America Against Poverty* (Routledge and Kegan Paul).

JENKINS, S. P. (1991) 'Poverty Measurement and the Within Household Distribution: Agenda for Action', *Journal of Social Policy*, 20.4.

JOHNSON, N. (1990) *Reconstructing the Welfare State: a Decade of Change 1980–1990* (Harvester/Wheatsheaf).

JOHNSON, P. and WEBB, S. (1990) *Counting People with Low Incomes: the impact of recent changes in official statistics* (Institute for Fiscal Studies).

JORDAN, B. (1987) *Rethinking Welfare* (Basil Blackwell).

JOSEPH, K. (1972) 'The Cycle of Deprivation', Speech to Pre-School Playgroups Association, 29 June.

JOSEPH, K. and SUMPTION, J. (1979) *Equality* (John Murray).

JOSHI, H. (1988) *The cash opportunity costs of childbearing* (Centre for Economic Policy Research), Discussion Paper 208.

JOSHI, H. (1992) 'The Cost of Caring', in Glendinning, C. and Millar, J. (eds), *Women and Poverty in Britain: the 1990s* (Harvester/Wheatsheaf).

LAND, H. and ROSE, H. (1985) 'Compulsory altruism for all, or an altruistic society for some?', in Bean, P., Ferris, J. and Whynes, D. (eds), *In Defence of Welfare* (Tavistock).

LE GRAND, J. (1982) *The Strategy of Equality* (Allen and Unwin).

LEES, R. and SMITH, G. (eds) (1975) *Action Research in Community Development* (Routledge and Kegan Paul).

LEVITAS, R. (ed.) (1986) *The Ideology of the New Right* (Polity).

LEWIS, J. and PIACHAUD, D. (1992) 'Women and Poverty in the Twentieth Century', in Glendinning, C. and Millar, J. (eds), *Women and Poverty in Britain: the 1990s* (Harvester/Wheatsheaf).

LEWIS, O. (1965) *The Children of Sanchez* (Penguin).

LEWIS, O. (1968) *La Vida* (Panther).

LIEBFRIED, S. (1991) 'Towards a European Welfare State', paper to Anglo–German Conference, University of Nottingham, April.

LISTER, R. (1975) *Social Security: the Case for Reform* (CPAG).

LISTER, R. (1987) *There is an Alternative – Reforming Social Security* (CPAG).

LISTER, R. (1990) 'Women, Economic Dependency and Citizenship', *Journal of Social Policy*, 19.4.

LISTER, R. (1991) 'The Overhaul of Maintenance', *Poverty*, no. 78.

LISTER, R. and BERESFORD, P. (1991) *Working Together Against Poverty: Involving Poor People in Action Against Poverty* (Open Services Project/ University of Bradford).

LISTER, R. and FIMISTER, G. (1980) *The Case Against Contribution Tests* (CPAG).

LONEY, M. (1983) *Community Against Government: the British Community Development Project 1968–78* (Heinemann).

LONSDALE, S. (1992) 'Patterns of Paid Work', in Glendinning, C. and Millar, J. (eds), *Women and Poverty in Britain: the 1990s* (Harvester/ Wheatsheaf).

LONSDALE, S. and WALKER, A. (1984) A *Right to Work: Disability and Employment* (LPU).

LOW PAY UNIT (1992) *Poor Britain – Poverty, Inequality and Low Pay in the Nineties* (LPU) pamphlet no. 56.

MACGREGOR, S. (1981) *The Politics of Poverty* (Longman).

MACK, J. and LANSLEY, S. (1985) *Poor Britain* (George Allen and Unwin).

MACK, J. and LANSLEY, S. (1992) *Breadline Britain 1990s: the Findings of the Television Series* (London Weekend Television).

MACNICOL, J. (1987) 'In Pursuit of the Underclass', *Journal of Social Policy*, 16.3.

MANCHESTER LAW CENTRE (1984) *From Ill Treatment to No treatment. The New Health Regulations: Black People and Internal Controls* (Manchester Law Centre).

MANN, K. (1992) *The Making of an English 'Underclass'? The Social Divisions of Welfare and Labour* (Open University P).

MANN, K. and ANSTEE, J. (1989) *Growing Fringes: Hypotheses in the Development of Occupational Welfare* (Armley).

MARRIS, P. and REIN, M. (1974) *Dilemmas of Social Reform* (Penguin).

MARSHALL, T. H. (1950) *Citizenship and Social Class* (Cambridge UP).

MARTIN, J., MELZER, H. and ELLIOTT, D. (1988) *OPCS Report 1, the Prevalence of Disability among Adults* (HMSO).

MARTIN, J. and WHITE, A. (1988) *OPCS Report 2, the Financial Circumstances of Disabled Adults living in Private Households* (HMSO).

MARTIN, J., WHITE, A. and MELTZER, H. (1989) *OPCS Report 4, Disabled Adults: Services, Transport and Employment* (HMSO).

MARX, K. (1952) *Wage Labour and Capital* (Progress).

MATTHEWS, A. and TRUSCOTT, P. (1990) *Disability, Household Income and Expenditure: a Follow–up Survey of Disabled Adults in the Family Expenditure Survey*, DSS Research Report no. 2 (HMSO).

MCCARTHY, M. (1986) *Campaigning for the Poor: CPAG and the Politics of Welfare* (Croom Helm).

MCCLELLAND, J. (ed.) (1982) *A Little Pride and Dignity: the Importance of Child Benefit* (CPAG).

MCDONNELL K. (1982) 'Working in Housing Aid', *Critical Social Policy*, 2.1.

MCLAUGHLIN, E. (1992) 'Mixed Blessings? The Invalid Care Allowance and Carer's Income Needs', *Benefits*, issue 3.

MILLAR, J. (1988) 'The Costs of Marital Breakdown', in Walker, R. and Parker, G. (eds), *Money Matters: Income, Wealth and Financial Welfare* (Sage).

MILLAR, J. (1989a) *Poverty and the Lone Parent Family: the challenge to Social Policy* (Avebury).

MILLAR, J. (1989b) 'Social Security, Equality and Women in the UK', *Policy and Politics*, 17.4.

MILLAR, J. (1991) 'Bearing the Cost', in Becker, S. (Ed.), *Windows of Opportunity: Public Policy and the Poor* (CPAG).

MILLAR, J. (1992) 'Lone Mothers and Poverty', in Glendinning, C. and Millar, J. (eds), *Women and Poverty in Britain: the 1990s* (Harvester/Wheatsheaf).

MILLAR, J. and GLENDINNING, G. (1989) 'Gender and Poverty', *Journal of Social Policy*, 18.3.

MITCHELL, D. (1991) *Income Transfers in Ten Welfare States* (Avebury).

MOORE, J. (1989) 'The End of the Line for Poverty', speech to Greater London Area CPC, 11 May.

MOORE, R. and WALLACE, T. (1975) *Slamming the Door* (Martin Robertson).

MORRIS, A. E. and NOTT, S. M. (1991) *Working Women and the Law: Equality and Discrimination in Theory and Practice* (Routledge).

MORRIS, L. (1989) *The Workings of the Household* (Polity).

MORRIS, L. (1991) 'Women's Poor Work', in Brown, P. and Scase, R. (eds), *Poor Work: Disadvantage and the Division of Labour* (Open University P).

MORRIS, L. and RUANE, S. (1989) *Household Financial Management and the Labour Market* (Gower).

MOYNIHAN, D. P. (1965) *The Negro Family: the Case for National Action* (Office of Policy Planning and Research, US Department of Labor).

MURRAY, C. (1984) *Losing Ground: American Social Policy 1950–1980* (New York: Basic Books).

MURRAY, C. (1990) *The Emerging British Underclass* (IEA).

NACAB (1991) *Barriers to Benefit: Black Claimants and Social Security* (NACAB).

NATIONAL CONSUMER COUNCIL (1976) *Means-tested Benefits: a Discussion Paper* (National Consumer Council).

NOVAK, T. (1984) *Poverty and Social Security* (Pluto).

NOVAK, T. (1988) *Poverty and the State: an Historical Sociology* (Open University P).

O'HIGGINS, M. (1985) 'Inequality, Redistribution and Recession: the British Experience 1976–1982', *Journal of Social Policy*, 14.1.

O'HIGGINS, M., BRADSHAW, J. and WALKER, R. (1988) 'Income Distribution over the Life Cycle', in Walker, R. and Parker, G. (eds), *Money Matters: Income, Wealth and Financial Welfare* (Sage).

OLIVER, M. (1990) *The Politics of Disablement: a Sociological Approach* (Macmillan).

OLIVER, M. (1991a) 'Speaking Out: disabled people and state welfare', in Dalley, G. (ed.), *Disability and Social Policy* (PSI).

OLIVER, M. (1991b) 'Disability and participation in the labour market', in Brown, P. and Scase, R. (eds), *Poor Work: Disadvantage and the Division of Labour* (Open University P).

OPPENHEIM, C. (1990) *Poverty: the Facts* (CPAG).

ORSHANSKY, M. (1965) 'Counting the Poor: Another Look at the Poverty Profile', *Social Security Bulletin*, vol. 28.

ORSHANSKY, M. (1969) 'How Poverty is Measured', *Monthly Labour Review*, vol. 92.

PAHL, J. (1980) 'Patterns of Money Management within Marriage', *Journal of Social Policy*, 9.3.

PAHL, J. (1984) 'The Allocation of Money within the Household', in Freeman, M. (ed.), *The State, the Law and the Family* (Tavistock).

PAHL, J. (1988) 'Earning, Sharing, Spending: Married Couples and their Money', in Walker, R. and Parker, G. (eds), *Money Matters: Income, Wealth and Financial Welfare* (Sage).

PAHL, J. (1989) *Money and Marriage* (Macmillan).

PARKER, G. (1988) 'Indebtedness', in Walker, R. and Parker, G. (eds), *Money Matters: Income, Wealth and Financial Welfare* (Sage).

PARKER, G. (1990) *With due care and attention: a review of research on informal care* (Family Policy Studies Centre).

PARKER, H. (1989) *Instead of the Dole: an Enquiry into the Integration of the Tax and Benefit Systems* (Routledge).

PARKER, H. and SUTHERLAND, H. (1991) *Child Tax Allowances? A comparison of child benefit, child tax reliefs, and basic incomes as instruments of family policy* (LSE/STICERD).

PEN, J. (1971) 'A Parade of Dwarfs (and a few Giants)', in Preston, T. S. (ed.), *Income Distribution* (Penguin).

PHILLIPS, K. (1990) *The Politics of Rich and Poor: Wealth and the American Electorate in the Reagan Aftermath* (New York: Random House).

PIACHAUD, D. (1979) *The Cost of a Child* (CPAG).

PIACHAUD, D. (1981a) 'Peter Townsend and the Holy Grail', *New Society*, 10 September.

PIACHAUD, D. (1981b) *Children and Poverty* (CPAG).

PIACHAUD, D. (1982a) *Family Incomes since the War* (Study Commission on the Family).

PIACHAUD, D. (1982b) 'Patterns of Income and Expenditure within Families', *Journal of Social Policy*, 11.4.

PIACHAUD, D. (1984) *Round about 50 hours a week: the time costs of children* (CPAG).

PIACHAUD, D. (1986) 'Disability and Unemployment', *Journal of Social Policy*, 15.2.

PIACHAUD, D. (1987) 'Problems in the Definition and Measurement of Poverty', *Journal of Social Policy*, 16.2

PIACHAUD, D. (1988) 'Poverty in Britain 1899 to 1983', *Journal of Social Policy*, 17.3.

PIVEN, F. and CLOWARD, R. (1972) *Regulating the Poor: the Functions of Public Welfare* (Tavistock).

PLOWDEN REPORT (1967) *Children and their Primary Schools*, Report of Central Advisory Council for Education, vols I. and II (HMSO).

PRESCOTT–CLARKE, P. (1990) *Employment and Handicap* (Social and Community Planning Research).

PURDY, D. (1988) *Social Power and the Labour Market* (Macmillan).

QURESHI, H. and WALKER, A. (1989) *The Caring Relationship: Elderly People and their Families* (Macmillan).

REX, J. (1973) *Race, Colonialism and the city* (Routledge and Kegan Paul).

REX, J. (1979) 'Black Militancy and Class Conflict', in Miles, R. and Phizaklea, A. (eds), *Racism and Political Action in Britain* (Routledge and Kegan Paul).

REX, J. and TOMLINSON, S. (1979) *Colonial Immigrants in a British City* (Routledge and Kegan Paul).

RHYS WILLIAMS, B. (1989) *Stepping Stones to Independence: National Insurance after 1990* (Aberdeen University P).

RINGEN, S. (1988) 'Direct and Indirect Measures of Poverty', *Journal of Social Policy*, 17.3.

ROBINSON, V. (1990) 'Roots to Mobility: the Social Mobility of Britain's Black Population 1971–87', *Ethnic and Racial Studies*, 13.2.

ROLL, J. (1986) *Babies and Money: Birth Trends and Costs* (Family Policy Studies Centre).

ROLL, J. (1989) 'Social and Economic Change and Women's Poverty', in Graham, H. and Popay, J. (eds), *Women and Poverty: Exploring the Research and Policy Agenda* (Thomas Coram Research Unit/University of Warwick).

ROOM, G., LAWSON, R. and LACZKO, F. (1989) ' "New Poverty" in the European Community', *Policy and Politics*, 17.2.

ROOM, G. *et al*: (eds) (1991) *National Policies to Combat Social Exclusion: First Annual Report of the European Community Observatory* (CRESEP, University of Bath).

ROSSITER, C. and WICKS, M. (1982) *Crisis or Challenge? Family Care, Elderly People and Social Policy* (Study Commission on the Family).

ROWNTREE, B. S. (1901) *Poverty: a Study of Town Life* (Macmillan).

ROWNTREE, B. S. (1941) *Poverty and Progress: a Second Social Survey of York* (Longman).

ROWNTREE, B. S. and LAVERS, G. (1951) *Poverty and the Welfare State* (Longman).

ROYAL COMMISSION (1978) *Royal Commission on the Distribution of Income and Wealth – Report no. 6* (HMSO).

ROYAL COMMISSION (1979) *Royal Commission on the Distribution of Income and Wealth -- Report no. 7* (HMSO).

ROYAL COMMISSION (1980) *An A to Z of Income and Wealth, Royal Commission on the Distribution of Income and Wealth* (HMSO).

RUBENSTEIN, W. D. (1986) *Wealth and Inequality in Britain* (Faber).

RUNCIMAN, W. G. (1966) *Relative Deprivation and Social Justice: a study of attitudes to social inequality in twentieth-century England* (Penguin).

RUTTER, M. and MADGE, N. (1976) *Cycles of Disadvantage* (Heinemann).

RYAN, W. (1971) *Blaming the Victim* (Orbach and Chambers).

SANDFORD, C. (1980) 'The Tax Credit Scheme', in Sandford, C., Pond, C. and Walker, R. (eds), *Taxation and Social Policy* (Heinemann EB).

SEABROOK, J. (1984) *Landscapes of Poverty* (Blackwell).

SEN, A. (1983) 'Poor, Relatively Speaking', *Oxford Economic Papers*, 35.1.

SHEFFIELD CPAG (1989) *Out of Sight, Out of mind* (Sheffield Libraries and Information Services).

SHERRADEN, M. (1991) *Assets and the Poor: a New American Welfare Policy* (New York: Sharpe).

SMEEDING, T., O'HIGGINS, M. and RAINWATER, L. (eds) (1990) *Poverty, Inequality and Income Distribution in Comparative Perspective: the Luxembourg Income Study (LIS)* (Harvester/Wheatsheaf).

SMITH, A. (1776) *An inquiry into the nature and causes of the wealth of nations*, 1892 ed. (Routledge).

SMITH, R. (1985) 'Who's Fiddling? Fraud and Abuse', in Ward, S. (ed.), *DHSS in Crisis: Social Security – Under Pressure and Under Review* (CPAG).

SMYTH, M. and ROBUS, N. (1989) *OPCS Report 5, The Financial Circumstances of Families with Disabled Children living in Private Households* (HMSO).

SOLTOW, L. (1980) 'Long-Run Changes in British Income Inequality', in Akinson A. B. (ed.), *Wealth, Income and Inequality* second ed. (Oxford UP).

SPICKER, P. (1990) 'Charles Booth: the examination of poverty', *Social Policy and Administration*, 24.1.

SQUIRES, P. (1990) *Anti-Social Policy: Welfare, Ideology and the Disciplinary State* (Harvester/Wheatsheaf).

STEDMAN JONES, G. (1971) *Outcast London* (Oxford UP).

STEPHENS, M. (1990) *Community Law Centres: a Critical Appraisal* (Avebury).

STOKER, G. (1988) *The Politics of Local Government* (Macmillan).

SWANN REPORT (1985) *Education for All: the Report of the Committee of Enquiry into the Education of Children from Ethnic Minority Groups*, Cmnd 9453 (HMSO).

TAWNEY, R. H. (1913) 'Inaugural Lecture "Poverty as an Industrial Problem"', reproduced in *Memoranda on the Problems of Poverty*, vol. 2 (William Morris Press).

TAWNEY, R. H. (1931) *Equality* (Allen and Unwin).

TAYLOR GOOBY, P. (1991) *Social Change, Social Welfare and Social Science* (Harvester/Wheatsheaf).

TEAGUE, P. (1989) *The European Community: the Social Dimension. Labour Market Policies for 1992* (Kogan Page).

TEEKENS, R. and VAN PRAAG, B. (eds) (1990) *Analysing Poverty in the European Community: Policy issues, Research Options and Data Sources* (Eurostat).

THANE, P. (1982) *The Foundations of the Welfare State* (Longman).

THERBORN, G. (1984) 'The Prospects of Labour and the Transformation of Advanced Capitalism', *New Left Review*, no. 145.

THERBORN, G. and ROEBROEK, J. (1986) 'The Irreversible Welfare State: Its Recent Maturation, Its Encounter with the Economic Crisis, and Its Future Prospects', *International Journal of Health Services*, 16.3

THOMPSON, P., BUCKLE, J. and LAVERY, M. (1988) *Not the OPCS Survey: Being Disabled Costs More Than They Said* (DIG).

THOMPSON, P., LAVERY, M. and CURTICE, C. (1990) *Short Changed by Disability* (DIG).

TITMUSS, R. M. (1955) 'Age and Society: Some Fundamental Assumptions', in *Old Age in the Modern World*, Report of the Third Congress of International Association of Gerontology, Edinburgh (Livingstone).

TITMUSS, R. M. (1958) 'The Social Division of Welfare', in Titmuss, R. M., *Essays on the Welfare State* (Allen and Unwin).

TOMLINSON, A. (1986) 'Playing away from home: leisure, disadvantage and issues of income and access', in Golding, P. (ed.), *Excluding the Poor* (CPAG).

TOPLISS, E. (1979) *Provision for the Disabled* second ed. (Blackwell Scientific with Martin Robertson).

TOPOROWSKI, J. (1986) 'Beyond banking: financial institutions and the poor', in Golding P. (ed.), *Excluding the Poor* (CPAG).

TOWNSEND, P. (1954) 'The Meaning of Poverty', *British Journal of Sociology*, June.

TOWNSEND, P. (1979) *Poverty in the United Kingdom: a Survey of Household Resources and Standards of Living* (Penguin).

TOWNSEND, P. (1984) *Why are the Many Poor?*, Fabian Tract 500 (Fabian Society).

TOWNSEND, P. (1987) 'Deprivation', *Journal of Social Policy*, 16.2.

TOWNSEND, P. (1991) T*he Poor are Poorer: a Statistical Report on Changes in the Living Standards of Rich and Poor in the United Kingdom 1979–1989* (University of Bristol).

TOWNSEND, P. and BOSANQUET, N. (1972) *Labour and Inequality* (Fabian Society).

TOWNSEND, P., CORRIGAN, P. and KOWARZIK, U. (1987) *Poverty and Labour in London: Interim Report of a Centenary Survey* (Low Pay Unit).

TOWNSEND, P. and DAVIDSON, N. and WHITEHEAD, M. (eds), (1988) *Inequalities in Health: the Black Report and the Health Divide* (Penguin).

VAN PARIJS, P. (ed.) (1992) *Arguing for Basic Income: Ethical Foundations for a Radical Reform* (Verso).

VAN PRAAG, B., HAGENAARS, A. and VAN WEEREN, H. (1982) 'Poverty in Europe', *Review of Income and Wealth*, 28.

VEIT–WILSON, J. (1986) 'Paradigms of Poverty: a Rehabilitation of B. S. Rowntree', *Journal of Social Policy*, 15.1.

VEIT–WILSON, J. (1987) 'Consensual Approaches to Poverty Lines and Social Security', *Journal of Social Policy*, 16.2.

VINCENT, D. (1991) *Poor Citizens: the State and the Poor in Twentieth Century Britain* (Longman).

WALKER, A. (1980) 'The Social Creation of Poverty and Dependency in Old Age', *Journal of Social Policy*, 9.1.

WALKER, A. (1982a) *Unqualified and Underemployed: Handicapped Young People and the Labour Market* (Macmillan).

WALKER, A. (ed.) (1982b) *Community Care: the Family, the State and Social Policy* (Blackwell/Martin Robertson).

WALKER, A. (1986) 'Pensions and the Production of Poverty in Old Age', in Walker, A. and Phillipson, C. (eds), *Ageing and Social Policy: a Critical Assessment* (Gower).

WALKER, A. (1990a) 'Poverty and Inequality in Old Age', in Bond, J. and Coleman, P. (eds), *Ageing in Society: an Introduction to Social Gerontology* (Sage).

WALKER, A. (1990b) 'The strategy of inequality. Poverty and income distribution in Britain 1979–89', in Taylor, I. (ed.), *The Social Effects of Free Market Policies: an International Text* (Harvester/Wheatsheaf).

WALKER, A. and PHILLIPSON, C. (eds) (1986) *Ageing and Social Policy: a Critical Assessment* (Gower).

WALKER, A. and WALKER, C. (eds) (1987) *The Growing Divide: a Social Audit 1979–87* (CPAG).

WALKER, A. and WALKER, L. (1991) 'Disability and financial need – the failure of the social security system', in Dalley, G. (ed.), *Disability and Social Policy* (PSI).

WALKER, R. (1987) 'Consensual Approaches to the Definition of Poverty: Towards an Alternative Methodology', *Journal of Social Policy*, 16.2.

WALKER, R. (1988) 'The Costs of Household Formation', in Walker, R. and Parker, G. (eds), *Money Matters: Income, Wealth and Financial Welfare* (Sage).

WALKER, R. (1991) *Poverty and Poverty Dynamics* (Centre for Research in Social Policy, Loughborough University).

WALKER, R., LAWSON, R. and TOWNSEND, P. (eds) (1984) *Responses to Poverty: Lessons from Europe* (Heinemann EB).

WALKER, R. and PARKER, G. (eds) (1988) *Money Matters: Income, Wealth and Financial Welfare* (Sage).

WARD, R. and CROSS, M. (1991) 'Race, employment and economic change', in Brown, P. and Scase, R. (eds), *Poor Work: Disadvantage and the Division of Labour* (Open University P).

WARD, S. (1986) 'Power, politics and poverty', in Golding, P. (ed.), *Excluding the Poor* (CPAG).

WHEELER, R. (1986) 'Housing Policy and Elderly People', in Walker, A. and Phillipson, C. (eds), *Ageing and Social Policy: a Critical Assessment* (Gower).

WHITE PAPER (1990) *The Way Ahead: Benefits for Disabled People*, Department of Social Security, Cmnd 917 (HMSO).

WHITELEY, P. and WINYARD, S. (1983) 'Influencing Social Policy: the Effectiveness of the Poverty Lobby in Britain', *Journal of Social Policy*, 12.1.

WILLIAMS, S. (1986) 'Exclusion: the hidden face of poverty', in Golding P. (ed.), *Excluding the Poor* (CPAG).

WILSON, W. J. (1987) *The Truly Disadvantaged: the Inner city, the Underclass and Public Policy* (University of Chicago P).

WOLFE, T. (1971) *Radical Chic and Mau-mauing the Flak Catchers* (New York: Bantam Books).

YOUNG, J. (1986) *The Islington Crime Survey* (Gower).

YU, A. C. S. (1992) *Low Cost Budget Standards for Three Household Types* (Family Budget Unit).

Index

accounting period 93, 107
Adam Smith Institute 204, 235
Age Concern 207
aggregation 98–9, 130–2, 136
Anomalies Act 129
arithmetic tradition 102, 114, 202–6
Association of Metropolitan
    Authorities 252
Attendance Allowance 181, 183,
    185, 230

Basic Income 234, 236–7
Beveridge, Lord 8, 96, 130, 141,
    164, 166, 202, 219–25, 229, 230,
    234, 237, 259
'Five Giants' 259
Bismarck 218, 221
Black Report 81, 154
Blue Books 103
'Breadline Britain' 71, 116–17
budget standards 63, 116
Bureau of Labor Statistics, US 64

Campaign for the Homeless and
    Rootless 248
capitalism 10, 23, 33, 40, 202, 257,
    265
'Cardboard City' 60, 80
'Cathy Come Home' 116, 209
Centre for Policy Studies 204
Charity Organisation Society 218
Child Poverty Action Group 7, 16,
    27, 65, 85, 97, 104, 108, 114, 115,
    127, 132, 134, 144, 191, 203–10,
    222, 229, 239, 248, 250
Citizens' Advice Bureau 151, 247
Citizens' Rights Office 248
claimants' unions 211

community action programme 242,
    244, 245
community care 135, 182
    grants 182

Community Development
    Project 244–6, 251–3
concertation 49, 53
conservatism 35
culture of poverty 29, 77, 193, 196,
    240, 253
cycle of caring 135
cycle of deprivation 29, 194, 197,
    240, 253

'dependency culture' 262, 264
deprivation indicator 63, 69
destitution 8, 14, 205
Diamond Commission 104, 158
Disability Aliiance 180, 183, 248
Disability Living Allowance 148,
    183, 185–6, 230
disability trap 183
Disability Working Allowance 183
Disablement Income Group 175,
    176, 182, 183, 207
Disabled Persons Act 1944 179
double shift 129
dual labour market 128–9

econometrics 109
Educational Priority Areas 194, 243
Engel curve 67, 92
Equal Pay Act 1970 127
equivalence scales 89, 91–2, 97

Fabianism 7, 59, 201, 204–6,
    258–61, 265–6
Family Budget Unit 65
fiscal welfare 85, 260
Fisher Committee 21
friendly societies 218, 219

gerontic ratio 172
Gini coefficient 112
'golden triangle' 44
Griffiths Report 182

284

head count 108–9
horizontal equity 25, 96–7, 215
households below average
    income 16, 90, 91, 103, 108

ideology 19–23
income proxy measures 63, 66
Independent Living Fund 182
Institute of Economic Affairs 195,
    204, 261
Institute for Fiscal Studies 16, 90,
    234–5
Invalid Care Allowance 131–2, 148,
    185–6
Invalidity Benefit 180

less eligibility 11, 217, 225
London School of Economics 7,
    106, 201–3
Lorenz curve 111–3
low-income families 16, 90, 91, 108
Low Pay Unit 13, 207
Luxembourg Income Study 14, 39,
    41, 105–6

Manpower Services Commission 247
marginal tax rate 233
Married Women's Property Act
    1964 124
Mobility Allowance 181, 183, 230

National Assistance 130, 165, 219,
    220, 225
    Board 225
National Association of Citizens'
    Advice Bureaux 151, 152, 247,
    248
National Consumer Council 228
National Council for One Parent
    Families 207
National Health Service 222, 259
National Unemployed Workers'
    Movement 211
'new poor' 26, 44, 48
'new right' 34, 58, 204
New Society 209
Non-contributory Invalidity
    Pension 131, 180

occupational welfare 85, 132,
    166–8, 179
Office of Economic
    Opportunity 242
Office of Population Censuses and
    Surveys 174–6, 178, 181–5
opportunity costs 136, 186
outdoor relief 11, 217

panel studies 94, 108
passport checking 149
pathology 23, 28–9, 192–8, 240,
    242, 245, 253, 262
Plowden Report 194, 243
pockets of poverty 239–41
Policy Studies Institute 142, 145–6,
    151, 153, 155, 248
Poor Law 11–12, 129, 164, 217, 219,
    221, 225, 234
poverty gap 108–9
poverty lobby 205, 208
poverty trap 183, 232–3, 236
public funds, no recourse to 149–50

replacement ratio 227–8
residence test 148
retirement 161–4

scrounging 21, 232
severe disablement allowance 148,
    180–1
Sex Discrimination Act 1975 127
Shelter 207
snapshot measures 93, 107–8
social assistance 225–9, 234
Social Charter 46, 48, 50, 51, 268
social democracy 35–6
'social dumping' 44, 48
Social Fund 182
social insurance 219, 220–5, 229,
    234, 237–8
Social Security Act 1986 167, 228
socialism 36–7
Speenhamland 11, 258
'Spongers, The' 209
sponsorship 150
State Earnings Related Pension
    Scheme 95, 122, 167–8, 171–2,
    224

Statutory Maternity Pay 132
Statutory Sick Pay 132
subsidiarity 53
subsistence 8, 58, 61, 223, 255
superannuation 166
Supplementary Benefit
    Commission 205, 227
Swann Report 154

take-up 152, 181, 183, 186, 227,
    228, 231–2, 233, 235, 247, 248,
    252, 254
    campaigns 249–50
Tax Credits 234–6
TAXMOD (LSE Welfare State
    Research Programme) 106
'thirteenth state' 49

time poverty 99, 125, 136
'trickle down' 262

Unemployment Assistance 130, 219
unemployment trap 227
Urban Aid Programme 243–4

vertical equity 25, 96, 215, 216

wage stop 207, 228
welfare rights 246–50, 252, 253, 254
welfare state capitalism 265
Widow's Benefit 130
window of observation 107
'Woopies' 169
workhouse 11, 12, 129, 164, 217
Workmen's Compensation
    Acts 180